'The b
read si
Alan Bleasdale

Linnell, **Daniel**, obituary writer.
Married: Laura Jardine, free spirit, bar
owner, parachutist, American. *Children*:
Jack, toddler and ice-cream connoisseur.
Publications: Who's Who in Hell, the
definitive encyclopaedia of evil-doing.
Recreations: writing about dead people,
collecting music, travelling, imbibing
alcohol.
Phobias: Heights. Infidelity. Death.

WHO'S WHO IN HELL
The brilliant, bittersweet debut from
Robert Chalmers

British publication: Atlantic Books, April 02
US publication: Grove Press, October 02

 New York • London

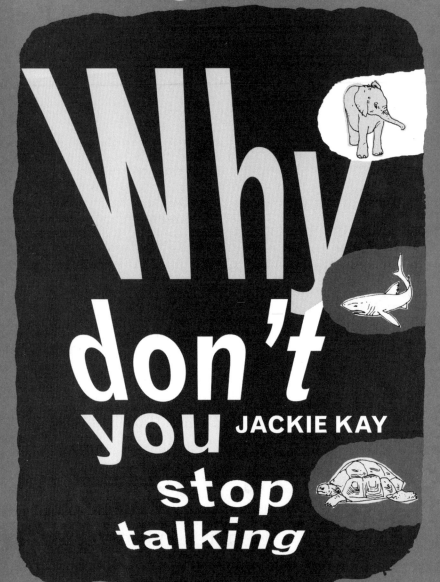

DON'T
LET'S GO
TO THE
DOGS
TONIGHT

AN AFRICAN
CHILDHOOD

ALEXANDRA FULLER

PICADOR

GRANTA

GRANTA 77, SPRING 2002
www.granta.com

EDITOR *Ian Jack*
DEPUTY EDITORS *Liz Jobey, Sophie Harrison*
EDITORIAL ASSISTANT *Fatema Ahmed*

CONTRIBUTING EDITORS *Neil Belton, Pete de Bolla, Ursula Doyle,*
Will Hobson, Gail Lynch, Blake Morrison, Andrew O'Hagan, Lucretia Stewart

ASSOCIATE PUBLISHER *Sally Lewis*
FINANCE *Geoffrey Gordon*
SALES *Frances Hollingdale*
PUBLICITY *Louise Campbell*
SUBSCRIPTIONS *John Kirkby, Darryl Wilks, Chris Bennett*
PUBLISHING ASSISTANT *Mark Williams*
ADVERTISING MANAGER *Kate Rochester*

PUBLISHER *Rea S. Hederman*

Granta, 2–3 Hanover Yard, Noel Road, London N1 8BE
Tel 020 7704 9776 Fax 020 7704 0474
e-mail for editorial: editorial@granta.com

Granta US, 1755 Broadway, 5th Floor, New York, NY 10019-3780, USA

TO SUBSCRIBE call 020 7704 0470 or e-mail subs@granta.com
A one-year subscription (four issues) costs £26.95 (UK), £34.95 (rest of Europe) and £41.95 (rest of the world).

Granta is printed and bound in Italy by Legoprint. The paper used in this publication meets the minimum requirements of American National Standard for Information Sciences—Permanence of Paper for Printed Library Materials, ANSI Z39.48-1984.

Granta is published by Granta Publications.
This selection copyright © 2002 Granta Publications.

Design: Random Design.
Front cover photograph: Lorraine Molina/Photonica; back cover photograph: The Old City, Kabul, December 2001 by Thomas Dworzak.

Lyrics from Let's Do It (Let's Fall in Love) on page 197 of Blake Morrison:
Words and music by Cole Porter. © Harms Inc, USA. Warner Chappell Music Ltd, London W6 8BS.
Reproduced by permission of International Music Publications Ltd. All rights reserved.

ISBN 0 903141 50 7

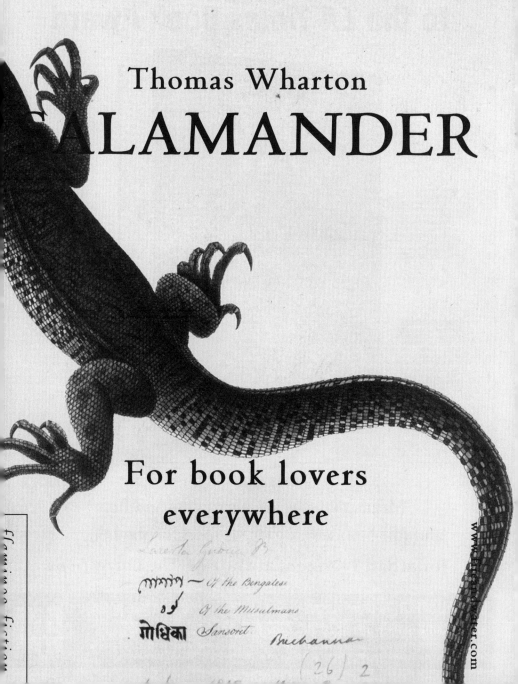

A glorious odyssey in search
of the infinite book

Thomas Wharton

ALAMANDER

For book lovers
everywhere

ffamingo fiction

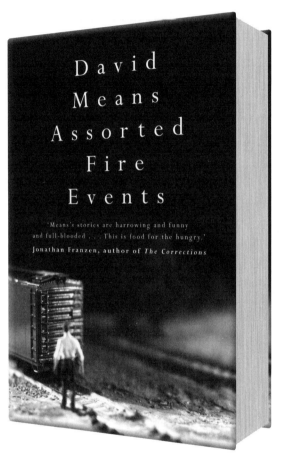

GRANTA 77

What We Think of America

EPISODES AND OPINIONS FROM TWENTY-FOUR WRITERS

Hanan al-Shaykh, Ian Buruma, Amit Chaudhuri,
Haim Chertok, Aleksa Djilas, Ariel Dorfman, Benoît Duteurtre,
Hans Magnus Enzensberger, John Gray, Ramachandra Guha,
Lu Gusun, James Hamilton-Paterson, Michael Ignatieff,
Ivan Klíma, Doris Lessing, Yang Lian, David Malouf,
Fintan O'Toole, Orhan Pamuk, Harold Pinter,
Karim Raslan, Raja Shehadeh, Tara Bray Smith, Ahdaf Soueif

ELSEWHERE

Pankaj Mishra	JIHADIS	83
J. M. Coetzee	YOUTH	121
Francis Spufford	THE HABIT	141
Thomas Dworzak	AUTUMN IN AFGHANISTAN	161
Blake Morrison	HAVE YOU DECIDED TO LOVE ME YET?	193
Ziauddin Sardar	MECCA	223

NOTES ON CONTRIBUTORS   256

What *we* think of America and its ally...

CLASH OF FUNDAMENTALISMS Crusades, Jihads and Modernity
Tariq Ali
The visible violence of September 11 was the response to the invisible violence inflicted on countries by the United States and its allies. In this wide raging book that provides an explanation for both the rise of Islamic fundamentalism and the new forms of Western colonialism, Tariq Ali argues that many of the values proclaimed by the Enlightenment retain their relevance, while portrayals of the American Empire as a new emancipatory project are misguided.

April 2002 • 160 pages • £15/$22 • hdbk • 1-85984-679-3

PARIAH Misfortunes of the British Kingdom • **Tom Nairn**

'A corrosive polemic. It seems obvious now that his has been the most forceful and original mind to confront, demask and anatomise the British State.' Neal Ascherson, *London Review of Books*

April 2002 • 100 pages • £13/$22 • hdbk • 1-85984-657-2

COUNTERPUNCH The Journalism that Rediscovers America
Edited by Alexander Cockburn & Jeffrey St. Clair

'Probably the most gifted polemicists writing in English today.'
David Rieff, *Times Literary Supplement*

'Without writers like Cockburn and St. Clair...the official version is the only one that survives.' *LA Weekly*

April 2002 • 400 pages • £12/$26 • pbk • 1-85984-455-3

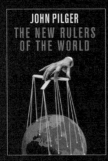

THE NEW RULERS OF THE WORLD • **John Pilger**

'John Pilger's work has been a beacon of light in often dark times. The realities he has brought to light have been a revelation, over and over again, and his courage and insight a constant inspiration.'
Noam Chomsky

May 2002 • 160 pages • £10/$19 • hdbk • 1-85984-393-X

VERSO

UK: 6 Meard Street, London W1F 0EG
USA: 180 Varick Street, New York, NY 10014-4606
www.versobooks.com

GRANTA

WHAT WE THINK
OF AMERICA

'...a fully-fledged, award-winning, gold-plated monster...it knows only one language—bombs and death' —Harold Pinter

'...the only country whose citizenship is an act of faith, the only country whose promises to itself continue to command the faith of people like me, who are not its citizens' —Michael Ignatieff

New York, September 2001

What We Think of America

A merica shapes the way non-Americans live and think. Before the Cold War ended, that had been true of half the world for several decades. Now, with the possible exceptions of North Korea and Burma, it is true of all of it. American cultural, economic and political influence is potent almost everywhere, in every life. What do we think of when we think of America? Fear, resentment, envy, anger, wonder, hope? And when did we start to think it?

By way of introducing the twenty-four writers in this collection of personal story and opinion, I offer two scenes from my own boyhood in Scotland in the 1950s.

The first: a lovely ship at anchor in the firth, perhaps half a mile from our village in Fife. This is the liner *Caronia* on its annual cruise to northern Europe from New York. Little black launches are coming and going from its pale-green hull to take tourists back and forth to Edinburgh on the further shore. At our feet, strewn along the beach's tideline and soggy with salt water, lie hundreds of half-eaten half-grapefruits. These have been tossed overboard by the *Caronia*'s kitchen crew. This is what Americans have had for breakfast—often neglecting (unbelievably, or so it seems to us) to eat the decoration of glacé cherries, which now also lie so abundantly on the sand. Where have I seen so many decorative cherries before? It must be in the back-page full-colour ad of *National Geographic* magazine, where they are spiked across something called a York Ham. Possibly some kind of pudding? All these luxuries are coming to us, or to some of us, but not quite yet.

The second: a crowd of boys on another beach, not far away from the first. In the middle is an American boy, who has somehow landed up in Fife. The crowd is taunting him, 'Hank the Yank! Hank the Yank!', and he is red-faced, bewildered and crying. Why are we being so awful to him? Possibly because of some boastfulness on his part, or some argument over whether Britain or the US has the largest number of warships. Impossibly, we insist that Britain has; as a country, we are already living historically (a fact which is illustrated a summer or two later when the USS *Wisconsin* sails up the firth and drops anchor at the same spot as the *Caronia* usually does; the *Wisconsin* is one of a whole fleet of battleships, and Britain by now has none).

I remembered 'Hank the Yank' in the weeks after September 11, when so much anti-American feeling suddenly rose to the surface of newspaper columns and ordinary conversation—and not only in Hebron or Cairo or Lahore. Throughout Europe, even at the supper tables and bars of America's most loyal ally, you could hear (and, let's face it, speak) twin sentiments joined by that dangerous conjunction, but. What has happened is terrible, but it's...*hardly surprising* or *hubris surely* or, the most extreme, *they had it coming to them.* Two months later, the *International Herald Tribune* reported that in a poll of 275 'opinion leaders' throughout the world—a poll, as it were, of pollsters—more than two-thirds of the non-American respondents agreed with the proposition that it was 'good that Americans now know what it's like to be vulnerable'. More than half of these 'opinion leaders' outside the US also agreed to the idea that many or most people believed that 'American policies or actions in the world were a major cause of the September 11 attacks'.

The pieces that follow are not about that day, nor are they excuses for it. They are about how America has entered non-American lives, and to what effect, for good and bad and both.

Ian Jack

Hanan al-Shaykh
Lebanon

I am the one visiting America this time, but I still remember America coming into our neighbourhood, our house, when I was a child. I remember pushing aside all the heads bending eagerly over it and the hands trying to touch it until I was face to face with it: a red satin cushion with a statue of a good-hearted woman on it, wearing a crown on her head and holding a lamp, a torch. The cushion was accompanied by a greetings card of high buildings which looked like the wooden art deco column in our sitting room, whose glass middle I once saw lit up.

My cousin sent America to our home after he went there to study aeronautical engineering. When he returned, four years later, sheep were slaughtered in his honour and he became an overnight celebrity. Our house was the focus of attention, as if we were all famous.

Years later, I come to visit my sister in America, in a state full of palm trees. As soon as we arrive, I hear my mother sighing bitterly, and wonder why the sun isn't ashamed to shine. My mother sighs from the depths of her heart, as if she hopes this will find my sister and her three children a place to live. They are going to be made homeless the day after tomorrow. My mother has never been homeless in Beirut, despite the war and the violence. 'It's as if we're born with our houses on our backs in our country, like tortoises,' she says.

My nephews and niece try to collect all their things together, but what about their posters, and the walls which have echoed to their music and their voices? My sister goes round gathering up clothes and books as if she is harvesting wheat, parcelling up bale after bale, only to have new shoots sprouting before her eyes. I see a belt that used to be mine among the clothes and handbags. Instead of rejoicing in the memories it evokes of happy times in Beirut, I feel sad for it, because it too has no home now.

My nephews shout at my sister because she's throwing away papers, falling to bits with age, which they had put in a corner, ready to take with them. Their noise alarms my mother, and my sister threatens to call the police. All this does is remind everyone that it was the police who came to evict them in the first place, after the neighbours complained. It wasn't the first time. My sister's children can only relax when they listen to rap. Its rhythm restores their equilibrium. They are talented musicians who write their own lyrics and set them to music. If this were a different kind of area, this unsolicited music might be seen as nourishment for its audience's soul.

In the past my sister used to send me photos of my niece and nephews from time to time. Americans, except for their Arab eyes. Don't ask me what Arab eyes are like. They have a kind of wariness, perhaps, with a hint of mischief in it. I would smile as I pictured them leaping through a mist, carrying lunch boxes and baseball bats, munching popcorn in an aura of cookies and Kool-Aid—that distinctive smell of their school lockers—and their rooms at home like toy departments, and later like caves where as teenagers they would take refuge with their dreams and pimples.

But here in reality I see cautious expressions, eyes that are dull yet rebellious, and the children living in rooms which are almost like garages or temporary refuges, where the body can rest, but not the soul.

The clock ticks. Tick tock. Tick tock. My mother climbs on top of her seven big suitcases and covers them with sheets so she can forget they exist. She is regretting having bought presents for her neighbours, friends, relatives and the local baker in Beirut, all of them expecting something from America, even just a tin ashtray from McDonald's. Everyone wants something from America, non-disposable nappies among other things, as if the bowels won't do what they are supposed to do if they're exposed to the wrong kind of fabric. People want bedcovers, medicines, children's toys, nail varnish, nighties, shoes of all sizes. I picture my mother throwing everything into the middle of the sitting room on her return: 'Go on. Try them on. Take them if they fit.'

My mother puts a hand to her forehead as if trying to dig out a name to contact in America. In vain. People here are like silkworms wrapped in their cocoons. Why is America empty? Where are the people? I want to see the owner of the property. My mother urges my sister to talk to him: 'He's a human being after all. You can beg him to be kind to you for your children's sake, and let you stay on here. We'll tell him how all this country meant to your husband was women's breasts, blonde hair and alcohol, from the moment he set foot on American soil. How he left you for one of them, so it's hard for you to raise your children. We can promise the landlord that the children won't play instruments or listen to music from now on. This is meant to be the land of freedom...shouldn't freedom extend into the homes and streets, like blood and oxygen flowing round the body?'

My mother is pleased with her analogy and keeps repeating it until my sister tells her to be quiet. She's ringing round, trying to find another flat. To no avail: my sister has become well known among letting agencies, moving her children from one place to another like a cat.

After numerous attempts she slams the phone down.

'Collateral, collateral. That's all they want. That's what held me back before, and nothing's changed.'

My sister used to picture herself disembarking from a passenger liner and being received by official welcomers, taken by the hand, patted on the shoulder, starting her new life in this model country warmed by their encouraging smiles. America was the land of dreams, stretching to infinity, resembling no other country on earth. It had no antiquated laws. Its constitution was founded on equality and justice. Now she finds herself like a fish trapped in a net if she can't come up with some collateral. But if she does find some, they'll drown her in debt. Debts will rain down on her from all sides, once she starts the ball rolling.

She's discovered that her hands are tied. Bureaucracy has injected her with a deadly substance, sapping her resolve. As an immigrant, she has to have ready cash, or she's dead. She who came to the land of dreams like Venus emerging from the sea, naked except for her long hair. She had no references allowing her to open a bank account, no permanent address, no acquaintances with influence or status or property, who could give her credit and support her until she found her feet, equip her to rent a flat, buy a car, open a bank account.

She had to find a job at once, and it was impossible. The competition for jobs was like a war, showing her what a harsh society she was living in. She pleaded for a little time to become acquainted with the surroundings, the new culture, the unfamiliar way of life. It all reinforced her sense of insecurity and stripped her of her self-confidence. She went through one interview after another.

Now the whole process is repeating itself in front of me and my mother. Finally one of the letting agencies responds positively and a few hours later an employee from the agency arrives to negotiate the

contract. My mother and I feel pleased that this woman has come
in person from the agency, but my sister takes it as a bad sign: 'She
must want to make sure that I'm not a vagrant.'

The woman sits in the middle of the room, cradling her laptop,
looking around her apprehensively. She refuses my mother's offer of
coffee and asks my sister if she really has a job, as she has tried her
office number and had no luck. My sister replies that she didn't go
into work today. My mother interrupts. 'Sick,' she explains, pointing
at her heart.

'If your mother's sick, does that mean she'll be living with you
too?'

My sister answers that my mother is just visiting, and will be gone
next week.

'But how do you know that? Perhaps your mother will change
her mind and stay in the United States.'

'Me?' interrupts my mother again. 'Stay here? I'd rather die.'

The woman doesn't understand what she means, and asks my
sister to produce her driving licence. My sister replies awkwardly, 'I
don't have a car. I don't know how to drive.'

'So how do you get to work then? You just told me you have a
job!'

'I go by bus.'

'What? By bus! Surely only old people take the bus!'

The woman casts her eyes round the empty room, unable to believe
her ears, pleading with the few remaining objects and my mother's
seven suitcases to tell her the truth. Then she asks my sister again, or
rather interrogates her: 'Is it possible that you don't have a car?'

'Did you hear the joke about the man who was given a ticket by
the police because they caught him walking?'

The woman doesn't smile. She asks my sister to give her the names
of the people she works with. My sister flushes and turns as red as
a pomegranate, especially when the woman refuses to accept two
months' rent and demands four months, in advance because she
doesn't have collateral.

After the woman has left, my mother sighs. 'Ah! If that taxi driver
in Beirut only knew what was happening to you and your children.
I don't even know why I'm visiting you. I knew you'd be walking
on shifting sands, being buried bit by bit, hardly able to keep your

heads above the surface. If only he knew what really goes on in America...but he'd never believe it.'

The taxi driver had struck his face in a torment of envy when he found that his passenger had a return ticket to the States, and an entry visa.

'Why doesn't your photo with Reagan save us?' we say jokingly to my mother. This is a photo of her with a poster of Reagan behind her, looking so real that some simple people in Beirut believe my mother is friendly with him, and have asked her to use her influence with him to get them a US visa.

We sleep, or rather close our eyes to relax, so that we can make decisions.

My mother and sister take refuge with a friend. Although my nephews assure us that one of their friends will put them up, they are going to sleep on the beach as they have often done before, warmed by the bright stars and wept over by the dew.

My niece will sleep in a friend's car. My mother's heart will be on fire, and icy cold. And I will no longer cling to my memory of an old American woman with earrings like little birds in cages, who gasped in wonder at the Roman ruins in Baalbek, and made me want my grandmother to be able to travel abroad like her. I will forget the feel of the 'cowboys', as we used to call jeans, which my father borrowed for me from a friend of his who owned a clothes store. He made me promise only to wear them at the school party. In the end, I never dared wear them at all, but was content to look at them and touch them. When I saw them, I saw a piece of America running ahead of me, disregarding the cries of 'Shame!'

Translated from the Arabic by Catherine Cobham

Ian Buruma
Germany/Holland/Britain

Los Angeles, in 1971, was the most exotic place I had ever visited. Despite the faint familiarity of mock-Tudor, faux-Loire chateau, fake-Spanish/Moorish, cod-King Arthur's castle mansions in Beverly Hills, the city looked unlike anything I'd seen before. Looking down upon the giant sprawl from the Hollywood Hills, where I was staying with an alcoholic brain surgeon who raided his dispensary for all kinds of hitherto untested recreational goodies, the place was like a mirage shimmering in the palm-fringed distance. If the whole thing had suddenly evaporated it would have come as no great surprise. Of course I loved it.

Being a fairly conventional young man, I did the conventional things, for that time. One memorable evening was spent at Disneyland in the company of two Japanese-American brothers named Bruce and Norman. Being, as I say, conventional types, we were high on LSD. We watched the Supremes shimmering in and out of different costumes at the rate of about one a minute, or so it seemed. Being attacked from all sides by singing gnomes in national dress, Mexican, French, Japanese, German, American, Greek, African and so on, was less agreeable. But the living ghost of Abraham Lincoln speaking the Gettysburg Address into my ear was very fine.

The thing I remember most clearly from that night, however, is the long, supercharged conversation of my companions. The subject, loosely, was 'identity'. Norman, the elder brother, was fascinated by his native California, its ethos, its many tribes, its culture, its vapid good life and the sheer looniness of it all. An LA intellectual, driving a Volkswagen Beetle, Norman lapped it all up, while keeping a sardonic, analytical distance. His goal was to make serious movies in Hollywood, which he was not yet ready to regard as a complete contradiction. To make money in the meantime, he made porno. His family roots in Japan barely interested him. Norman had never bothered to learn Japanese. His culture was American. He felt comfortable with the freedom of American rootlessness.

Bruce was different. He talked that night of 2,000 years of Asian culture, which could not just be thrown away like old clothes. It was part of one's identity. Unlike Norman, he did speak some Japanese, was interested in Japanese art, and adopted the general demeanour of a man in touch with Zen. This, too, was a part of Californian culture, one might say, but Bruce made much of his difference from white Americans. There was in him still a residual hankering for blood, tradition, family, the things many immigrants come to leave behind. The old world still existed for him.

This particular conundrum was as new to me as the cityscape of southern California. Assimilation played a part in my family background. But the way my mother's family of cultured German

Jews had become cultured British Jews was not the same as the common American experience. For them, it had meant assimilation into another old European culture with its own customs and traditions, which were, however, not so very different from those of the country they came from. My grandparents did not lose very much, not even their love of Richard Wagner. America, especially California, holds out a more radical promise to its new citizens. The US, too, has its national customs and traditions, but underlying them is the ideal that each person is free to choose his own destiny, unfettered by the social chains of whatever old world one had escaped from. Rather than adopting the ready-made identity of another settled tradition, the idea is to start afresh, to make oneself up again and, as far as possible, forget the past. America gives every man a second chance. Success or failure are not determined by family origins, or bound by the rules of class. The pursuit of personal happiness is not just a right, but almost a duty.

This is an ideal America, to be sure, a New Jerusalem without racial prejudice, religious bigotry or social inequality. But it is an ideal that doesn't exist in quite the same way anywhere else. Some of us in the Old World despise Americans for their lack of historical or tragic sense, but that is to miss the point, for the promise of freedom in America is precisely to be liberated from the past. The price for some is to feel cast adrift in a constant present, forever in pursuit, like a modern Tantalus, of elusive gratifications. Our aspirations may be narrowed by continuity, history and traditions, but at least we are not alone, and the limitations of fate offer a certain cold comfort. This, perhaps, is the main basis of tension between the Old and the New Worlds, or indeed between Bruce and Norman.

In fact, however, this tension exists everywhere. The pull to cut loose, to reinvent ourselves, to shake off the past, and to want instant gratification, sexual, material, spiritual, is something most of us have felt. That is why 'America', the ideal, expressed in Hollywood movies, rock music, advertising and other pop culture, is so attractive, so sexy and, to some, so deeply disturbing. All of us want a bit of 'America', but few of us can have it, and even those who do still hunger for more, and more.

A character in a German movie by Wim Wenders exclaimed that 'America has colonized our minds'. It is a glib statement, typical of a German of the 1968 generation, but to some extent it is true. Hundreds of millions of people, from London to Tokyo, are tantalized by the desire for 'America'. I myself have felt it ever since my father sent me a postcard of the Manhattan skyline while on a business trip to America in 1959. There was something about that forest of Babylonian towers, gleaming in the starry night, that had the power to excite even the mind of an eight-year-old.

I still feel a schoolboyish thrill every time I go to America, and an exhilarating sense of lightness when I get there. Chatting to strangers somehow becomes easier. The burden of European caginess, and of the snobberies and class prejudices left behind, like crusty scales, by a European education, appears to be lifted. The feeling never entirely wears off, even when the drawbacks of American society—the sentimentality, the conformism, the insularity—become more apparent.

But then I am privileged. I don't have to start at the bottom, like a penniless immigrant, and I can move in and out of America at will, picking those bits of 'America' that I like and ignoring the bits I don't, always in the safe knowledge that I can return to the comfortable, democratic European world which is still my home. The idea of 'America', as a possible refuge, as a place where one might have a second chance, and as a defender of our freedom, is reassuring to me.

America, however, is a very different place to those who live in places where 'America' is only a mirage, a kind of guilty wet dream in dry desert lands, a promise which can never be fulfilled. If you live under a tyranny, with no personal freedom and no hope of advancement, in a country that feels abandoned and perhaps even betrayed by the modern world, the pull of family, tribe and tradition may be all that is left. Then a very different utopia beckons the embittered pilgrim, one built on a mirage of purity, sacred community and self-sacrifice. In such a state of mind, it is not enough to avert your gaze from those seductive towers of Babylon. You might have to tear them down.

Amit Chaudhuri
India

When we were children, we played cowboys and Indians sometimes. We rather liked being cowboys; we instructed ourselves that the

Indians were 'Red' Indians—the term 'American Indian' was still not in currency—not remotely like us, who enacted our make-believe in the large basement garages of a building on Malabar Hill in South Bombay. It was while looking for us, we noted, that Columbus had lighted upon America. The enormity of the accident—and the relatively unacknowledged but not inconsiderable part we had played in it!

In many places and ways, Bombay echoed, and still echoes, America. This is not to say it is an imitation; its America is to be found *there*, in its streets, and nowhere else. But this echo also sets it apart from every other Indian city; gives it its own melancholy destiny to fulfil.

There is, first of all, the allure of tall buildings. They cluster around Nariman Point—what might probably be called Bombay's 'financial district': the Air India building (where a bomb went off in 1993), the Indian Express building, the Oberoi Towers. This is reclaimed land; I remember when Nariman Point was still a 'point', a strip of land petering out into rocks and the sea. But tall buildings are everywhere in South Bombay. Some of them are as famous as famous people; a few, like some Bombay celebrities, have less than impeccable reputations. Some time in the late Seventies or early Eighties a building called Kanchenjunga, designed by the architect Charles Correa, came up on the hilly incline of Peddar Road, a giant, off-white rectangular box, with large perforations made in it, coloured violently red on the inside (the perforations were the balconies of duplex flats). For a long time, no one occupied those flats. The building had been erected on a disputed site. No matter; the building became a star—if a slightly shunned one—and a part of the skyline of jostling high and low, young and old structures, the all-night party of the Bombay skyline. Years later, occupants appeared on the balconies; but you are not really meant to see people in the tall Bombay buildings.

There is more than a hint of New York here. The tall buildings are, literally, 'upstarts'; they are mainly post-Independence social climbers; their altitude suggests the precedence of desire over the genteel evasions of the colonial age.

But, in the perpetual sunshine, in the sea, in the palm trees, is also something of California. The pleasures of the body; the body standing in the sun.

21

And so, all those beaches; in Chowpatty, Juhu, Marve, not to speak of the Governor's private beach, which children from the Cathedral School used to visit once a year. The children taken for pony rides; the men, some of them frauds, racketeers or embezzlers, gambolling on the sand; semi-nude, back to a second infancy. The image crystallizes for me Bombay's mixture of the childlike and the grown-up, of naivety and ruthlessness, a mixture that, as I now know, is also peculiarly American. Childhood fantasy and adult knowingness, innocence and violence, inhabiting the same space, even the same mind and body.

I was introduced to America through the comic book. My Bengali parents had taught me no English before I went to school; settled outside Bengal, in Bombay, they had longed to make me intimate with the Bengali language. I was admitted into the school— on what basis, I don't know; I knew no English. The headmistress suggested an unusual two-pronged approach to my mother: to familiarize me with the language by giving me both Ladybird and comic books to read. Through the Ladybird books I was brought to a world of English families and landscapes; this education in English continued with Enid Blyton, whose cocooned universe contained strange cruelties and snobberies as well as buttered scones and picnic hampers.

That world, although close to us historically in many ways, felt remote; but American comic books, which taught me to read, somehow entered our lives in Bombay and became indistinguishable from them; we didn't know where one ended and the other began. The much thumbed and perused copy, in the 'circulating library', of the Archie Comics Digest; the thin line separating us from Riverdale. The monthly purchase of Gold Key comics; the 'friendly' ghosts and witches; Richie Rich, that Fitzgeraldian cartoon character, who, with swimming pools, butlers, chauffeurs, was still not completely happy. Superheroes who led dull lives as employees in tall buildings, to whom the simple act of putting on spectacles conferred an impenetrable aura of ordinariness and guaranteed a foolproof disguise; or led reclusive lives as tycoons in opulent mansions with vast underground garages in which a single car was kept; or even, like Elastic Man, turned sad, congenital deformities into a prodigious talent for fighting crime. If Gregor Samsa had been born in America, would his 'metamorphosis' have made him famous, like Spiderman or the Incredible Hulk?

Our American childhood in Bombay happened during the Cold War, when one part of the world was under the canopy of Brezhnev's enormous eyebrows. We were in that part of the world. Although India is a democracy, it was certainly a political and strategic ally of Russia; Russia gave us an idea of moral and economic rectitude, while America provided us with a sort of illicit entertainment. As for Soviet entertainment, there were the astonishing films. We went to watch Sovexport films for two reasons. The first was that Russian films emerged from a more consciously artistic tradition of cinema than anything to be found in Hollywood. The other reason was less high-minded: our political friendship led to an odd indulgence on the part of the National Board of Film Censors, and the nudity in bad Sovexport films went largely uncut. The cuts in Hollywood films were clumsily, even insultingly, made—a woman might be unbuttoning her blouse; she seemed to suffer a brief spasm or convulsion; then she was seen to be buttoning her blouse. We, in the Seventies, studied that spasm closely but hopelessly. Nakedness in American movies was kept from us by a wall of propriety harder to penetrate than the Iron Curtain.

Superheroes; but also villains. For a generation, Henry Kissinger was the most hated man in India. In 1975, Sanjay Gandhi would overtake him in loathsomeness; but that bureaucratic suit, those thick glasses and that heavy accent would always make Indians shudder. And Nixon, too, who, with Kissinger, presided over the Bangladesh war; the way the American government always seemed to be on the wrong side of everything. Nevertheless, the young men and women queued up for application forms at the USIS in Marine Lines. The lines were long and exhausting; later, they left for the States. Returning for holidays, the men wore shorts, and T-shirts with the logos of obscure universities. Even their fathers began to wear shorts. On the rear windows of cars in Bombay, they pasted stickers with the names of those unheard-of universities, which others would be obliged to memorize in a traffic jam. What was it that took them there? Was it a desire for success and assimilation that Europe could not offer? And was it the ability, and desire, to merge (but not quite) with those crowds in Manhattan, or settle down in some suburb, or relocate themselves in the vast spaces in between?

Haim Chertok
America/Israel

As an unrepentent citizen of both the Zionist Entity and the global Gulliver-state, I am exquisitely aware of the disesteem, both spontaneous and ritualistic, in which I am held by much of the rest of world. Or, in any event, by their self-appointed spokesmen. From the intellectual fringes of the Occident to the fanatical centres of the Levant, my dossier constitutes an automatic double-whammy of reproach and contempt.

It was when I was hitch-hiking around France in the late Fifties, a time when the French—enforcing the fiction that Algeria was an integral part of France—were suppressing nationalists with Gallic flare and industry, that I first was confronted by vacuous anti-Americanism. Upon discovering they had made a temporary American captive, salesmen, farmers, truck drivers seemed driven to challenge the teenager in the passenger seat: 'How do *you* explain Selma?' As though I were Bull Conners incarnate or the French were not themselves torturers.

If the weather turned nasty, the attack was oblique. *'C'est le bomb atomique.'* Another American sin. I learned to prevaricate: I was from Toronto. Yes, yes, a Canadian. As often as not my new pal would buy a beer for another victim of the nasty Americans.

Things change. Always. In time I too learned to mindlessly condemn my native land. In 1976 I bid the US farewell and Israel *shalom*. I disengaged myself from what I took to be America's overweening chutzpah by vamoosing in the very midst of its bicentennial self-glorification. I imagined that my American critical mass might be consigned to a black hole and I felt very good about assuming a new identity as an instant Israeli.

How had a pure product of the Bronx come to such a pass? Vietnam, of course. Three years of military service, mostly in the Far East, had undone my mindset. In January 1964 I was discharged. Two months later Secretary of Defense McNamara voiced the possibility of activating the reserves, to which I had been assigned involuntarily. Nothing could persuade me to don an American uniform ever again.

Two weeks later I descended upon the Israel Immigration Center in San Francisco. A process was initiated that reached fruition twelve years later. At first as a refuge, later as an alternative vision, Israel,

I conjectured, would serve me well. Never did I anticipate that, six years after leaving America, I would be serving in an army again, this time wearing Israeli fatigues, at the airport in Beirut. It was September 1982. From Vietnam to Sabra and Shatila, obscenity to obscenity.

The wheel of my dual citizenry has ratcheted twenty years. As I write, exemplary Belgium, in its heyday the most barbarous of all colonial powers, considers whether to try Israel's prime minister as a war criminal for actions perpetrated by Israel's erstwhile Maronite cohorts. And M. Bernard, the emissary of French civilization to London, indicts a certain shitty little entity as a threat to world peace primarily for defending its citizens from terrorist incursions.

On balance, Israel has served me well enough. I am of the party of compromise for peace. Of course I recognize Israel is partly responsible for this region's endemic suffering. I also appreciate that until Palestinians accept a measure of responsibility for their own pain and humilation, neither compromise nor peace will be achieved. In recent years I have eaten a lot of crow. In all the enlightened world, only my spurned homeland could be relied upon for a reasonably nuanced perspective of events here. Only America vetoes deranged resolutions in the Security Council. And only American adminstrations have seriously endeavoured to nudge Palestinians from their skewed sense of the realities of our region.

For all of which I thank the former Gullivers of Arkansas and Texas and duly honour the civilized values of the republic for which they stand.

Aleksa Djilas
Serbia

I first came to the United States in 1987 to work at a university. As a sociologist and historian in my mid-thirties I of course already knew something about American politics. But what I had to say, and unfortunately often did say, was unoriginal, cautious and dreadfully reasonable. I bored my friends and colleagues. I console myself, however, that any inclination towards tedious moderation in politics may, after all that happened in the 1990s, be seen as a great virtue in someone from former Yugoslavia.

I have improved somewhat since then. I now live in my native

Belgrade and occasionally comment in the Serbian media on American affairs. I always underline that I am not an expert. But in Serbia you overhear people in the streets, on buses, in grocery stores, discussing without hesitation the ultimate goals of American global strategy and revealing to each other the most arcane secrets of American diplomacy and espionage. So since everyone knows everything, my moderate estimates of my own knowledge are perceived as either false modesty or an attempt to conceal something.

In the liberal milieu of my American East Coast university, my only attention-grabbing views were on American–Soviet relations. I was firmly and infuriatingly 'conservative': America was neglecting its defences and making too many concessions during détente, the loyalty of its NATO allies was suspect, the neutron bomb was a good idea, and so on. Few people with a PhD from the London School of Economics could boast of having ascended such Reaganite heights. But then, I had the advantage of being from a communist country.

Actually, I was a veteran defender of the United States of America. In the first grades of my Belgrade elementary school, some of us pupils divided into two opposing groups: 'Americans' and 'Russians'. It was mostly the boys who played this game of Cold War propaganda, since the girls, while better pupils, were less politically opinionated. The battles we fought for the hearts and minds of our uncommitted schoolmates were truly titanic and I was one of the most vocal champions of American democracy and all other things American. Even Yuri Gagarin's orbit in 1961 could not slow down the flow of my eloquence about the superiority of American space technology.

Whenever we lacked knowledge or information (and that was most of the time) we boys relied on our fertile imagination to supply ammunition for our debates. One particular story I invented described the greatest May Day military parade in history, which supposedly took place in the United States. Though I knew that Washington was the capital, I placed it in New York because I wanted the skyscrapers in the background.

Of course, Americans had never celebrated that international holiday in honour of workers with any display of military might. But we were just back to school after the May 1 holiday, and like the rest of the world had been either favourably impressed with or terrified by the annual Soviet display of cannons, tanks and rockets traversing

Red Square. Those giant ICBMs with their thermonuclear innards dazzled me: ultra-modern but somehow primordial, they looked beautifully evil as they moved across the television screen. The 'Russians' in my classroom were bursting with pride and the questions they posed were painful: Why didn't the Americans stage such a spectacular procession? Wasn't this proof that they were weaker?

The silent majority of pupils became even more silent. Then I heard a voice coming to the rescue. It was mine: the Americans had once had a military parade so magnificent no other could ever come close to it. They therefore needed no repetition.

Then I began describing this parade to end all parades. Among the many wonders I was imagining, and trying to make my classmates imagine, was a cruiser, complete with guns and rockets, sailors and flags, being carried through New York on gigantic trucks.

Children are supposed to be the first to see when the emperor is naked, but for me imperial America was always beautifully dressed. And the things that reminded me of her were beautiful too: the colour light-blue, ice cream, birthday parties, the new swimming pool in my neighbourhood, a tall tree with smooth bark in my yard that I liked to climb.

Such was my belief in American goodness and might that when President Kennedy was shot I was only partly upset. Part of my ten-year-old heart was thrilled because I believed we were about to witness a dramatic turnaround and a happy ending to the story. I knew, after all, that heroes in American movies were immortal— bullets either missed them or injured them only slightly, and even the heaviest punch on their faces never left a mark. So I expected brilliant American doctors to perform miraculous surgery and save the movie-star president.

When it was officially announced an hour later that Kennedy was dead, I was deeply sad. But at school it turned into a big victory for us 'Americans'. Even though a few 'Russians' said it proved America was a wild country, most pupils commiserated with it in its tragedy.

No 'Russian' preserved his identity into adulthood and the reasons for his disenchantment with communism and the Soviet Union need no explaining. America remained popular with many people in Serbia until it helped Croatian forces to expel about a quarter of a million Serbs from Croatia in 1995. Indeed even we 'Americans' lived through the 1990s with the painful impression that the United States had one set of standards for the misdeeds of Serbian forces and another for those of non-Serbian ones. Whatever the truth may be, America bombed Serbia in 1999 and the love was gone for good.

But what were the views of us 'Americans' and 'Russians' towards internal Yugoslav politics when our country began to disintegrate in the late 1980s and then descended into the bloodshed of the 1990s? I would like to be able to say that all of us 'Americans' had grown up to be the kind of liberal opponents of Serbian nationalism any *New York Times* editorial could be proud of, while all 'Russians' became grim supporters of Slobodan Milosovic. But often neither was the case.

On the one hand, childhood 'Russians' were not necessarily power-worshipping Stalinists, but sincere believers in equality, both social and national. And they remained so later in life though, of course, freed from naive faith that communism would bring this about. On the other hand, many 'Americans' did not have deep attachment to democratic values, but were greedy for chunks of American wealth or saw the United States as a global supporter of right-wing, reactionary anti-communism. Throughout Serbian history such anti-communism has always allied itself with policies of Serbian domination over other nations of Yugoslavia. So both 'Russians' and 'Americans' contributed to the government and the opposition, to nationalism and anti-nationalism.

In fact, we boys shared the views and values of our parents, and in our quarrels mostly repeated in a childish and childlike form what we heard at home. My father, Milovan Djilas, for example, spent nine years in jail for his criticism of the rule of the communist bureaucracy, in particular for his book *The New Class* which was published in 1957. Before he became a dissident he had been a government minister himself, second, third or fourth in the party hierarchy to President Tito, depending on whom you ask (he said fourth).

Back in those days American and other Western diplomats in Belgrade showed little interest in human rights and democratic reforms in Yugoslavia. And they strictly avoided contact with dissidents, my father included. Since its conflict with Stalin in 1948 Yugoslavia had been independent from Moscow and the United States considered it wise to be on good terms with Tito. Indeed several American presidents publicly flattered the communist dictator.

Many in the West and especially in the United States now believe that it was a mistake to deny even cautious, limited support to the democratic opposition.With the benefit of hindsight, it seems obvious that Tito's repressive policies (though moderate when compared to Eastern Europe) created conditions for the alliance of conservative communism and radical nationalism that pushed Yugoslavia into the civil war.

In my teens I freed myself from my idolatry of America and began thinking critically about its political life, though, as I have already confessed, with a tiresome avoidance of any exceptional or strong opinions. I remained, however, staunchly anti-Soviet and therefore clearly committed to the American side in the Cold War. Although officially America was not supporting us democrats in Yugoslavia, we felt that we were fighting the same global battle for democracy and against communist one-party rule. In a sense we loved America because we feared the Soviet Union. The land of camps for political prisoners was America's beautician; its crimes and evil intentions made the wrinkles on America's face much less noticeable.

Ultimately, the Soviet Union wisely decided to give up fighting the Cold War. While I think it is wrong to say the United States won, America undoubtedly played a crucial role in the containment and disintegration of communism. But the democratic opposition in Eastern Europe and in the Soviet Union itself had paid a much higher price. So if I now feel a lingering gratitude to America, it is mostly for developing my childhood imagination. Would it not still be a great idea to have trucks carry a huge ship down Fifth Avenue, though this time one without weapons?

Ariel Dorfman
Chile

More than thirty years later, what I remember above all is the blond American brat at the pool in Jahuel. He couldn't have been more than three years old, but he was ruining the calm and wonder of our lazy Chilean afternoon. His *gringa* mother made no attempt to control him. She slept in her bikini, tummy down on a sunbed under a giant eucalyptus, while her son screamed and ran about. My then girlfriend Angelica (she was not yet my wife, so that means this happened before 1966) kept her eyes tight shut in the hope that, somehow, this would reduce the fanfare. As for me, I tried to concentrate on the sunset as it lit up the slopes of the Andes. Angelica had been brought up a few miles from here, in the small town of Santa María, and I had been looking forward to this visit and the promise of a quiet time among the rocks and ridges and scrub highlands of the Valle del Aconcagua, which had blessed her childhood and adolescence. I'd just spent half an hour in the pool, which was fed by a mountain spring and icy cold; I remember thinking that my endurance of this temperature was a sign that I was becoming truly Chilean. When I first arrived in Chile from the States in 1954, as a twelve-year-old unable to speak a word of Spanish whose only desire was to return to the New York from where he had been banished, the fierce chill of the Pacific and southern Chile's equally glacial rivers and lakes struck me as a personal affront. How could I become part of a country which made my body so cold? And yet gradually I had fallen in love with it: evidence that I belonged here came from my new relish for bone-chilling swims.

That may have been the real reason for my annoyance with the kid. If he'd been brown-skinned and yelped in Spanish, I'd probably have forgiven him; who was I to deny him the right to be exasperating in his own land? Instead, he reminded me of who I had been, of my deep and recently forsaken allegiance to the United States and John Wayne, of my ten joyful years in Manhattan, of the Yankee identity which I was trying so hard to repudiate. So I pretended that I didn't understand a word he aimed in my direction and tried to make myself into a monolingual Spanish speaker, a *chileno* whose terrain was being invaded by this foreign spawn. This was the fanatical 1960s. Everything was coloured by politics. The odious American boy and his inconsiderate American mother had taken over this serene Chilean pool as if they owned it. Absurd, perhaps, to think this now, but they symbolized to me the many ways in which the US had dominated Latin America: its ownership of mines and fields and banks and ships, its proconsuls in Mexico and Buenos Aires and Bogotá, its invasions of Nicaragua and Cuba and Guatemala, its training of torturers, its coups in Brazil and Bolivia and Honduras, its barely concealed idea that the only thing Latin Americans understood was a kick in the pants; and also, of course, as for all my generation, the horror of Vietnam. But what was most irritating about Americans—to me, who had been one, who had been just as unconscious and insensitive in my own day—was their blind innocence, their inability to grasp how their intrusive bodies and loud mouths and naive incomprehension grated on the world. Their professed unconcern—'What? Me Worry?'—about what was done in their name seemed to me more outrageous than the deeds themselves.

Does this explain what happened next?

A few feet away from me, the boy teetered at the edge of the pool and then fell in.

May God forgive me—or if there is no God, may my two-year-old American-born granddaughter forgive me when she is old enough to read these words—but I hesitated. It isn't easy now to return to that sliver of time to reconstruct what went through my mind, but how I remember it is that for a couple of seconds I let myself lapse into a murderous passivity. The boy didn't flail out; he sank into the blue, icy water, silently. Just his body sinking slowly and my eyes watching just as slowly. What comes back to me is the pang of indifference I felt at the sight—that it was none of my business, that in some perverse sense the kid had it coming to him, as had his mother. It would have been so easy to let those two seconds stretch into three and then four and then more, it would have been so simple for that coolness to devour the world.

I can't be sure that this is what I felt, because I may be associating later events with what happened that day. The CIA had still to engineer a coup against the democratic government of Chile; Washington had still to arm the Contras in Nicaragua, and train the death squads in El Salvador. Still, my paralysis must have been born of a deep turmoil of grievance and resentment—maybe it was time for them to experience what we experience, maybe they shouldn't presume that when their kids fall in the pool we will rescue them. My anger was on behalf of millions of unfortunate others; it wasn't because my own affluent self had suffered. But that mysteriously made it all the more intense; it was easier to blame the Americans for all the misery that surrounded me than to really do something about it myself.

I plunged in and scooped the boy out, and deposited him sputtering (and screaming again) on the rim of the pool. His mother woke up—there must have been some special urgency in his shrieks—and I was so embarrassed by her gratitude that I forgot to

31

pretend that I didn't speak English. She turned out to be a jazz enthusiast. We'd been to the same Louis Armstrong concert in Santiago, which had been sponsored by the then-suspect US Information Service, though that hadn't stopped me bebopping in a most unChilean way in the aisles. (That is how effortless it was, and still is, to cross over from Yankee-basher to enthralled lover of American culture, a zigzag, back-and-forth path of detestation and adoration that millions of my fellow humans around the world have also been treading for many decades.)

In the years since I've come to realize how comfortable it is to employ anti-Americanism as a way of avoiding the faults and deficiencies of our own societies, even though such self-criticism should not prevent us from assigning blame to Americans when that blame is due, which it often is. The United States has such incommensurate power to do good or evil, and has set itself high standards of freedom and tolerance by which to be measured. But I am wary today, so many years later, of the automatic response of the kind that briefly, as I recall that afternoon, led me to deny our common humanity as that child descended into the cold quiet maelstrom of those waters.

Benoît Duteurtre
France

For several years now French conversation has been invaded by the same expressions for the United States: 'Disneyland', 'Land of Coca-Cola and McDonald's'. So-called intellectuals have denounced 'America's subculture' as the supposed antithesis to Europe's 'exception culturelle'. And now a terrible tragedy striking the city of New York has been enough to trigger a resurgence—after the initial gestures of compassion—of the old leftist line about 'American imperialism', according to which the attacks of 11 September are a logical outcome of US policies.

What worries me about this is certainly not that someone might criticize America, but that a pattern is emerging which is essentially nationalistic: one that entitles France, for instance, as a self-proclaimed bastion of human rights, to pass lofty judgement on Yankee power. It's as if, by adopting this stance, Europe hopes to disguise from itself the fact that it belongs to exactly the same world as America and is mired in identical contradictions: subject to the same economic tyranny and the same social turmoil, yet claiming to uphold all that is right and good.

Paradoxically, the neo-nationalism evident in the current European criticism of America is a nationalism of the left. In the Sixties, progressive movements were bitterly opposed to any shows of patriotism. Since they have come to power—in the media and, to a certain extent, in politics—they no longer hesitate to espouse a kind of national pride. They're not fighting for the French flag but for humanist values which apparently French society alone can defend (even when reality proves the opposite).

So America's aim is to impose its economic system on the whole world? In fact Europe voluntarily chose this system and now in turn imposes it on countries that want to enter the EU. So the violence of American society couldn't be further from Europe's welfare system? Rhetoric aside, over the last thirty years France has allowed the growth of urban ghettos comparable to the worst of the American inner cities. So the European mind rejects the levelling-down effects of American culture? Yet it was a French socialist government that invited and financed the creation of Euro Disney. And besides, one might do well to wonder about the seductive power of American cinema or music, which have such a grip on the contemporary world, whereas European art can seem imprisoned in its cultural pretensions.

I love Paris and New York. I travel regularly between the two cities; but I more often come across New Yorkers able to criticize a certain kind of American horror than Parisians capable of defining a particular French horror: that mixture of a pristine conscience always ready to criticize and an unquestioning acceptance of the need to adapt and modernize. This arrogance strikes me as particularly abhorrent since September 11.

At the same time as expressing their friendship and solidarity, the eternal moralizers (who had shown themselves so indulgent towards totalitarianism in Russia or Cambodia) couldn't find words harsh enough for America. With his mind on self-promotion, President Chirac for his part preached greater understanding between religions and peoples. Ringing through his unconvincing phrases, I heard the inferiority complex of a Europe deprived of its role as a world leader (whose various imperialisms remain the source of many contemporary conflicts) but still quick to judge good and evil, while at the same time seeking to dissassociate itself completely from the power—America—that has replaced it.

'Is the death of a Rwandan any less important than the death of an American?' ask the sceptics, exasperated by the media's compassion. Of course all massacres are atrocities. But for me the collapse of the Twin Towers was more moving than any of the other tragedies of the last decade. Because in my eyes Europe and America are intimately linked by history, by way of life and thought; and because we belong to the same society which we should learn to transform together—rather than maintaining an artificial opposition, on either side of the Atlantic, between the province of power and the province of the mind.

Translated from the French by Will Hobson

Hans Magnus Enzensberger
Germany

The first time I saw an American was in 1945. He sat in a jeep, looking well-fed, confident and even dashing in his freshly pressed uniform, cruising through a landscape of rubble with his left hand lazily hanging out, holding a cigarette. An armada of benign aliens had finally arrived to deliver Germany from its twelve years' nightmare. Overnight the rats had scurried away and hidden in the ruins, and suddenly some of us felt free to do as we liked. Why these liberators had first bombed us and then imposed democracy on a reluctant population was not quite clear to me. A sort of cargo cult developed when CARE parcels, a free press, Benny Goodman records and the first westerns were dropped on us instead of explosives. Fraternization with the enemy, though strictly forbidden, was a popular pastime for bored GIs (witness black children now pushing sixty walking the streets of Munich, broad Bavarian dialect their native tongue).

Only later did it dawn on me that we owed the generous terms of the *pax americana* to the Russians and the beginning of the Cold War. Germany turned into an American protectorate. It was a huge relief and a respite from a long tradition of subservience to authority. For a few decades we lived under the American umbrella, and the place became, as they say, an economic giant while remaining a political dwarf. Only the most hardened Nazi could fail to feel gratitude and admiration for the invaders from outer space.

I spent a lot of time in the capital. Its name was neither Bonn nor Berlin, it was New York. That was where the action was, and like most of my generation, I was under the illusion that it was an easy place to hang out and have some fun—just like home, only less fraught with guilt, more open, full of energy and promise.

It was the Vietnam war which finally shattered this naive and rosy image. More or less reluctantly we had to take leave of the mirage we had embraced so eagerly. Our America was not the real thing, it was a projection in more than one sense: both a road movie and a psychological trick played upon us by our own delusions. The turbulent crowd of '68 lost no time in denouncing their former object of desire. 'USA—SA—SS,' they shouted. 'Imperialism' was their rallying call, the CIA took the place of the Devil, and at the end of the day a few desperadoes on the left went so far as to throw bombs at the very US bases which had protected us from the Soviets.

Even the more level-headed of us began to realize that our friends from overseas had some embarassing habits: a penchant for dictatorships in many parts of the world, a fair supply of double standards, a curious mix of ruthless self-interest and missionary rhetoric, and, at home, a bizarre gun cult and a relish for the death penalty. It took us more than two decades to discover most of these traits. We had only ourselves to blame for our disillusionment.

The silliest outgrowth of German and West European Anti-Americanism had to do with *Kultur*. There were those who minded Coca-Cola more than Pinochet, and fast food more than My Lai. Rock and roll invaded the sugary world of homegrown kitsch, soap operas replaced brain trust programmes, and ads and TV spots were couched in an idiom aping English. A phantom called Americanization stalked Paris, Milan and Berlin.

I confess that it took me quite some time to realize that nothing of the sort was in the offing. Quite the contrary: our little continent actually became more European, and the United States more exotic than ever. Gradually it dawned on me that the better I knew the place, the less familiar it looked. Just because they speak a language rather similar to the one we had listened to during the war, thanks to the BBC, and consume much of the same stuff from the same kind of department stores, it does not follow that we think and feel alike. And I find the strangeness of America a relief, if not a blessing. Different rules and habits, different cities, different beliefs and obsessions. Think of a place where cigarettes are perceived as more of a threat to human health than machine guns, where a casual acquaintance will offer you the use of their apartment with all their belongings included, where almost everyone believes in some god or other and where the outside world, unless it intrudes with bombs, is largely ignored! Surely we cannot pretend to understand such a society entirely. It will always be something else, a world unto itself, a Western Heavenly Empire, a China of our imagination, a place to admire, to be grateful to, and to be baffled by forever.

John Gray
Britain

It's hard to think of a place that's less like the America we think we know than New Orleans. In the monocular vision of many Europeans, America is a nation of death-obsessed puritans, too overworked and too intimidated by risk to savour life's passing pleasures. It is a land of doctrinaires, naively devoted to a stupefying array of world-improving projects and life-changing therapies, where even politicians are judged by how sincere they seem to be, and literature and philosophy are used to inculcate an unyielding optimism about human possibilities. In this common European stereotype, America is a desperately earnest place, where irony and the tragic sense of life are as unfamiliar as the nonchalant pursuit of pleasure.

If so, New Orleans can only be the most extraordinary—and delicious—anomaly. When I began visiting the city in the Eighties, its hedonism and fatalism charmed me at once. It wasn't just the jazz and the recklessly spicy food. What captivated me was that no one took life very seriously. Meals could start late afternoon with cocktails and extend far into the night. Drinking and smoking were done with a passion that left no place for worries about health—or regrets. One evening, eating in a small restaurant I knew well, I was surprised to hear the plaintive tones of Edith Piaf. I asked the owner what she thought of the singer. She replied: 'She regretted far too much.' Her reply expresses an attitude to life that takes its pleasures more seriously than its tragedies, and views high-minded moralizing with a disbelief bordering on disdain. I thought that an admirable stance then, and I do still.

Some will say New Orleans is only a singularity, an extreme case of Southern alienation from the mainstream of American life, but to my mind this is to miss the point. It's not just that the European view of American culture is in many respects the reverse of the truth. After all, how do H. L. Mencken, Ambrose Bierce or Dorothy Parker fit the stereotype of a culture without irony? How does the American genre of film noir tally with an inability to perceive tragedy? Isn't *Moby-Dick* an encounter with nihilism and the limits of intelligibility that's superior to anything produced in Europe—precisely because it's more playful? In fact, as D. H. Lawrence recognized in his marvellous essays on American literature, it's in American writing that one finds the most intrepid exploration of the extremes of human experience. If there is a comparable European literature, it can only be Russian.

There is a larger point, which I think is more important. America is too rich in contradictions for any definition of it to be possible. For every attitude that is supposed to be distinctively American one can find an opposite stance that is no less so. I suppose it's true that the rightwing Christian fundamentalist Pat Robertson is a recognizably American figure. But so are William Burroughs and Camille Paglia. Among philosophers, perhaps there is something identifiably American about William James, the brother of the novelist and the greatest of the Pragmatists. But it was an American philosopher, George Santayana, who produced the most devastating criticism ever made of American Pragmatism. In truth, there is no such thing as an essentially American world view—any more than there is an essentially American landscape. Anyone who thinks otherwise shows they have not grasped the most important fact about America, which is that it is unknowable.

This may seem an esoteric point, but I think it bears directly on America's present condition. Like many others, I have admired the dignity with which Americans have responded to the events of September 11. Perhaps more unusually among Europeans, I have been impressed by the restraint and sobriety with which the US has conducted the war. There may be a case against waging it (though I've yet to hear one I'm at all persuaded by). But if the war must be fought, it had better be by people with cool heads. I don't think anyone can fault American policy on that count.

The familiar stereotypes of America are demonstrably mistaken. Even so, there is a sense in which September 11 has brought about the meltdown of a particular American self-image. Until then, American policies could be based on the belief that history had ended, and with it any threat to peace and prosperity. Free markets were spreading inexorably, and with them American-style democracy. These were absurd notions, and not only because a great many people beyond America's shores didn't share them. They embodied a ridiculously impoverished view of America itself. Devotion to the free market has never been particularly strong in American politics, even on the Right. The idea that it is peculiarly American is belied by American history, in which protectionism and populism have been more enduring traditions, and the power of government has been vigorously used to deal with economic crises. The same is true today, with the Bush administration casually tossing aside the economic orthodoxies of the past.

In the Eighties and Nineties, the cult of the free market succeeded in passing itself off as the one true American faith. Today it belongs in an irrecoverable past. As a side effect of September 11, no one any longer imagines that American values will spread irresistibly across the world. More subtly, and more significantly, few people believe American values can be identified with the narrowly sectarian philosophy that held power over the past couple of decades. Quietly, almost imperceptibly, another America is being born—one as creative, contradictory and indefinable as any that has existed in the past.

Ramachandra Guha
India

At a garden party in Calcutta sometime in the late Fifties, a football kicked by the host's son broke a whisky bottle. Fragments of glass entered the exposed arm of the Consul General of the United States of America, who was taken to the hospital to be stitched up. As he went off, the biologist J. B. S. Haldane broke an embarrassed silence with this comment: 'A little Bengali communist has successfully attacked an American imperialist.'

By the time I moved to Calcutta twenty years later, a communist government had come to power in Bengal. One of its first acts was to name the street on which the US Consulate stood after Ho Chi Minh. Otherwise too the intellectual climate was suffused with hostility to America. Our heroes were Marx and Mao, and, moving on, writers who had taken our side in the Cold War, such as Jean Paul Sartre and Gabriel García Márquez.

I became a member of the local British Council, but would not enter the library of the United States Information Service. Then my wife got a scholarship to Yale, and I reluctantly followed. I reached New Haven on a Friday, and was introduced to the Dean of the School where I was to teach. On Sunday I was taking a walk through the campus when I saw the Dean park his car, take a large carton out of the boot, and carry it across the road to the School and up three flights to his office.

That sight of the boss as his own coolie was a body blow to my anti-Americanism. My father and grandfather had both been heads of Indian research laboratories; any material they took to work or back—even a slim file with a single piece of paper in it—would be placed in the car by one flunkey and carried inside by another. (Doubtless the Warden of an Oxford College can likewise call upon a willing porter.) Over the years, I have often been struck by the dignity of labour in America, by the ease with which high-ranking Americans carry their own loads, fix their own fences, and mow their own lawns. This, it seems to me, is part of a wider absence of caste or class distinctions. Indian intellectuals have tended to downplay these American achievements: the respect for the individual, the remarkable social mobility, the searching scrutiny to which public officials and state agencies are subjected. They see only the imperial power, the exploiter and the bully, the invader of faraway lands and the manipulator of international organizations to serve the interests of the American economy. The Gulf War, as one friend of mine put it, was undertaken 'in defence of the American way of driving'.

On the world stage America is not a pretty sight. Even between its various wars of adventure, its arrogance is on continuous display. The United States has disregarded strictures passed on it by the International Court of Justice, and defaulted on its financial obligations to the United Nations. It has violated the global climate change treaty, and the global biodiversity treaty. It has not signed the agreement to abolish the production of landmines. The only international treaties it signs and honours are those it can both draft and impose on other countries, such as the agreement on Intellectual Property Rights.

The truth about America is that it is at once deeply democratic and instinctively imperialist. This curious coexistence of contrary values is certainly exceptional in the history of the world. Other democratic countries, such as Sweden or Norway at the present time, are not imperialist. Scandinavian countries honour their international obligations, and (unlike the Americans) generously support social welfare programmes in the poorer parts of the world. Other imperialist countries, such as France and Great Britain in the past, were not properly democratic. In the heyday of European expansion men without property and all women did not have the vote. Even after suffrage was extended British governments were run by an oligarchy. The imagination boggles at the thought of a Ken Starr examining the sexual and other peccadilloes of a Benjamin Disraeli.

Historically, anti-Americanism in India was shaped by an aesthetic distaste for America's greatest gift—the making of money. When Jawaharlal Nehru first visited the United States in 1949, as Prime Minister of a free India, he was given a banquet in New York where the host told him: 'Mr Neroo, there are fifty billion dollars sitting around this table...' Naturally, the Brahmin schooled by British socialists was less than impressed.

Within India, the austere socialism of Nehru's day has now been replaced by the swaggering buoyancy of consumer capitalism. In cultural terms, America, rather than Britain, has become the locus of Indian emulation. Politically, too, the countries are closer than ever before. Yet the new enchantment with America—which is perhaps most manifest amongst politically minded Hindus—seems to have as shallow a foundation as the older disgust. Subliminally, but sometimes also on the surface, it is premised on the belief that America and its ally Israel have taken a tough line with the Muslims. (They take no nonsense from the Palestinians, as we should take no nonsense from the Pakistanis.) The prosperous Indian community in America models itself on the Jewish diaspora, whose influence it hopes one day to equal, and even exceed.

The current admiration for the United States has all to do with power. Strategic thinkers in New Delhi have little time for America's experiments with transparency of governance; they ask only that it recognize India as the 'natural' leader of this part of the world—as, in fact, the United States of South Asia. That it already is. Like its new-found political mentor, India is more reliably democratic than the other countries of South Asia; at the same time, it seeks to bully and dominate them. At least in the short term, the prestige attached to the term 'democracy' in the post Cold War (and post September 11) world will make India even more insolent in its dealings with its neighbours. Echoing a famous President of Mexico, King Gyanendra might well say: 'Poor Nepal! So far from God, so near to the Republic of India.'

Lu Gusun
China

Mr G, my collaborator at the University of California at Berkeley, where I was carrying out research and lecturing as a senior Fulbright Scholar between 1984 and '85, invited me to house-sit for him as he was taking his family on vacation. We agreed that I would move in after they had left, picking up the keys from under the doormat.

I duly arrived at his house after dark. The porch light was on so I had no difficulty finding the keys and letting myself in. It was an uneventful night.

When I woke the next morning and stepped on to the porch to survey the view of the distant Bay, the sun was high in the sky, rendering the porch light conspicuously superfluous. 'Waste not, want not': accustomed as I was to my frugal Chinese way of life, I was bothered by this waste of electricity. I looked for a light switch.

I looked in all the places where you'd expect to find a light switch but found none. It was a good couple of minutes before I spotted something incongruous on the whitewashed wall. It was a garishly coloured caricature of Ronald Reagan, the sitting president of the United States. It appeared to have been clipped from some tabloid newspaper and glued to a piece of cardboard for support before being hung on the wall. Grinning foolishly, poor Ronald was completely naked, without a stitch on—not even a G-string!

And then, hidden in his private parts, what should I notice but the switch, pointing skyward as if the President had a king-size hard-on.

From the Staten Island Ferry, September 2001

'O man!' I cried, outraged. Several months earlier Reagan had visited my university in Shanghai, China. He had been my guest. He had come to my class, exchanged pleasantries with me, answered questions from my students and finally autographed the picture his men had taken of him and me together. I knew that the Chinese revere authority and respect friends—sometimes to a fault. I also knew about the radicalized student movement at Berkeley in the Sixties, which had won the university the reputation of being a bastion of free speech. Mr G had been a youthful professor of English at the time, very vocal and visible in his partisan politics. But wasn't a switch in the private parts too uncouth a joke? Or was I 'underdeveloped' in my cultural taste?

Incidentally, Mr G has since become one of the founders of a new literary critical school and is known not only to the two coasts of the United States but also worldwide.

James Hamilton-Paterson
Britain

Since my life encompassed much of the Second World War, as well as the entire Cold War, I grew up with the shibboleths of the democratic West ringing in my ears. Their dire antithesis was totalitarianism: secret police surveillance, the gulag, Big Brother. 'Our' cause, despite Hiroshima, was championed from the moral high ground by the United States and was supposed to be based on secular political principles deriving ultimately from the Enlightenment, rationalism and the French Revolution. This duly sanctified version of democracy, anti-imperialism and free speech has taken some hard knocks these last fifty years. There was always something hysterical about the Vietnam War, just as there has been something equally gross in Washington's installation and support of sundry atrocious regimes around the world—regimes sometimes even worse than anything offered by what Ronald Reagan called 'the Evil Empire', complete with their own gulags. This notorious 'hold-the-nose' strategy said something too bleak and disillusioning for us to ignore: that beneath the rhetorical invocations of freedom and democracy America's foreign policy was as much driven by expediency and ruthless self-interest as anyone else's. The moral high ground turns out to be mostly swamp land. Seen with hindsight by the flickering light of marsh gas, Vietnam now looks to have been more consistent than it was a tragic aberration. Might is right. Onward and upward. It is no accident that it is the American *military* who are planning to be the first to colonize the moon.

Time and again I'm struck by the extraordinary disparity between the United States's global face and the many individual Americans I know and love. Their sophistication, generosity of spirit, intellectual honesty and subversive humour seem wholly at odds with their country's monolithic weight on the world. Why is it, I wonder, their government is never represented by people like themselves? President after president, administration after administration: all embody the ethos of the far right. Can these frightful incumbents of the White House and Foggy Bottom *really* express the median view of the commonsensical American electorate, bearing in mind that in this famous democracy only about fifty per cent bother to vote? Are my friends in some way disenfranchised: part of a vital, intelligent and quintessentially American constituency doomed to be forever unrepresented in their Congress and Senate? And if so, why?

A recent visit to the Philippines—the latest in a series that now stretches back twenty-two years—has as usual prompted me to as many thoughts about the United States as about its former colony. The political system the Philippines inherited from its self-imposed mentor in 1898 now often looks like a parody of Washington, dominated as it is by a relatively hermetic political elite and Tammany Hall malpractices. In both countries it is impossible to accede to any worthwhile elected position without a huge 'war chest' of campaign funds. If it is true that behind every great fortune there lies a great crime, this scarcely augurs well for democracy. You can forget the Founding Fathers' noble ideal of citizens in leather jerkins or dungarees stepping forward to lead the Republic with clear draughts from deep wells of folk wisdom. Certainly in the Philippines the only time a true man of the people has made it to the presidency was in 1998, when the ex-action movie star Joseph Estrada was elected by a landslide so overwhelming that even the traditional expedients of ballot-rigging and intimidation were rendered pointless. It took the snubbed and rancorous elite a scant two years to cut him down by engineering his removal from office on charges of malpractice which, if consistently brought against Philippine presidents, would leave that office almost permanently vacant. Twenty-five years ago the same elite were overwhelmingly content with Ferdinand Marcos, who had taken office with the CIA's help and who remained president for twenty years with the support of five different American presidents mainly because the US needed reliable bases and facilities during the Vietnam War. Keep holding that nose! (I'm beginning to see why my American friends stay clear of politics.)

This last trip I read Mark Twain's radical travelogue *The Innocents Abroad*, in which he began his lifelong task of defining his American identity by chartering a steamer with a party of travellers and sailing to the Mediterranean. To read between his exuberantly irreverent lines, Twain had tired of the Old World's cultural hegemony long before he set foot in it in 1867, irritated by its lofty assumptions of superiority. His own affectation of being a bit of a hick and proud of it—a sort of Missourian Crocodile Dundee at large in Naples rather than New York—is occasionally wearisome. But he is mostly refreshing and clear-sighted about such dread cultural millstones as the Renaissance and the Holy Land. Following the United States's modest appropriation of the entire twentieth century as 'the American century' the rest of the world can now return the compliment and remind itself that America, too, is not immune to a Twainian jaundiced eye. Twain was rightly offended that Europe didn't take America seriously. These days we may find equally offensive the degree to which America remains staunchly ignorant and dismissive of the ninety per cent of the planet that is not the United States. (In this respect the US media mostly play a dismal role. The Evil Empire's citizens were often far better informed about the world than Americans generally are.)

To someone old enough to remember, the ironies abound. Today the Western democracies' forms of social control and surveillance, dominated as they are by US agencies and technology, far exceed Big Brother's wildest dreams. We of the free world are constantly spied on and monitored, always in the name of our own security, and this process can only intensify. Meanwhile, the bogus commonality endlessly invoked by American media phrases such as 'the world community' fits entire nations and cultures for their white (Our Allies) hats or else for the black hats of 'pariah' states. It is the insidious currency of English—a language now spoken with consummate crudeness and imprecision almost everywhere—that bolsters these illusions of shared views. As I appreciate each time I visit the same Philippine hamlet (which is hardly even part of that country's polity, let alone of a 'global village'), cultures *au fond* comprehend practically nothing of one another. Yet it is in increasingly anglocentric, CNN-soundbite terms that countries are internationally 'understood' and, it often seems, in which US foreign policy is made. The hubris is as rank as it is disastrous.

Still, the fatal flaw of arrogance need not be dignified by references to Greek tragedy. It is enough to remember that Twain's trip to Europe was dominated by ruins. America, too, will not last in its present form. In due course, and by means as yet unknown, the United States's global hegemony will go the way of the British, Spanish, Roman and all other empires. Byzantium? Babylon? The one is suing to join the EU, the other is in the grip of Saddam Hussein. Forget the ethical hand-wringing. It's about power, stupid; and power eventually sifts through a nation's grasp like sand.

Michael Ignatieff
Canada

We had come from all over the country to march against Richard Nixon on the day he took his second oath of office on the steps of the Capitol. There might have been a quarter of a million of us, and the March route was sealed off from the rest of Washington by a solid steel wall of buses parked nose to tail. We never got close to Nixon. In the pauses between our chanting, we could hear his inaugural address blaring out over loudspeakers. It pleases me to think, thirty years later, that nobody now remembers a thing he said.

Even then we knew this was the last of the great demonstrations. The pulverization of Cambodia would continue and the carnage on the way to the eventual defeat of America would not be stopped. But we marched anyway, arm in arm or alone with our thoughts, looking at the spire of the Washington Monument or looking down at the marching feet moving through the debris. I, a bourgeois class enemy if there ever was one, marched behind a coven of Trotskyites who were carrying a banner proclaiming WORKER'S REVOLUTION IN BROOKLYN.

The fall of Saigon was three years down the road; the genocide in Cambodia came later. We had no idea what would happen if any of our slogans came true, if the NLF or the Vietcong did win. What happened was that they were massacred, and the North Vietnamese imposed a tyranny over the whole of the south that endures to this day. But I am still glad I was there. It still seems like the right thing to have done.

I'm a Canadian, but it was inevitable that the great cause of my growing up was an American war, not a Canadian wrong. I loved my own country, but I believed in America in a way that Canada never allowed. I was against the war because I thought it betrayed something essential about the country. I marched because I believed in Jefferson and Lincoln.

When the march ended, thousands of us gathered at the Lincoln Memorial, at the feet of Lincoln's statue, sitting there, until darkness and cold drove us away, looking out, like him, with those intense eyes, down the length of the Mall. The words of Lincoln, carved on the walls of the Memorial, were still just legible in the ebbing light:

> That we here highly resolve that these dead shall not have died in vain—that this nation, under God, shall have a new birth of freedom—and that government of the people, by the people, for the people, shall not perish from the earth.

On another wall of the monument, you could just make out the words from Lincoln's Second Inaugural, written as the Civil War advanced to its terrible victory:

> With malice toward none; with charity for all; with firmness in the right, as God gives us to see the right, let us strive on to finish the work we are in.

He was a country lawyer, and the language that was native to him came from *Blackstone's Commentaries on the Laws of England*, Shakespeare's plays and the Old Testament prophets. Out of these elements, forged together in a hundred stump speeches to his fellow citizens, he created American scripture, the prayers the country offers to believe in itself.

The invention of American scripture is not the prerogative of presidents. In 1945, on the battlefield of Iwo Jima, a rabbi from the US Marines buried his marines with these words:

Too much blood has gone into this soil for us to let it die barren. Too much pain and heartache have fertilized the earth on which we stand. We here solemnly swear: it shall not be in vain. Out of this will come, we promise, the birth of a new freedom for the sons of men everywhere.

The rabbi was burying Jews and Christians in the same soil. He was burying blacks and whites who had served in a segregated army. He knew, as Lincoln had known, that if citizens are willing to die together, then their descendants must live in freedom together.

I teach students from twenty countries in my class at Harvard. During this autumn of September 11 I thought they should hear American scripture. I played them the speech that Martin Luther King gave on the steps of the courthouse in Montgomery, Alabama, after he had led his people to the end of the Selma March to secure their rights as American voters:

I know you are asking today, 'How long will it take?' I come to say to you this afternoon: however difficult the moment, however frustrating the hour, it will not be long, because the truth pressed to earth will rise again. How long? Not long, because no lie can live forever. How long? Not long, because you will reap what you sow. How long? Not long, because the arm of the moral universe is long, but it bends toward justice. How long? Not long, cause mine eyes have seen the glory of the coming of the Lord, trampling out the vintage where the grapes of wrath are stored. He has loosed the fateful lightning of his terrible swift sword. His truth is marching on... Be jubilant my feet. Our God is marching on.

The power of American scripture lies in this constant process of democratic reinvention. First a wartime president, then a battlefield rabbi, then a black pastor—all reach into the same treasure house of language, at once sacred and profane, to renew the faith of the only country on earth that believes in itself in this way, the only country whose citizenship is an act of faith, the only country whose promises to itself continue to command the faith of people like me, who are not its citizens.

Ivan Klíma
Czech Republic

I belong to that dwindling number of people who still remember the Second World War. I regard it as a quirk of fate that the very day we were carted off to concentration camp (I was ten at the time), Nazi Germany went to war with the United States. It was paradoxical: in the middle of their despair at what had happened to them, the people around me embraced each other. They believed that with America's entry into the conflict, the decisive moment had arrived and the war would soon be over—Hitler had no hope of victory.

The fighting didn't come to an end as quickly as we imagined, but I well remember during the last year of the war squadrons of Flying Fortresses flying over the town where I was interned. I stood in the barracks yard and watched them with a sense of exalted terror and joy, because their clearly undisturbed flight heralded the German defeat that was now just round the corner.

Unlike my compatriots in West Bohemia, I didn't encounter the Americans as liberators. Terezín camp was liberated by the Red Army, like Prague, to which I then returned.

I loved American war films, although I was less enamoured of the sickly film musicals of the day—they seemed to me to belong to a different world to the one I knew. I later realized that musicals and war films symbolized the two extremes of the Americans' attitude to life.

Soon after the war, all American films disappeared from Czechoslovakia, the war films and the sickly musicals alike—it was the beginning of the communist era. Along with them went books by all modern American authors with the exception of the communist Howard Fast. Nevertheless, in a lane not far from the Botanical Gardens in Prague I came across a sort of stationer's-cum-bookbinder's shop that had remained in private ownership. I used to chat to the owner about literature and one day he declared mysteriously that he had something to show me. From the depths of his shop he brought out two novels: one by Steinbeck, the other by Hemingway. In those days such books were something like contraband. I paid for the two treasures and took them away with me. I was hooked. Later, when censorship was relaxed, I got to read Dos Passos, Faulkner, Wilder, Heller, Mailer, Roth and others. They had a lifelong influence on me. I know that for many people American culture means Hollywood films and endless TV serials. For me American culture means above all its literature, which in the last century was undoubtedly among the most remarkable in the world.

I first visited the US in 1968, to attend the premiere of my play *The Castle*. I recall being overwhelmed by New York, which seemed to me like a city from another planet, from another culture. (That is precisely why I subsequently came to dislike it: it seemed to me that in that enormous agglomeration of concrete and asphalt, people, and particularly children, must either go crazy or suffer deprivation.) A year later I was invited to take up a visiting fellowship at the University of Michigan in Ann Arbor. By then, the Soviet army of occupation was well ensconced in Czechoslovakia. The purges began, rigid censorship was reintroduced and culture was driven underground. I left the day before the frontiers were closed. At that moment I perceived the US chiefly as a land of freedom. (On the bridge I had to cross each day on my way to the faculty, someone had painted an enormous red hammer and sickle—a paradox for someone who had managed to escape the land of communist symbols for a short while.) Something else I'll never forget is how, straight after a TV programme in which President Nixon eloquently defended the Vietnam War, a commentator came on the screen and started to take the president to task in a manner that seemed unbelievable to me. It was all part of the democracy and freedom that I still admire about America.

I have been told many times how superficial Americans' relationships are—shallow because they are simply social convention. In my view this is not true. The Americans mostly live at peace, but the moment an accident or even a disaster occurs, they act. It needn't be a terrorist attack. I once drove off the road into a ditch in a blizzard and got stuck in a snowdrift. It was about twenty degrees below zero and there was such a gale blowing that anyone out in the open would have started to freeze. Nevertheless, within moments a lorry pulled up and the driver ran over to make sure no one in the car was injured and to ask if we needed help. He gave one of my companions a lift to go and arrange for the car to be towed out. The next driver to pass by, a few seconds later, tried to pull us out with a chain. I don't think drivers in our country would behave with such concern and self-sacrifice.

We returned from America six months later when the neo-Stalinist era in Czechoslovakia was at its height. America became the embodiment of freedom for all of us: we received uncensored news from there, and its journalists came and took an interest in our circumstances, and their interest and their reporting about the state of affairs in our country helped inhibit the inclinations of the communist regime to stamp on anyone who resisted them. And from time to time we actually visited the free territory of the American Ambassador's residence. It was a great encouragement to me to know that there existed an entire continent where one could live freely, where they didn't jail people because of their attitude to the regime, where they didn't confiscate books or ban authors and where they didn't expel professors from universities for rejecting a totalitarian (or any other) ideology.

For more than a century now there has existed a sort of American dream. For some it means boundless affluence, for others freedom. I am not a devotee of hypermarkets or of grandiose mansions containing dozens of rooms for just two or three people and a few pedigree dogs and cats. I've never yearned for more than one car or a private plane, jet-engined or otherwise. I have an aversion to profligacy, but I don't share the view that there is an indirect relationship between America's affluence and Third World poverty. Without idealizing the policies of the big monopolies (either American or European), I am convinced that America's wealth, which derives from the work of many generations, is chiefly the result of the creative activity of free citizens. The Americans are not to blame for Third World poverty, which is mostly due to the circumstances in the Third World and the demoralizing lack of freedom that most of the people there endure.

On my visits to the United States over the past ten years, I have discovered that freedom continues to prevail there as it did years ago and there is even greater affluence. That affluence is certainly provocative with the world in the state it is. It would be better if the

Americans—and we Europeans—exercised rather more restraint.

Freedom also tends to be viewed in different ways. For some it represents freedom of spirit and independence from authority, for others it signifies vice and spiritual and moral depravity. Freedom can indeed have paradoxical consequences. One of them is the unbridled cult of entertainment, which increasingly nowadays seems to be the supreme social value: witness the astronomical sums paid to hockey and basketball players, pop singers, and film and TV stars. And the tide of violence, horror and perversion, catering for the basest instincts, which streams every day from the gutter press and from film and television screens seems to me not so much an expression of freedom as a manifestation of moral decline that is ultimately a threat to the freedom of the citizen. In this respect I do not agree with the message of Forman's celebrated film about Larry Flint.

Nevertheless I regard attacks by fanatics on American citizens in New York or anywhere else in the world as being, above all, an attack on the civic freedoms that America embodies and thus an attack on my own freedom too. To view them in any other way ultimately means siding with the reactionary and totalitarian forces which spurn democracy, civil rights, racial and sexual equality and the freedom to live according to one's own convictions and to profess—or not—any belief.

Translated from the Czech by Gerald Turner

Doris Lessing
Britain

Busily promoting my book *African Laughter* I flitted about (as authors do) on the East Coast, doing phone-ins and interviews, and had to conclude that Americans see Africa as something like Long Island, with a single government, situated vaguely south ('The Indian Ocean? What's that?'). In New York I had the heaviest, most ignorant audience of my life, very discouraging, but the day after in Washington 300 of the brightest best-informed people I can remember. To talk about 'America' as if it were a homogenous unity isn't useful, but I hazard the following generalizations.

America, it seems to me, has as little resistance to an idea or a mass emotion as isolated communities have to measles and whooping cough. From outside, it is as if you are watching one violent storm after another sweep across a landscape of extremes. Their Cold War was colder than anywhere else in the West, with the intemperate execution of the Rosenbergs, and grotesqueries of the McCarthy trials. In the Seventies, Black Power, militant feminism, the Weathermen— all flourished. On one of my visits, people could talk of nothing else. Two years later they probably still flourished, but no one mentioned them. 'You know us,' said a friend. 'We have short memories'.

Everything is taken to extremes. We all know this, but the fact is seldom taken into account when we try to understand what is going on. The famous Political Correctness, which began as a sensible examination of language for hidden bias, became hysterical and soon afflicted whole areas of education. Universities have been ruined by it. I was visiting a university town not far from New York when two male academics took me out into the garden, for fear of being overheard, and said they hated what they had to teach, but they had families, and would not get tenure if they didn't toe the line. A few years earlier, in Los Angeles, I found that my novel *The Good Terrorist* was being 'taught'. The teaching consisted of the students scrutinizing it for political incorrectness. This was thought to be a good approach to literature. Unfortunately, strong and inflexible ideas attract the stupid...what am I saying! Britain shows milder symptoms of the same disease, so it is instructive to see where such hysteria may lead if not checked.

The reaction to the events of 11 September—terrible as they were—seems excessive to outsiders, and we have to say this to our American friends, although they have become so touchy, and ready to break off relations with accusations of hard-heartedness. The United States is in the grip of a patriotic fever which reminds me of the Second World War. They seem to themselves as unique, alone, misunderstood, beleaguered, and they see any criticism as treachery.

The judgement 'they had it coming', so angrily resented, is perhaps misunderstood. What people felt was that Americans had at last learned that they are like everyone else, vulnerable to the snakes of Envy and Revenge, to bombs exploding on a street corner (as in Belfast), or in a hotel housing a government (as in Brighton). They say themselves that they have been expelled from their Eden. How strange they should ever have thought they had a right to one.

New York, September 2001

Yang Lian
China

'The full moon's fuller in America.' In China before 1949, this was a way of referring to the much-coveted lifestyle in the 'gilded imperium' on the other shore of the Pacific. After '49, of course, it became a way of satirizing the absurdities of capitalist 'running dogs'. Whatever. It was a powerful image: silvered, shining. And don't forget, in modern Chinese the round 'fullness' of the moon is a perfect pun for the round fullness of a dollar.

In the early 1980s this illusion was shattered for me by an evening meal at a Beijing restaurant. A visiting university professor from America had invited me, then a novice poet, to eat out. As usual the conversation never strayed from the cruelty of the contemporary political situation in China and the hardships of practising 'underground literature'. After we'd finished eating, there were considerable leftovers on the table. 'Do you want to take them home?' asked the professor. 'Sorry? Why would I want to do that?' In China there is no sense that the remains of a meal has any 'surplus value', and no one uses the phrase 'doggie bag'.

'If this were the States, a poet would have no qualms about taking one back home. It's not to feed the dog, you know; it's to feed yourself'.

American poets surely can't be poorer than their Chinese counterparts? That would just be too far beneath the 'American moon'!

After the mid-autumn festival of 1992 I made my first visit to New York as an exile. Standing at the end of a street in Chinatown, I was just getting a sense of the incomprehensibility of fate when the sound of a greeting made me jump. 'Yang Lian!' It turned out to be another Chinese poet, one who had migrated somewhat earlier. In the middle of the usual pleasantries, he said, 'You must stay in New York.'

'Why New York?' I asked.

'Because if you've made it in New York, you've made it in the world.' He looked utterly serious. In the emptiness above the bright lights of the city, the great wheel of the moon, perhaps a little overstuffed, was rising. So this was the 'American moon'. I didn't know whether to be envious or amused.

In this same New York: 'My God. By the end of next month, my bank account will be completely cleared out!' This wasn't the first or last time I'd heard such a cry of despair while talking on the phone with my American poet friend L.S. But here he was describing his circumstances while writing poetry from a flat in Greenwich Village. What was to be done?

'Why don't you come and have dinner here with me? At least you'd save the money for a meal.' I had begun to appreciate the importance of the 'doggie bag'. In America, after all, my novelist wife was obliged to work as a maid to earn a little money, and I was running myself ragged at universities, giving readings here, there and everywhere, no matter how far away, for a couple of hundred dollars a performance. 'Capitalism' was not only a slogan, it was a steely logical network, which held everything in its mesh. We had, in the past, been the happy beneficiaries of the 'socialist rice bowl' while talking up the high principles of 'individuality' and 'identity'. Now we faced up to the concrete realities: putting bread on the table, paying the rent, buying medicine, a glass of beer…the tyranny of money: terrifying and sweet. The oppression of survival made the seductions of 'success' loom ever larger. I forced my translator to create a new form for a word, so that the poems I had written in America could, as a series, be called *Darknesses*, as a sequel to the old saying about the moon, a 'realization' concerning American poets, that they were in dire straits compared with us: here, no one was going to put up money for the love of art, let alone to raise a halo over the head of political opposition. So you want to write poetry? Be prepared to regret it. A dog that could write poetry would dream of 'doggie bags', and in the dream it would see the American moon, but as full and round as a filling meat pie. My father had warned me, 'You know, poets always die in poverty.' I guess the fathers of American poets will be even more intimate with such worries.

Of course American culture means Hollywood, McDonald's, all manner of credit cards, crowds of ravenous consumers, and so on. But for me it means 'doggie-bag art'. And as for those, like me, who cannot even begin to have faith in the doggie bag—who keep on writing, reciting—I suppose they continue to do so for an audience of one: that unchanging moon, hanging at the edge of the sky.

Translated from the Chinese by John Cayley

David Malouf
Australia

One morning early in 1908, some half a million people lined the foreshores of Sydney Harbour to see sixteen battleships of the United States navy steam grandly through the Heads, the Great White Fleet as it is known in our national mythology. Three years earlier, the Japanese had destroyed the Russian navy in the straits at Tsushima. The Great White Fleet was a demonstration—and to Australians, forever anxious about their isolation in the Asian hemisphere, a welcome assurance—that the Pacific, our Pacific, was still a white man's lake.

Thirty-three years later, on a morning in March 1941, my father took me to Newstead Park to see the occasion repeated, on a smaller scale but with something like the same importance: the arrival on the Hamilton Reach of our own Brisbane River of two ships of the American Pacific fleet. I was just seven. I can still recall, after more than sixty years, the quality of the occasion, the clarity and freshness of the morning as it was embodied in the lines of white-uniformed sailors on the decks, the sense I got from the excitement around me of a moment that was 'history'. To appreciate any of that you must understand how isolated Australia was in those days at the end of the Thirties and what it was that a child such as I was understood by 'America'.

America was what I lost myself in at the Lyric Pictures every Saturday afternoon. A world sufficiently like our own as to be entirely familiar, but so unlike, with its skyscrapers, its freeways and flyovers, its limousines, its fast-talking 'babes', its uniformed cabbies and bellboys and gangsters, as to be explicable only as a vision of a more sophisticated and glamorous future that we had not yet caught up with. It was a promise of what our world too would be when the sprawling weatherboard town we lived in, where farmers still sold day-old chicks in laneways off Queen Street in the city and every suburban house had a chook-house at the bottom of the yard, broke free of its subtropical torpor and became part of that exciting Twentieth Century, of which the world up there on the screen was the visible and shining image. Those sailors in their dazzling white uniforms and bucket caps were its forerunners and emissaries. To be in their real rather than their screen presence was to be in direct communion with the world to come.

In fact it came more quickly than any of us could have thought possible. Dawdling home from school a few months later I saw the headlines on the afternoon newsboards, JAPS BOMB PEARL HARBOR, and ran to bring the news to my mother and her bridge ladies. Three weeks after, at New Year, our prime minister, Mr Curtin, made the announcement that was to change our lives forever—or that part of them that is lived in 'history'. 'Without any inhibitions', he told us, 'I make it quite clear that Australia looks towards America, free of any pangs as to our traditional links and kinship with the United Kingdom.' He meant that it was the Americans who would come to save us. As he put it: 'They speak like us, they think like us, and they fight like us.'

Well, there were other ways in which they were *not* like us. Some of them were black. At first our government insisted that we should be saved only by white Americans—we were a white nation. When our saviours objected, we agreed that negroes *could* come, but only if they passed quickly through Sydney and Melbourne, were stationed only in the north, and if censorship was used to ensure that no one actually knew they were there.

We knew. The north was us. Brisbane, a town in those days of fewer than 400,000, became the operational centre of the Pacific campaign; over the next three years some two million Americans were either stationed there or passed through it. The city was segregated. Black Americans were confined to south Brisbane, once an area of grand weatherboard mansions but now a poorer working class and Aboriginal part of town, and armed MPs stood at the entrance to Victoria Bridge to stop them from crossing to the City.

So the Brisbane I grew up in was an Australian city with an American accent. Hershey Bars and Babe Ruths joined Cherry Ripe and Hoadley's Violet Crumble Bars as our favourite lollies. General MacArthur and Mrs MacArthur and their little boy became our resident royalty. The older sisters of our schoolfriends developed American boyfriends, 'escorts'. Couples jitterbugged nightly at the Palm Grove and Cloudland and the Troc on the south side. Rough kids showed us American brands of 'frenchies'—Trojans, 'as thin as a shadow, as strong as an ox'. We learned to do American accents, played around with American personas and American slang.

The influence persisted. Sixty years later, Brisbane has the look of the middle-sized American metropolis we took from our afternoons at the Lyric and projected on to the unlikely reality of two-storeyed verandaed pubs and riverside woolstores and warehouses. Skyscrapers. Flyovers. Uniformed cabbies. Bellboys. Even gangsters. Done!

Australia, settled twelve years after the American Revolution, is a product of the Enlightenment, the English and Scottish Enlightenment. The American example was from the start a marker of what it was and was not to be. It was precisely to avoid the American experience that Australia was founded on the labour of convicts rather than slaves, and the White Australia Policy always had America in mind in its determination to protect Australian workers against cheap immigrant labour.

Australia arrived late on the scene. Its English was not the seventeenth-century English of the United States, with its roots in Evangelical dissent and the revolutionary idealism of the Quakers and the Diggers and the Levellers. It was the sober, serviceable language fashioned by writers like Addison and Steele and others to purge English of the violent and extreme expression, and political and sectarian hostilities, that had led to the Civil War. Young men would no longer go up to London, as Ben Jonson's Kastril does, 'to learn to quarrel', but to learn to be 'polite'. This was the language Australia inherited. The language of reasonable argument. Of balance. Of compromise. We may envy Americans the line of evangelical idealism that runs, say, from Jonathan Edwards to Jefferson, Emerson, Whitman and on to Martin Luther King, but we are not seduced by it. It is not our style. Idealism can also be murderous, and in the case of the United States, sometimes has been. The folds of eloquence can be a cover for intentions that are not at all idealistic.

We are ambivalent about 'America'—but isn't that so with all of us, even a good many Americans?—according to what 'America' most immediately suggests to us: The United Fruit Company, McCarthyism, Vietnam, the CIA subversion of Allende, the tanks at Waco; or the words of the Declaration and Lincoln's address at Gettysburg, the Marshall Plan, the Civil Rights Movement, our own delivery from European Fascism, Communism or the Japanese.

'America' is a phenomenon large enough to contain contradictions, also large; to contain in the sense of holding them in tension as a necessary element in the sort of society it sets out to be and the extraordinary energy it produces: that world of possibility and inventiveness and elan that is in the cultural richness of American cities, Chicago or LA or New York, the excellence of American universities and research institutions, the generosity of American foundations, and in the many glories, early and late, of jazz and popular music, the movies, American painting, architecture, poetry. Our recognition of the way these things have coloured our lives and changed us is also part of the story.

Fintan O'Toole
Ireland

Leafing through Charles Hepworth Holland's *Geology of Ireland*, I discover that North America starts somewhere on a line between Dingle and Newry. Four hundred million years ago, Ireland lay at the point where the part of the earth's crust on which North America now sits was sliding underneath the part that supports Europe. Bits of the two continents were pushed together somewhere around the middle of Ireland. In the south and east, the underlying rock belongs to Europe. But if you stand in the north or west of the island, the ground beneath your feet belongs to the North American Plate. In this, tectonics gives a more accurate sense of the world I grew up in than politics or history.

In 1963, when I was five, President John F. Kennedy came to Ireland. I remember a new colour coming into our field of vision: a gorgeous man's irridescent tan radiating out from an open-topped car. I remember too seeing him on television in County Wexford, where his people and my grandfather came from. Kennedy told a joke to the adoring locals. A New Ross man emigrates to the States. He is doing all right, but not as well the myth of American abundance requires. So he takes a trip to Washington, and stands in front of the White House. He gets a passer-by to take a picture of him. When the folks back home turn the photograph over they find the words: 'This is our summer house. Come and see it.'

The joke was masterfully judged. It flattered the teller, of course, reminding us of how much better he had done than most of our uncles, aunts and cousins who had made the same voyage. The White House really was his house. It acknowledged the depth of our gullibility and the height of our fantasies about America without breaking the spell of God's Own Country. The joker was, after all, an Irish Catholic who became president—apparently tangible proof that the dream could come true. And it reflected a keen understanding of the way America shone most directly into our lives. The sitcoms and thrillers, the movies and the music, created the magic. But the intimate grip was exerted by the family photographs from Springfield Massachusetts, Hackensack, New Jersey, Portland, Maine. This is our car. This is our ice-box. This is our porch. This is our pool. That the images might, as Kennedy slyly acknowledged, be illusions, merely added to their allure.

Did he know what he was doing, telling this story to us? Did he know that the photographs of his visit, packaged in the special newspaper supplements we kept for years, would be like the photograph in his joke: a message to ourselves back home in our dreary lives, to pretend to ourselves that we were doing well? Did he know that the unwritten words on the backs of those photographs of our faces in the crowds, beaming at him in beatific bliss, pressing towards him as towards a messiah, were 'This is my cousin. He came to see me'? Was he savouring the secret triumph of his power, that he was inside the White House, while we, poor Paddys, were standing outside the railings concocting false images to hide our failures?

Looking back on those souvenir brochures, I am struck by the utterly unabashed rapture with which Kennedy was greeted, even by the famously stern old revolutionary who was still our president. Eamon de Valera, a man who had made a career as a nationalist hero out of addressing foreign leaders from a lofty height of righteousness, spoke to him with the awed obsequiousness of a priest addressing God from the altar.

He hailed the much younger Kennedy like the chief of a remote tribe who has just been presented with a looking-glass and a necklace of cheap beads by a captain of the Royal Navy who is all the while eyeing his island for signs of removable wealth. He greeted Kennedy, not as President of America, but as 'the first citizen of the great republic of the West, upon whose enlightened, wise and firm leadership hangs the hope of the world'. The great republic of the West—the great white kingdom beyond the sea whose leader offers the natives fatherly protection and in return asks only for breadfruit.

Had it been *Mutiny on the Bounty*, Kennedy would then have been offered a tribal dance and a choice of the plumpest virgins. Knowing what we now know, we can be sure he would have taken the lot.

The aftermath of such intoxicated expressions of desire is usually self-contempt. I sometimes think that much of the public life of my country since 1963 has been an attempt to fill the hole in our self-image that Kennedy's visit had exposed. We were supposed to be a deeply spiritual people, concerned with God, the land and the nation. The ecstasy evoked by the appearance among us of the first citizen of the great republic of the West revealed to us how utterly bedazzled we were by all the things we were not meant to want: his cool, sexy, glamour, his impregnable aura of wealth and his ability to embody the fridges and TVs, the porches and pools that our American cousins conjured up in those family photographs. We were embarrassed by our sudden, naked impulse to worship the golden calf.

It helped, for a while, that JFK was shot a few months later. The unfolding of the Kennedy tragedy with Bobby's murder five years after that allowed us to haul the shameful desires back into the confines of the old religion. I remember my grandfather's bedroom in our council house in Dublin, with its mass-manufactured triptych on the wall: JFK, Bobby and Pope John the twenty-third, the three Catholic saints of 1960s modernity. But even this veneration could not forever keep at bay the knowledge that we had disgraced ourselves by being so gormlessly awestruck in our adoration of America.

In the end, the only force big enough to fill the hole that had been exposed was America itself. We brought America down to size by becoming America. We made ourselves sexy and cool. We got tans. We got porches. We built Nevada-style ranch houses in Connemara. Some of us got pools, though the weather being what it is, they soon succumbed to dank weeds and wind-blown detritus. We went to work making Viagra in Cork and microchips in Maynooth. We got so used to living an American life that it ceased to be such a big deal.

When I went to live in New York for a while in the late 1990s, I was slightly disappointed by how much like home it felt. We had broken America's tantalizing spell by turning it into our own, living it out day by day. We are no longer tormented by the illusion, because it is, for us, no longer an illusion but our mundane reality. And if we sometimes feel the tectonic plates shifting beneath us and wonder where we are, it is simply because America is now the ground on which we now stand.

Orhan Pamuk
Turkey

My first encounters with Americans took place in an atmosphere of childhood simplicity yet bore traces of complex desires and envy that later developed in me.

In 1961 my father's job took us to Ankara, where we lived in an expensive apartment, across from the nicest park in the city, which had a man-made pond in whose waters swam two weary swans. Sometimes we heard our upstairs neighbours moving about. They were Americans—their blue Chevrolet was parked in the garage. We were curious about them.

We weren't curious about American culture. We didn't know or care whether the films we saw at the Ankara cinema, packed with children each week for the Sunday discount matinee, were American or French. It was enough that the films, speaking through subtitles, came to us from the West.

What we were curious about was the Americans themselves. At that time, in this new and relatively affluent part of Ankara, there were a lot of Americans and we found them interesting for what they carried, and what they threw away. The most interesting American thing that we collected, pulled out of rubbish bins, or smashed flat with an angry stomp, were empty Coca-Cola cans. We called all such tins 'kukas', although sometimes they'd be empty beer tins or cans left over from different soft drinks. Even though we played games with the cans—most often what was called 'kuka hide-and-seek'— even though we cut them up and made metal signs out of them, even though we used their tabs as play money, I had never tasted Coke or any other canned drink.

We often hunted for 'kukas' in a large dustbin belonging to one of the new apartment buildings. In this building there lived a young American woman whose beauty was renowned. One day, in a gesture we had seen only in films, her husband pulled out of their garage, interrupting our football match as he slowly drove by, and kissed the tips of his fingers, sending a kiss to the beautiful woman wearing a nightgown and waving her hand on the balcony. We were overcome with silence. No matter how much love the adults we knew shared, they never revealed their happiness and privacy in front of others with such ease.

The things that the Americans owned, which often passed to those who befriended them, were purchased from a large shop I'd never seen—it was forbidden to Turks—'P/X', which we referred to as 'Piyeks.' Things like blue jeans, Chicklets, Converse All-Stars, the latest American albums, nauseating sweet and salty candies, coloured hairslides, baby food, toys. Many of these items were 'smuggled' out of Piyeks and sold under the counter in certain Ankara shops at exorbitant prices. My older brother and I were mad about marbles, and we would save up and buy American marbles from one of these shops. They were made of white porcelain and we treated them like jewels beside our own Turkish mica and glass ones.

We discovered that the son of our upstairs neighbour, who went to school each day in a big orange school bus, like the ones I would later see in American films, had a stock of these porcelain marbles. He was a lonely boy, with no friends. He was about our age, with his hair cut in the American style, short and standing up straight on top. He must have seen us playing marbles with our friends in the yard; at any rate, he'd bought himself many, many marbles from Piyeks. It seemed like he had thousands. He'd empty them all out of a bag at once and the dizzying sound of hundreds of marbles hitting the floor above us drove my brother and me crazy.

Soon, news of this abundance spread to our friends. Two or three of them took to standing in our backyard and calling up to the window of the American, 'Hey, boy!' After a long period of calling and waiting, he'd suddenly appear on his balcony and angrily toss a handful of marbles down to those waiting below. He'd watch them grab and scuffle for the marbles, then disappear again. He was a cross and lonely king tossing gold pieces to the masses! Sometimes he didn't come out for an entire day; then the news that the king's bus had brought him back from school or that his parents had gone out and left him alone would quickly spread. Once a crowd had assembled, he would begin dropping marbles, not by the handful, but one by one, and my friends would run about the backyard and push each other as they picked them up.

One afternoon, the king began to toss marbles down to our balcony. They fell like hard rain, some of them bouncing off our balcony and on to the ground below. My brother and I couldn't stop ourselves. We rushed out to our balcony and started picking them up. When the downpour intensified, our scramble got rougher.

'What's going on here?' said my mother, coming to the balcony door. 'Get inside—now!'

We shut the balcony door and from inside watched the continuing rain of marbles with embarrassment and sorrow. Then the rain slackened and stopped. The king had understood that we couldn't go out on the balcony. He started pouring marbles on to the floor of his room instead. The sound excited us again. As soon as no one was around, we guiltily collected the marbles from the balcony and sombrely divided them between us.

The following day, heeding our mother's instructions, we called up to the king when he appeared on his balcony: 'Hey, boy, do you want to exchange?' We held up our own glass and mica marbles. Five minutes later he rang our doorbell. We gave him five or ten Turkish marbles and he extended a handful of his expensive American ones. We traded in silence. He told us his name and we told us ours.

More than the profitable trade, we were struck by the fact that his name was Bobby, that his squinty eyes were blue and that his knees, like ours, were dirty from playing. Then he ran back up the stairs to his own apartment.

Harold Pinter
Britain

On September 10, 2001 I received an honorary degree at the University of Florence. I made a speech in which I referred to the term 'humanitarian intervention'—the term used by NATO to justify its bombing of Serbia in 1999.

I said the following: On May 7, 1999 NATO aircraft bombed the marketplace of the southern city of Nis, killing thirty-three civilians and injuring many more. It was, according to NATO, a 'mistake'.

The bombing of Nis was no 'mistake'. General Wesley K. Clark declared, as the NATO bombing began: 'We are going to systematically and progressively attack, disrupt, degrade, devastate and ultimately—unless President Milosovic complies with the demands of the international community—destroy these forces and their facilities and support.' Milosovic's 'forces', as we know, included television stations, schools, hospitals, theatres, old people's homes—and the marketplace in Nis. It was in fact a fundamental feature of NATO policy to terrorize the civilian population.

The bombing of Nis, far from being a 'mistake', was in fact an act of murder. It stemmed from a 'war' which was in itself illegal, a bandit act, waged outside all recognized parameters of International Law, in defiance of the United Nations, even contravening NATO's own charter. But the actions taken, we are told, were taken in pursuance of a policy of 'humanitarian intervention' and the civilian deaths were described as 'collateral damage'.

'Humanitarian intervention' is a comparatively new concept. But President George W. Bush is also following in the great American presidential tradition by referring to 'freedom-loving people' (I must say I would be fascinated to meet a 'freedom-hating people'). President Bush possesses quite a few 'freedom-loving' people himself—not only in his own Texas prisons but throughout the whole of the United States, in what can accurately be described as a vast gulag—two million prisoners in fact—a remarkable proportion of them black. Rape of young prisoners, both male and female, is commonplace. So is the use of weapons of torture as defined by Amnesty International—stun guns, stun belts, restraint chairs. Prison is a great industry in the United States—just behind pornography when it comes to profits.

There have been and remain considerable sections of mankind for whom the mere articulation of the word 'freedom' has resulted in torture and death. I'm referring to the hundreds upon hundreds of thousands of people throughout Guatemala, El Salvador, Turkey, Israel, Haiti, Brazil, Greece, Uruguay, East Timor, Nicaragua, South Korea, Argentina, Chile, the Philippines and Indonesia, for example, killed in all cases by forces inspired and subsidized by the United States. Why did they die? They died because to one degree or another they dared to question the status quo, the endless plateau of poverty, disease, degradation and oppression which is their birthright. On behalf of the dead, we must regard the breathtaking discrepancy between US government language and US government action with the absolute contempt it merits.

The United States has in fact—since the end of the Second World

What We Think of America

War—pursued a brilliant, even witty, strategy. It has exercised a sustained, systematic, remorseless and quite clinical manipulation of power worldwide, while masquerading as a force for universal good. But at least now—it can be said—the US has come out of its closet. The smile is still there of course (all US presidents have always had wonderful smiles) but the posture is infinitely more naked and more blatant than it has ever been. The Bush administration, as we all know, has rejected the Kyoto agreement, has refused to sign an agreement which would regulate the trade of small arms, has distanced itself from the Anti-Ballistic Missile Treaty, the Comprehensive Nuclear-Test-Ban Treaty and the Biological Weapons Convention. In relation to the latter the US made it quite clear that it would agree to the banning of biological weapons as long as there was no inspection of any biological weapons factory on American soil. The US has also refused to ratify the proposed International Criminal Court of Justice. It is bringing into operation the American Service Members Protection Act which will permit the authorization of military force to free any American soldier taken into International Criminal Court custody. In other words they really will 'Send in the Marines'.

Arrogant, indifferent, contemptuous of International Law, both dismissive and manipulative of the United Nations: this is now the most dangerous power the world has ever known—the authentic 'rogue state', but a 'rogue state' of colossal military and economic might. And Europe—especially the United Kingdom—is both compliant and complicit, or as Cassius in Julius Caesar put it: we 'peep about to find ourselves dishonourable graves'.

There is, however, as we have seen, a profound revulsion and disgust with the manifestations of US power and global capitalism which is growing throughout the world and becoming a formidable force in its own right. I believe a central inspiration for this force has been the actions and indeed the philosophical stance of the Zapatistas in Mexico. The Zapatistas say (as I understand it): 'Do not try to define us. We define ourselves. We will not be what you want us to be. We will not accept the destiny you have chosen for us. We will not accept your terms. We will not abide by your rules. The only way you can eliminate us is to destroy us and you cannot destroy us. We are free.'

These remarks seem to me even more valid now than when I made them on September 10. The 'rogue state' has—without thought, without pause for reflection, without a moment of doubt, let alone shame—confirmed that it is a fully-fledged, award-winning, gold-plated monster. It has effectively declared war on the world. It knows only one language—bombs and death. 'And still they smiled and still the horror grew.'

Karim Raslan
Malaysia

When I was six years old television—*Lassie, Hi Chaparral* and *The Monkees*—was launched in Malaysia. It happened on the same day that a wooden crate containing the twenty-three volumes of the *Encyclopaedia Britannica* was deposited outside our house in Kuala Lumpur. Or maybe I'm mistaken? No one in the family can remember now. But whatever the case, TV shows like *Bewitched* with Elizabeth Montgomery wrinkling her nose in order to cast her spells and the fat burgundy-coloured volumes were America for me: light, frivolous and deliciously silly on the one hand, sublime and serious on the other.

Thirty-two years after the encyclopedia's unexpected arrival and sitting in here in an airless New York room, I have begun to realize how those unprepossessing books helped to shape the way I see the world, think and write. They started it. They made me question. They gave me a deep commitment to the power of rational thought, and an equally profound scepticism of the revelatory and of established authority (both secular and divine).

As the forces of Islamic conservatism gather strength and move to silence the singers, the poets and the writers there are times when I wish I'd never opened the wretched books and never known words like inquiry, doubt and enlightenment. But it is too late to relive the past—too late to change what we have done. What we have learned we cannot now unlearn.

At night, back then, the entire household, including the servants, would gather around the small flickering black-and-white television in my father's library. With the lights dimmed and bowls of crispy deep-fried salted anchovies smeared in chilli paste and stacks of prawn crackers to sustain us, we'd watch the evening's transmission. *The Man from U.N.C.L.E., Daktari*, reruns of *I Love Lucy*—anything at all—we weren't discriminating. The adults laughed at Barbara Eden's harem pants in *I Dream of Jeannie* and sighed whenever the film detective Charlie Chan said, 'This is Number One Son.'

While everyone was concentrating on the television I would move towards the bookshelves. I had developed a special game that only I could play. Quietly, with my eyes closed, I would take down one of the volumes of the encyclopedia. Opening the leather covers, I'd try and guess what I'd find: would it be Napoleon, Alliterative, Zug, Maharashtra or Ethiopia? Having found the subject, whatever it was, I'd read the entry, quickly, before my absence was noted.

What was it or who was it? Madach, Imre: Hungarian poet (1823–64). What did he do? He wrote *The Tragedy of Man*. Then I'd search for photographs—hoping to find ones I'd never seen before. I loved gazing at the images of other countries: Balinese dancers, homes in California, steel mills in Siberia, Thai temples and the Great Wall of China. Having satisfied my curiosity I'd return the volume to the shelves and start again, repeating the game.

The arrival of the crate containing the *Encyclopaedia Britannica* coincided with extraordinary and unsettling events. Neil Armstrong landed on the moon. In Malaysia, there were race riots between the Muslim Malays and the Chinese, following a hotly contested general election. Nineteen sixty-nine was an evil year for the country.

Unsurprisingly, though not disappointingly for my brothers and me, the schools were closed. We were confined to the house, where we grew extremely bored. Because we lived on the outskirts of the city in a hilly, wooded enclave, we had little real sense of what was taking place elsewhere in the country except when visitors turned up with stories of brutal killings and revenge attacks—stories that our parents tried their best to keep from us. The new encyclopedia was a welcome distraction from all the hushed and anxious conversations and I buried myself in its pages.

I found the name perplexing—Britannica but not British? No, my mother explained, definitely not British (although it had been once). Later I wondered how I could ever have made such a mistake. There was no way that something as vast and comprehensive and all-encompassing as the encyclopedia could have come from England, my mother's home. England was just too tired. It was small, quaint and tradition-bound. Houses were two-up, two-down: pinched and narrow. As far as I could tell from my father's library, the British had particular preoccupations: antiques, stately homes and Winston Churchill. America was different.

With so much time on my hands and no school, I spent the days poring over the pictures, maps and diagrams. The encyclopedia was interesting about anything and everything: temples in Thailand, dams in Egypt, coffee in Brazil, reproductive systems, nuclear fusion, steel production in Sverdlovsk as well as Sartre, Camus, and Jackson Pollock's squiggly paintings. I was amazed by their ambition and magnificence.

But I would be lying if I said that all the images were uniformly positive. There was one photograph from the encyclopedia that always left me with a sense of foreboding. It was a picture that showed a young mixed-race family sitting on the veranda of their 'spacious' Congolese bungalow in Leopoldville. The angular lines of the house and blinding whiteness of the sunlight reminded me of our home and Malaysia.

The father was African and a professional. From the way he held his head, erect and confident, I suspected that he might be a banker like my father. There was a small chocolate-coloured boy sitting by the European woman. They looked to all intents and purposes no different from us. They were modern, they were educated and they were prepared for the future. However, I knew the image was false. Malaysian troops had served in the UN peacekeeping mission and everyone had an uncle or cousin who'd been in Central Africa, who'd returned with stories. Congolese society had collapsed. Their lives had not fulfilled the promise held out by the encyclopedia. Something dark and evil had reclaimed their world.

Raja Shehadeh
Palestine
Ever since I was a child I have been losing friends and relatives to America. I remember one summer afternoon sitting on a green wicker chair, which had first to be cleared of dry pine needles, in the garden of the Ramallah Grand Hotel. Trees rustled in the breeze. I was just ten years old. My friend, Issa Mitri and I had been allowed to join a group of older guys who were saying farewell to Issa's brother. He was leaving the next day for the US, the first member of his family to emigrate.

What We Think of America

I had not heard that word before. Did it mean he would never come back? Issa solemnly confirmed that this was so. He was more proud than sad. I looked at his brother Elias, a tall, slightly stooped young man with a shy face. He didn't look particularly happy. I could not understand why. Travelling to America was to me then like going to heaven. I could not understand why he was not utterly blissful.

A few years later Issa left Ramallah to finish high school in America. This was soon after the 1967 war and Israel's occupation of the West Bank, and the Mitri family had decided he would be safer there. His mother went with him to keep house. His father, who reported for *Newsweek*, remained alone for a few months and then decided to pack his bags. I remember seeing him before he left and asking him if he was happy to be leaving. There was rancour in his voice as he told me: 'I have long been dreaming of the time when I would no longer have to follow your father around to get his comments on the situation.' My father was a political maverick. A few days after the war he had called for a peaceful resolution of the conflict based on the partition of the land into two states, Israel and Palestine, the Palestinian state to be created in the areas occupied by Israel in 1967. That was then a novel proposal, and it earned him few friends among Palestinians or Israelis.

There are tens of thousands of Ramallah people, like the Mitris, who have settled permanently in America. The few who come back for brief summer visits parade up and down Main Street in their Bermudas and baseball hats, stopping at the ice cream parlour to reminisce with its proprietor in an old accent that you hardly ever hear in Ramallah today. The migration has been going on since the end of the nineteenth century; today there are more Ramallah people in the US than in Ramallah. Before 1967 that was how most Palestinians related to America—via the good things about the country that they heard from their migrant friends and relations. After 1967, America entered our life in a different way.

After Israel occupied the Palestinian territories, it began almost immediately to claim large areas of land surrounding our towns and villages for the building of Jewish settlements. This was an expensive enterprise. Without American largesse, both official and private, this massive assault on our countryside would not have been possible.

When the British ruled Palestine during the Mandate period, they didn't expropriate Arab land to build Jewish settlements. They fulfilled the terms of the mandate that called for the creation of a national home for the Jews in Palestine in other less provocative and costly ways. The roads they built were cheap. They followed the contours of the hills. And they were still used well after the Mandate ended in May 1948. In the early Eighties, when I accompanied my father, whose driving was as perilous as his politics, to the court in Nablus I would hear him curse the British as he took the turns so abruptly that my stomach jumped. 'Instead of cutting through in a straight line they had to go around every damn hill,' he would complain. He had just returned from his first trip to the US and was captivated by the American spirit. He believed the Middle East should follow the American example and open up its borders for immigration. The influx of new blood would rid us of our interminable squabbles. How he proposed to convince Israel to abandon its dream of Jewish purity I never knew. In any case, I had no time to ask; it was only a passing fancy.

My father began his legal practice in Jaffa in 1935 when Palestine was still undivided. By the time I began to practise law, the West Bank was under Israeli occupation. On my way to courts in different parts of the country, I could see heavy Israeli machinery flattening the tops of hills. Many of the settlers were enthusiastic American Jews who dreamed of being pioneers. They used the tactics of colonizers everywhere: surveying, mapping, developing spurious legal arguments to justify their plunder, and terrorizing local Palestinians who stood in their way. 'Transfer' was the euphemism used by the Israeli parties which advocated ethnic cleansing. To many Palestinians it appeared that American money funded this settlement project just as America's pioneering history vindicated it.

Within a few years Israeli settlements came to dominate the Palestinian landscape. Next came the need for new roads to connect them to Israel; not the old British-style meandering roads but American-style straight four-lane highways that cut through the hills that stood in the way. Palestine is tiny and its countryside precious, yet by 1984 Israeli planners had developed a fully fledged road plan which superimposed on the old north–south road grid a scheme of east–west highways that would cut in half the commuting time between the West Bank's new dormitory settlements and the centre of Israel. The plan needed billions of America dollars to implement. Funding was again no problem.

In the context of the Middle East conflict, roads may seem a small thing, but they have done a kind of spiritual damage. Gone is that attractive stretch of serpentine road that meandered downhill into the lower wadi that led into Nablus, an ancient city cupped between the mountains of Ebal and Gerizim. Gone are the gorgeous, dramatic views. Now the expensive new highway cuts through the hill and all you can see as you drive is a cutting.

But American assistance did not stop at the funding of ideologically motivated programmes. Last July my cousin was at a wedding reception in a hotel on the southern outskirts of Ramallah when an F16 fighter jet dropped a hundred-pound bomb on a nearby building. Everything had been quiet. There had not been any warning of an imminent air attack. The young couple were exchanging rings. The wedding cake was about to be served. When the missile zoomed over the hotel, the aluminium frames of the large French windows were torn asunder, all the glass shattered, the powerful security doors burst out of their frames. The wedding cake became encrusted with glass and the guests along with the waiters all hit the floor. The target, an old house next to the hotel where the reception was being held, was obliterated. You could not tell that a house had ever stood on that land. Something happened to my cousin that evening. He felt he had been through the worst. He felt he had died and was surprised afterwards to find he was still alive. He was also emboldened. Fear had been wrested out of him. He did not hate America. He studied there. On his last trip to New York he had visited the Twin Towers in New York. He fully appreciated the immensity of the tragedy. When the bombing took place he was worried about his brother who often takes the Boston–Los Angeles flight in the course of his work. Yet when I asked him what he thought of the country he indicated that he dismissed it as a lackey of Israel, giving it unlimited military assistance and never censoring its use of US weaponry against innocent civilians.

Most Americans may never know why my cousin turned his back on their country. But in America the parts are larger than the whole. It is still possible that the optimism, energy and opposition of Americans in their diversity may yet turn the tide and make America listen.

Tara Bray Smith
Hawaii

In the early evening of September 10, just before sunset, I boarded a red-eye bound from Honolulu, my childhood home, to New York City, the place where I live today. I say 'place where I live today' because I've always had a problem calling anywhere besides Hawaii my home. Hawaii is where I was born; it's where my family lives, where my ancestors are buried, five generations back. Though I've now lived here almost as long as I once lived there (I'm thirty-one, I left when I was seventeen), I still carry a Hawaii driver's licence. It's white; a rainbow stretches across it. The computer-generated photo floating above the spectrum makes me look too tan, as if I'd just come up from the beach. The whole thing is so aggressively cheery it actually makes ticket agents laugh.

HNL–NYC: a trip members of my family have made many times before. Fleeing the plantation, they steamed to New York, not London or Paris. New York was our centre, our empire. Bright, independent women—always with a vaguely sapphic air about them—came to New York to make something of themselves.

They were great-aunts and great-great-aunts. Each floated about in her earnest, unmarried way, never leaving a family behind, never rooting herself in the city. Still, New York, and more specifically, Manhattan, probably seemed—as it seems to me now—like a kind of home. There are superficial similarities, of course: both are islands (New York's peaks and valleys a concrete version of Hawaii's eroded volcanic silhouettes); both breathtaking (the length of the city as seen from the FDR, glittering at night); both solipsistic, in the way only islands can be. But there's something more. New York reminded us of how we felt as *haole*—foreigners, white people—in Hawaii. Not so much in that we belonged, but in knowing that we never would. No one does. Belonging is a fiction easier to maintain, somehow, in the bulwark of the continental United States. In Hawaii, as in New York, everyone is an outsider, except maybe the Hawaiians themselves, and even they came from Tahiti.

It's what makes New York familiar, even lovable. On September 10 I was looking forward to returning. My flight, nearly direct, was set to arrive into LaGuardia at 10.49 the next morning. We landed, instead, in Detroit.

A deepening blue sky, and a setting sun, its sinking quickened by the fact that we are heading east. It's funny: when you're up in the air, questions of belonging seem much less confusing than on the ground. Places are just shapes strung together; you're too high to see any people. As the plane ascended over the blank Pacific that evening, the last thing I saw was a many-fingered turquoise blob, studded with grey, otherwise known as Pearl Harbor.

Rung round and pocked through with the once ominous, now strangely reassuring grey shapes of the US's Pacific industrial–military complex (turned to artists' studios and rollerblade paths in de-fortressed places like San Francisco and Seattle, still robustly defensive in Central Oahu, the centre of USPACOM, the US Pacific Command which orchestrates America's military movements over half the globe), Pearl Harbor in no way resembles a pearl, even from a distance, though in its 1,500 years of human history it did manage to cough up a few. Long known to Hawaiians for its supply of oysters, the estuarial river called Wai Momi, 'Water of Pearl', led into a reef-bound series of lagoons and inlets that, once dredged, would become modern-day Pearl Harbor. Within two decades after Contact (Captain Cook's first encounter with the natives in 1778) enough average-quality pearls were being secreted to make oyster-diving an activity punishable by death. It was, after all, like all land in Hawaii, entirely owned by the king: Kamehameha, uniter of all the islands and the first Hawaiian chief to use a cannon.

In 1819 Kamehameha died, and the right to harvest passed on to a Spaniard named Don Marin, said to have introduced the pineapple to Hawaii. By then, however, extensive cattle ranching and sandalwood logging in the uplands had begun to choke Wai Momi with silt. By 1840 whatever oysters hadn't been dug up simply disappeared. Ten years later, the Hawaiians in the area would also disappear, succumbing in the summer of 1853 to a smallpox epidemic that wiped away half of West Central Oahu's native population. In one summer, thousands of people, gone.

Then came sugar, and in 1876, reciprocity—the treaty whereby Kamehameha's successor David Kalakaua traded Pearl Harbor for a handful of colourful beads (OK, OK it was the right to sell sugar cane to the US tariff-free). James Campbell, owner and developer of the vast west-side Ewa Plantation, held a contest to rename the area around Wai Momi that had always been known, mundanely, as Puuloa, 'Long Hill', or, more poetically, as Awaawa-lei, 'Garland of Harbors'. 'Pearl City' won, sealing in a name.

Like Diamond Head, where, as the story goes, sailors coming into Waikiki mistook a worthless byproduct of volcanic activity called olivine (named for its colour, a dusty green) for diamonds, the name 'Pearl Harbor' made more sense in the abstract; latched on to, no doubt, by adventurers and sailors of the nineteenth century who, disillusioned and beat down by places like New York (in the throes of its own disease, typhoid, one of the reasons Herman Melville left Manhattan for points in the Pacific, including Honolulu), beheld in Hawaii a kind of Bunyanesque dream of paradise. What money there was to be made in Hawaii would, of course, come from traditional colonial sources: the bounty of the sea, in the form of whale oil, and the fruit of the land, in the form of sugar cane. Both unglamorous, back-breaking, extractive industries, and both wildly successful, for the largely white men who owned them.

Then came the ocean liners and pink hotels and consolidators, and Hawaii was resurrected as an ideal; resurrected so successfully, in fact, that rarely does anyone on the mainland think of Hawaii as anything but paradise, home to: breezes, tropical; palm trees, swaying; waters, crystal; and the Aloha Spirit. Except, of course, when they remember Pearl Harbor.

It has been, as Tom Brokaw reminds us, sixty years. The memorials started in June, with the opening of the movie, then escalated in the days and weeks following September 11, climaxing in a frenzy of interviews with Second World War veterans. (Still, type PEARL HARBOR into Google. What comes up first? Touchstone Pictures' official website for *Pearl Harbor*: 'December 7, 1941: A date which will live in infamy. From producer Jerry Bruckheimer and director Michael Bay.') Yet rarely in these advertisements and op-eds and articles and huzzas and remembrances and calls to arms is the story of the place that surrounds Pearl Harbor: the seven main islands and thousands of islets, atolls, shoals and reef formations that make up the modern entity known as the Hawaiian Islands, stretching more than a 1,000 miles from the Big Island in the south to Kure Atoll in the north. When you've got the pearl, of course, who cares about the oyster?

Perhaps this is deserved. Many people I know who are actually from Hawaii have never even visited the Arizona memorial. I haven't. The view of Pearl Harbor that is most familiar to those of us actually from the place is probably from on high, where it's rendered a study in grey (buildings and ships), blue (dredged, reefless seawater), and green (emerald mountains, Kelly military golf course). Down there Pearl Harbor is hard to get to: dominated by take-offs and landings; encircled by freeways (one wrong turn and you're at a strange checkpoint, very far from whichever Costco discount warehouse you were trying to visit). It's a place that's been effectively sliced away from the place around it, a place made distinct by war and American memory, not altogether unlike a certain sixteen square blocks at the tip of southern Manhattan, although the latter is, of course, minus the palm trees.

Ahdaf Soueif
Egypt

There was something so free, so untethered about them: 'The Daring Young Man on the Flying Trapeze', 'A Perfect Day for Bananafish'. The stories themselves were, perhaps, not so different from the stories of other nations, but their titles were more kooky, more exhilarating. *Tender Is the Night*. I was entranced that a book with a title that could have come off the cover of one of the Mills and Boon novels I was supposed to despise was considered serious— or in bookshop code, 'literary'—fiction. *Baby Doll* and *As I Lay Dying* opened up worlds that seemed at once more immediate and more dangerous than those of the European novels I was reading at the same time. *Giovanni's Room* was the first narrative I recognized as 'gay' and broke down more barriers in my mind.

While my mother's library shaped my fictive world my musical one had already been formed by my father's taste. Louis Armstrong's gentle growl had eased its way between Beethoven's Sonata No. 5 and Abd el-Wahhab's pre-1920 recordings and into my seven-year-old soul. I wondered at the undertow of sadness in even his happiest songs; where did it come from and how was it achieved? If the words and the rhythm were quite jolly what was that sorrow plucking at my heart? My first intimations of adult ambiguities.

Summer of 1966, the last 'normal' summer of my childhood, for the following June was to bring the Six Day War—and yet, not quite so normal. My youngest aunt, a doctor, has gone to New York to complete her medical training and the annual family migration to Alexandria has lost its first member. That was the summer 'Abd el-Haleem sang *'Ala hizb wdad galbi'* and I read Orwell's *Nineteen Eighty-Four* and rushed off, away from 'Room 101' and into the cool night air. Forever, now, a bar from that song will plant me back in the sand of Ma'mura beach at night-time, the orange and white paperback tucked under my arm, the music pounding out of the nearby palm-walled disco, the sea black and gently roaring ahead of me and beyond it no longer just the familiar Europe I knew but further, much much further beyond it: America.

The America we watched on television then was the America of *Bonanza* and *The Virginian*, neither of which, as far as I can remember, went much for the 'Cowboy and Injun' stuff that I found troubling. My problem, at that early age, was that the 'Indians' never got to put their side of the story. We were not expected to grieve when several of their yelling, galloping braves were cut down, nor did we ever see them in their 'normal' lives which, presumably, they had. Or had had before the righteous gun-toting (white) heroes came on the scene. At home in the Sixties one seemed to have no need to be aware or beware of political America—except for the CIA. There was a general sense that an American you met in Egypt would most likely be working for the CIA, and the CIA was implicated in the murder of Che Guevara. But then you didn't really meet Americans around Cairo. Not, anyway, in the way that you met British, French, Italian, German, Spanish and Russian people living and working in the city. I think that the first time I was struck by gross misuse of language was when I was told that the Peace Corps was really a tool of the CIA.

And yet, of course, I knew that we had a problem of some kind with America. I suppose I thought it was because Egypt was a leading player in the Non-Aligned group together with countries such as India, Indonesia and Yugoslavia. And the Soviets were helping us build the High Dam when Europe and America tried to block it. It seemed fair to me that we should get help where we could find it. I didn't understand, for example, why America had it in for Nasser. The bond between the US and Israel had not yet, I guess, become so starkly clear. When the June '67 war broke out many fingers pointed at America, speaking of its collusion with Israel, both in the setting up and in the execution of the war. Then films like *Z* and *Missing* spelled out the extent of CIA meddling in the affairs of other nations. But still, it was as though you could somehow disband the CIA and be left with the America of fiction and jazz, the America that seemed such fun, so democratic, so egalitarian and so free.

When it was time to go abroad to study for a PhD I chose not to go to America: it was too far from home. I studied in Lancaster in the UK instead. I had no idea how far from home that would turn out to be. It was in Lancaster that I first saw *Casablanca* and while the aficionados enthused about the film I wondered silently, underneath my liking for it, about the Arabs. Where were the Moroccans? And how come the only non-European character was a sleazebag? But maybe the longing for home was making me too thin-skinned.

Perhaps films were the reason why when, in 1978, I went to New York for the first time the city was entirely familiar to me. Which is not to say that it had no impact; it was electrifying. Electrifying and homey. Delis handed you your purchases in brown paper bags. The hot pretzels I bought on street corners were identical to our *semeet* and you were even given a twist of salt to dip the ends into. Paper and rubbish drifted across the streets. Small shops selling women's underwear displayed the same stolid, prosaic busts you saw in Cairo shop windows, and everywhere people talked and shouted and argued. It was at once like being at home and being inside a movie. The accent served as a distancing but endearing factor; I kept thinking everyone I spoke to was being ironic, sending themselves— or something—up.

On subsequent visits it seemed to me that there was plenty to send up. The TV programmes that were interrupted every ten minutes by commercials. The bizarre characters flaunting their personal problems on chat shows. The TV evangelists with their unabashed demands for donations. The fact that 'socialism' was a dirty word.

In the last two decades I've visited America many times and love its vibrancy, its variety, its playfulness. I've made strong and warm and—I hope—enduring friendships with Americans. But in the last two decades America's influence on the world and actions in it have become more and more distasteful. And what is unforgivable is that it is all done under the cover of 'freedom', 'democracy' and 'peace'.

Nowhere does the hypocrisy of American foreign policy seem more clear than in its unconditional support for Israel. This is generally explained by citing the power of the Zionist lobby, the misguided identification of 'Jewish' with 'Israeli' or 'Zionist'—an identification which many Jews now openly reject—and the wish to make amends for the Holocaust. But maybe the affinity goes deeper than that. The US too is a (relatively) young nation; a state that came into being at the hands of groups of white Europeans who 'discovered' a land and 'settled' it—never mind that there were people already there. Maybe America's fondness for Israel is like that of a parent watching a child follow in its footsteps. And now it looks as though the parent will be taught by the child: airborne attacks on civilian populations, illegal detentions, use of torture in interrogation, targeted assassinations worldwide, these have been the stock-in-trade of the Israeli state for fifty years and now America looks to follow suit. But Israel has a free press and Israel would not dare suggest subjecting its citizens—its Jewish citizens that is—to the infringements on their civil liberties that America is now proposing for Americans.

At the moment the world dominated by America looks like a pretty nasty place.

I still love my American friends; like the music and stories that captivated me all those years ago they're smart and funny and open and warm. Is it really the case that to be good for them America has to be bad for the rest of us? □

GRANTA

JIHADIS
Pankaj Mishra

Peshawar is a mess. And last winter—the winter before September 11 became a significant date, before the word 'Taliban' became part of the ordinary American vocabulary, when Osama Bin Laden, once resident in the city, was still merely infamous—it seemed at its worst. The smog above the city trapped the acrid smoke from the burning tyres that the Afghan refugees huddled around for warmth; Pakistani traffic policemen wearing new-looking gas masks flailed helplessly in the slow swirl of donkey carts, trucks, auto rickshaws and cars; and even the brighter carpets in the old bazaar blended into the greyness. I began to wonder, somewhat resentfully, if the romance of Peshawar, last renewed during the anti-communist jihad a decade before, had been an invention of jaded adventurers from the West, the predecessors of the eager white men and women I occasionally saw walking in the narrow alleys of the old quarters: visitors in the first flush of their enchantment with the Orient, for whom even the heroin addicts slumped on broken pavements could blend easily into the general quaintness of the East.

I felt oppressed by the city. Its shapeless squalor as well as its new aspirations to respectability reminded me too much of the small-town India of my childhood. Relief, along with proportion and order, seemed to lie only in the British-created cantonment, the military quarter: in the low red-tiled bungalows and whitewashed trees and brick-lined flower beds and the lone guard standing stiff before smoothly gravelled driveways. It was where I often found myself during the long evenings—browsing through the boldly pirated American and British paperbacks at Saeed Book Bank and visiting newspaper offices in Saddar Bazaar.

I was always nervous while visiting the cantonment. My visa for Pakistan said, NOT VALID FOR CANTT AREAS. I wasn't sure what this meant since Cantt areas in the cities of the subcontinent are impossible to avoid. I was expected to stay away from 'sensitive military installations', but since I didn't know what these were I had to play it safe. I never turned my head sideways when my rickshaw passed the grander-looking buildings, never made it apparent that I was curious about anything except the dreary progression of the well-paved road, and the proud replicas of new Pakistani missiles mounted on traffic islands—the missiles named provocatively after the Muslim conquerors of India.

This timidity was partly created by the three men in a beat-up Toyota who followed me every time I left my hotel. They would have been representatives of one or all of the three major intelligence agencies in Pakistan. Their interest in me seemed exaggerated: a reflex from the days of the spy-infested jihad. It would have mortified the very amiable Pakistani diplomats in New Delhi who arranged for my visa and gave me, an Indian writer, what I learned later was an unprecedented liberty of travel within Pakistan. But then to be an Indian in Pakistan—or, for that matter, a Pakistani in India—is to be trapped by the prickly nationalisms of the two neighbouring countries; it is to be automatically suspect.

Not that the spies did anything, or even looked, particularly ominous. The most visible among them, a plump, rosy-cheeked man in a pink salwar kurta, could have been one of the shopkeepers idle behind the open sackfuls of dry fruits in the narrow dark rooms of the old bazaar.

Still, if you are not used to being followed and watched, it can get stifling. The world seems full of a vague menace, the friendly, rather camp bellboy with slicked-down hair that you think you have tipped generously turns into an ungrateful informer, and the most variegated and lively street scene begins to look like an elaborate preparation for an arrest.

Paranoia was what the spies embodied and conveyed to me. But there was a deeper unease I felt throughout the first three weeks I spent in Pakistan, waiting to go to Afghanistan. It was an unease about Islam and Muslims I had so far attributed to others: something I sensed, while living in London, in the reports and outraged editorials (a few, even then) in the British and American press about the Taliban and Osama Bin Laden and other Islamic extremists, and to which I thought I could only be immune after my experience of Kashmir.

About 50,000 people—militants, soldiers and civilians—have been killed in the uprising that the Muslims of the Kashmir valley began against Indian rule in 1990. The Indian press prefers to describe the situation in the valley as a spillover from the jihad in Afghanistan, the timid Kashmiris having been overwhelmed by Pakistani and Afghan terrorists looking to wage fresh holy wars. This broad picture, which depicted Pakistan and Islamic fundamentalists as the major villains, blurred and then dissolved altogether during the several weeks I spent in Kashmir last year. Most Kashmiris still follow an unorthodox Sufi version of Islam. The brutalities of the 400,000 Indian soldiers in the valley was, in my view, what had pushed a small number of young Kashmiri Muslims into the kind of jihadi extremism promoted by religious groups in Pakistan and created popular support for the increasingly large number of Pakistan-backed militants fighting the Indian army in Kashmir.

The articles I published subsequently in an American magazine described the stages through which India, a Hindu-majority, if officially secular, nation, had become, despite many good intentions, a repressive colonial power for the four million Muslims of the Kashmir valley. Soon after the articles came out, officials from the Indian IB (Intelligence Bureau) visited my retired parents in India and interrogated them at some length about my 'pro-Pakistan' proclivities (which would have been confirmed for them when the Pakistani High Commissioner in New Delhi praised my articles in print and then, not long afterwards, arranged my exceptionally generous visa for Pakistan). Indian newspaper columnists denounced me as unpatriotic and, while wondering what would lead an apparently well-to-do upper-caste Hindu to betray his country in an American magazine, concluded that I was pandering to white pro-Muslim audiences in the West.

This was optimistic. You wouldn't have thought that such audiences existed, going by the little attention paid to Kashmir, or Chechnya—another place where Muslims led a popular but hopeless uprising against a powerful pro-West nation-state—in the British or American newspapers. Even the more detailed reports about Muslim terrorists turning up in the Philippines, Canada and Yemen barely mentioned, if at all, how the United States, during the Cold War, had helped establish the global network of Islamic militants that men like Osama Bin Laden now evidently controlled. Bereft of any recognizable context, the international news pages often seemed a kind of brisk atrocity-mongering. Islam in all its diversity appeared in them as little more than the West's 'other', in the same way communism had once been: the aggressive ideology of an unfree and dangerously deluded people.

Pankaj Mishra

I didn't expect that I would share this view of Islam and Muslims when I first thought, soon after returning from Kashmir, of travelling to Pakistan and Afghanistan. I wanted to find out more about the CIA-led jihad in the 1980s and the rise of the Taliban. I was curious about the much discussed, if always vaguely defined, conflict between Islam and the West. One evening in Srinagar, Kashmir, an old Muslim politician, routinely described as 'fundamentalist' in the Indian papers, had spoken to me of how the West feared Islam even more after the demise of communism because the religion, which a quarter of humanity followed, alone offered an alternative to the modern civilization of the West. It was hard for me then to work through such large generalizations. Later, when I began to read more Islamic history, it became clearer to me how quickly—in the past two hundred years, after several European centuries of cultural and technological backwardness—the West had caught up with the Islamic world, and then begun to subjugate it.

The India I had grown up in had also been radically and often traumatically reshaped by the great imperial power of the West, so I had some understanding of how people in demoralized societies could grow inflexible while trying to protect their older way of living. But in the case of Pakistan this understanding came from the books I read in London, before I had spent any time in a Muslim-majority country. In my first few days in Pakistan, I couldn't avoid feeling an almost atavistic fear of Islam and Muslims; and when, not long after I arrived there from London, Jamal in Peshawar said, 'They are all such fanatics here,' I immediately warmed towards him. For I had found myself silently nurturing this commonplace prejudice, although I wouldn't have wanted to articulate it myself. The sympathetic books I had read in London faded temporarily from my memory, and I forgot my high-minded suspicion of reporting in the Western press.

Jamal worked as a subeditor for *The Frontier Post*, one of Peshawar's English-language dailies. I got into the habit of dropping in to see him at his paper's offices, which were guarded at the reception desk by an old Pathan in a military coat, a Kalashnikov leaning against his wicker chair. Upstairs, low doors led to rooms lit by the dim screens of grimy computers. Delicate plumes of cigarette smoke hung in the air.

It was a difficult time for the newspaper. Its owner, a local Pathan businessman called Rahmat Shah Afridi, had been arrested in 1999 on a charge of drugs trading. His son, who ran the paper now, told me that the small amount of cannabis found in his father's Mercedes had been planted there by agents of Mian Nawaz Sharif, the then prime minister of Pakistan. It seemed like a typical Pakistani story of big men pursuing small private feuds and vendettas, and perhaps it wasn't entirely inaccurate: a few weeks after I left Pakistan, a special anti-narcotics court in Lahore sentenced Afridi to death. In any case, the smaller people were suffering: the staff had been working without salaries for three months.

But the shared austerity had made people jollier. The door to the room I usually sat in—really, a windowless box—opened every two minutes to reveal a new person with a joke, an anecdote, a filched cigarette, and a curious but friendly glance towards me, the visitor from India. A boy would regularly bring trays filled with chipped cups of milky tea which had been hastily poured. The cups were wet on the outside, and there were so many visitors that after three hours the dusty table glistened all over with small overlapping circles.

Jamal was as much of a cigarette-cadger and tea-drinker as anyone there. But he looked restless amid the bonhomie of his colleagues, and his face was alien to theirs—darker and blunter, not from this part of the world. I often felt his dull yellow eyes on me; there was, I sensed, something he wished to tell me in private, and when the moment came early one evening, it was this difference that he was keen to establish.

I hadn't been misled by his appearance. He was a Bengali, from Bangladesh, the country that had been East Pakistan until it came into being (with Indian help) as a separate nation in 1971. In 1975, as a young captain in the Bangladeshi army, he had taken part in the military coup against the government of Prime Minister Sheikh Mujibur Rahman. He had been present on the morning when Rahman and his family were gunned down at their official residence. 'An accident,' he said, 'we didn't mean to kill him.' Whether accidental or not, the moment was firmly in the past, part of Bangladesh's history. But Jamal had spent most of the quarter century since then dealing with the consequences.

He had spent four more years in Bangladesh, waging a futile insurgency against the government, before finally escaping to

Pakistan. There was no other choice: Pakistan, still bitter about its lost province, was the only country that wouldn't deport him straight back to Bangladesh where he was sure to be executed for Rahman's murder. He hadn't liked his new country one bit. He had arrived in Pakistan just as General Zia-ul-Haq was beginning his programme of Islamization; there was enough of the liberal Bengali, the reader of Tagore and Nazrul Islam, in him to be repelled by the brutal imposition of religion on everyday life. But he couldn't object too loudly; as a political refugee, he had to be grateful that he wasn't being hanged or shot. He managed as best he could, moving from job to job, city to city.

The story was refined and embellished over several evenings. I wasn't always sure how to respond to it, especially when he added that he felt he had a wonderful book inside him. But I didn't want to discourage or alienate him. He had known such a damaged life, only a kind of survival in Pakistan. And I felt he was on my side: a fellow stranger in Pakistan, adrift among the fanatics.

And Pakistan appeared, during my first days there, alarmingly filled with fanatics: there were the black-turbaned heavy-bearded leaders of the Taliban, arriving at their embassy in Islamabad in gleaming new Pajero cars; the retired general in Rawalpindi declaiming on the nobility of jihad; the crudely painted donation boxes for the jihad in Kashmir in the bazaars; the fundamentalist demagogues in small towns threatening to march upon Islamabad if sharia law and interest-free banking weren't immediately introduced; and the tribals in the so-called self-administering areas near the Afghan border cutting off hands in their attempts at proper Islamic justice. Almost every day, Sunnis murdered Shi'as and vice-versa, and a few young mujahideen achieved *shahadat*, or martyrdom, in Indian Kashmir. Against this background, it was easy to begin to sense, and fear, something hard and fierce even in the simple devotion of the skullcapped men half prostrate, on chilly evenings, on the streets of Peshawar.

But here I had to look out for my own prejudices. There had been many Muslims in the railway towns of North and Central India I had grown up in. I couldn't distinguish them from the low-caste Hindus among the railway labour gangs my father supervised. My father certainly had Muslim colleagues. But I cannot remember identifying any among the exhausted men in sweat-drenched white shirts and grey pants who returned home with my father for a cup of tea after a day out on the tracks, although the tea would have been served to them not in cups but in the special glasses kept aside in our kitchen for Muslims and low-caste Hindus.

Most of the Muslims were, in fact, very poor—much more so than us—and those were the ones I noticed. They lived in ghettos inside the older parts of the town, where, after the expansiveness of the British-built cantonment and Civil Lines and Railway Colony, the streets suddenly shrank. The houses were edged with open drains, the women disappeared behind sinisterly black burqas, flimsy rags curtained off the hanging carcasses at the butchers' shops, and the gaunt men with pointed beards looked quite capable of the brutality that our prejudices ascribed to them.

These prejudices were bred partly by our own lower middle class deprivations: anxieties about money, status and security that came to be related, in the usual unreflective way, to the alien-looking community in our midst. We weren't the kind of people who incited or took part in Hindu–Muslim riots, which in North India in the 1970s and 1980s occurred frequently, often cynically organized by out-of-power politicians wishing to destabilize an existing government, and which ended with the murders of scores of Muslims by an aggressively Hindu police. But we did accept the stereotype, and we had no trouble imagining the bearded Muslim as a violent aggressor who could murder a Hindu with as much relish as he might slaughter a cow.

Another, subtler cliché presented Muslims as backward-looking, a great drag on modernizing India, if not fifth columnists for Pakistan. Of course, the blunter dismissal was: Why don't these Muslims simply go to Pakistan? After all India had been partitioned in 1947 in order to create a new homeland for Indian Muslims. Pakistan was what most of them had asked for, so what were they doing in India?

It seems a crude question now, but it wasn't easy to answer then; and the assertion, made often by politicians and other privileged men, that India was a secular country which was open to people from all religions didn't convince us upper-caste Hindus who lived in straitened circumstances and practised as well as suffered discrimination. And so, feeling frustrated and demoralized ourselves, we unburdened upon the Muslims most of the pity and scorn with which we would have seen, if we could, our own lives. Hindu women probably deserved sympathy as much as Muslim women, but in our imagination it was Muslim women who led terribly oppressed lives.

The clichés bubbled up only when we noticed the Muslims. But mostly we didn't notice them—until the late 1980s, when Hindu nationalists began to agitate for the demolition of Babri mosque in Ayodhya, a town on the Gangetic plain in the state of Uttar Pradesh. It soon became a movement—and an argument—that swept across India. The Hindu nationalists claimed that the sixteenth-century Moghul conqueror of India, Babur, had built the mosque over the birthplace of Lord Rama after demolishing a Hindu temple on the same site. They saw a profound contempt for Hindus in Babur's decision, and they sought a kind of delayed retribution. They wanted the mosque, which was no longer used for prayers, demolished and a temple built in its place.

I was at university in Delhi by this time. On the campus, there were furious protests against what the Hindus in Ayodhya wanted to do. Student politicians organized demonstrations in which Hindus joined with Muslims and where one speaker after another denounced the Hindu nationalists for attempting to destroy the great Indian traditions of tolerance and accommodation. Still, in December 1992, the mosque was demolished by a Hindu mob. The student politicians in the campus raged for some weeks afterwards, but the Muslim students stayed away from their rallies. When I came across them in the dining room, I noticed they looked bitter, but I didn't feel involved. I had my own anxieties to deal with; a degree and then, with luck, a job that would help me climb out of the relative poverty my family had lived in for much of my childhood—relative, that is, to the newly moneyed middle class which was starting to flourish in India. Occasionally I would go to the after-dinner lectures by visiting left-wing journalists and academics—articulate, suave men who talked about the historical bonds between Hindus and Muslims and the uniquely syncretic civilization of India. These ideas about India's past and present didn't always match my experience—the sense I had of the distrust and hostility between Hindus and Muslims, and the keener sense I'd had, in the course of my travels through small-town India, of the stagnant resentments of the Muslim ghettos. But I didn't have the courage to contradict them then, and even now feel insecure before such powerful liberal pieties.

Pakistan has its own marginalized but vigorous liberals. They were the people who talked to me about the 'bearded fundos' and the imminent—or, according to some people, ongoing—Talibanization of Pakistan. It was a phrase I heard often, a new way of referring to troubles that had begun much earlier, in 1979, when Soviet troops entered Afghanistan to replace one faction of the ruling Afghan Communist Party with another, and the United States responded by arming anti-communist Afghans with the help of its ally, the military dictator of Pakistan, General Zia-ul-Haq.

Soon after his coup in 1977 against the elected government of Zulfikar Ali Bhutto, Zia had begun ostentatiously to declare his devotion to Islam. He announced his intention to create a pure Islamic society—that perennially undefined and therefore unfinished task which has given political legitimacy to many despots in Muslim countries. In April 1979 he hanged Bhutto—the populist demagogue who as prime minister used to describe Zia to visitors as 'my little monkey'.

Zia promptly began to channel military and other assistance from America and Saudi Arabia to the anti-communist radical Islamists based in Pakistan. He arranged for the smooth flow of mercenaries from Arab and other Muslim countries to Pakistan. He opened his country's borders to two million refugees escaping the proxy war in Afghanistan, and placed Pakistan in the forefront of what became an American-led global jihad against Soviet communism.

Pakistan was already quite an isolated country, as well as, almost from its beginning, an unhappy one. Very early in its history, its foundational myth had been broken: a shared religion, it turned out, couldn't solve the problem of how people with different ethnic and linguistic backgrounds were to live together. Urdu-speaking Muslims from India, arriving in large numbers in Sindh, found themselves resented by the poor Sindhis, who in turn felt themselves oppressed by the rich and dominant majority of Punjabi-speakers in the north.

Pankaj Mishra

The Pakistani army behaved brutally towards the separatist Bengalis
in East Pakistan, and then surrendered quickly to the invading Indian
troops in the short war that followed in 1971. There was international
shame and internal humiliation. The disastrous Pakistani obsession
with controlling events in Afghanistan grew out of the urgent need
to pacify the Pushtun separatists of the North-West Frontier.

India has its share of restless minorities, but it also has a consistent
political life. In Pakistan, the elected politicians have wrecked the
country's frail democratic structures, with the help of the army
officers and the bureaucrats who are the real rulers. Zia was anxious
to present Pakistan to America as a needy frontline state against
communist aggression, and to make himself invulnerable as a
dedicated anti-communist and Islamic holy warrior.

He was not without his Pakistani supporters. His Islamic zeal was
admired by the religious parties who received government patronage
for their so far unsuccessful attempt to Islamize Pakistan, and at
whose madrasas, or theological schools, thousands of young Afghan
refugees were to be fed, housed and educated. He was popular
among senior officers in the military, who were still smarting over
the surrender of 90,000 soldiers to the Indian army in 1971. They
sought to acquire, along with private fortunes, 'strategic depth'
against India by supervising the jihad in Afghanistan.

Lt General Hamid Gul was one of the first jihadis in the military.
He was much loved by Zia, who made him director of Military
Intelligence and then Director-General of the ISI, the Inter-Services
Intelligence Agency. In the 1980s Gul was one of the three or four
most powerful men in Pakistan—people who, under Zia's patronage,
could get away with just about anything.

But then in 1988 Zia and other senior army men died in a still
mysterious air crash. Benazir Bhutto, the daughter of the man Zia
had hanged, became prime minister of Pakistan. She got rid of Gul
at the first available opportunity, in 1989. Gul turned into an
intriguer: he led the frustrated power-hungry officers of the ISI who
conspired successfully with a few politicians to bring down Benazir
Bhutto in 1990.

I wanted to meet him, but he lived at the Chaklala airbase near
Rawalpindi. I told him on the phone that my shadows might stop

me travelling there. The galling awareness of his lost authority seemed present in his swift response. 'I'll see,' he said in a tight voice, 'who dares stops you from visiting my home.'

His house had Palladian columns—the mansions of military officers in Pakistan are always grand. The living room had framed photos of the Ka'ba on the walls and a suffocating excess of ornament: huge crystal decorations, shiny lifesize brass deer, green satin upholstery, rugs made from animal skins. A bearded man in a salwar-kurta sat uneasily on the big sofa, and then stood up hurriedly when another man, beardless, with a clipped moustache and wearing a tweed jacket, strode into the room. This was Gul, the jihadi, though his style suggested his original career as a cavalry officer. At times during our conversation he sounded like a graduate of Sandhurst. However, the facts of his early life as he told them, very reluctantly, were that his family came from the remote hills of Swat, and that he'd gone to a village school and then a government-run college in Lahore.

These were humble origins when compared to the 'brown sahibs' Gul was known for attacking at every opportunity—the men Anglicized and groomed to assume power at grander institutions such as Aitchison College in Lahore, and St Patrick's College in Karachi. They partly accounted for Gul's immodest ambitions and claims. In February 1989, when the Soviet army withdrew from Afghanistan, he was, as director-general of the ISI, leading the jihad. In fact, according to him, his role in the jihad had begun even while he was a lowly brigadier. Three weeks after the Soviet intervention in 1979, he wrote and circulated a policy paper, in which he advocated that Pakistan support a low-intensity guerrilla war against the Soviet Union and their Afghan allies, and gradually take it right into the Muslim-majority Central Asian provinces of the Soviet Union.

The paper reached Zia who was impressed by Gul's energy and ambition. A meeting with the general followed. 'I told General Zia,' Gul said, and the bearded man on the sofa nodded and smiled at the memory of the dead dictator, 'that if we defeated the Russians, and I was very optimistic that we would, then there was no reason why the borders of our great Islamic world should stop at the Amu Dariya.' (The Amu Dariya, or Oxus River, forms the boundary between Afghanistan and the former Soviet Union.)

Pankaj Mishra

Gul claimed his paper went on to be read by high-placed officials in the CIA, and formed the basis of later incursions into what William Casey, the director of the CIA, described as the 'soft underbelly of the Soviet Union'.

Much of this seemed like boasting. The Carter administration had long been waiting for the Soviets to slip up in Afghanistan. Zbigniew Brzezinski, National Security Advisor to President Carter, whose stated aim was to 'sow shit in the Soviet backyard', had arranged for clandestine aid to the radical Islamists in Pakistan a few months before Soviet troops arrived in Afghanistan. The Soviet intervention gave them the pretext they needed to up the ante. The day the Soviet army entered Afghanistan, Brzezinski wrote an exultant letter to Carter, 'Now we can give the Soviet Union its Vietnam War.' The CIA, under Casey, deepened this trap for the Soviets throughout the early and mid 1980s by providing billions of dollars worth of arms and aid.

In fact, Casey wanted the ISI to involve the Muslims of the Soviet Union in the jihad; he wasn't satisfied with the ISI-arranged smuggling of thousands of Qur'ans into what is now Uzbekistan and Tajikistan, or with the distribution of heroin among Soviet troops. An officer of the ISI I spoke to said that the ISI received plenty of unofficial encouragement from Casey to attempt more damaging stuff—but nothing that could be traced back to the CIA or the government of the United States.

Gul now had nothing but abuse for his former bankrollers in the CIA. 'A self-serving people. All they wanted was to turn Afghanistan into a Vietnam for the Soviet Union, they used us for this purpose, and then they lost interest after the Soviets withdrew.'

This was a commonplace sentiment in Pakistan: you heard it from liberal journalists who from the beginning had highlighted the folly and risk of fighting other people's wars; you heard it from the jihadis hoping to fight another day. American involvement in Afghanistan and Pakistan had become a story about the cynicism of cold warriors such as Brzezinski and Casey.

The jihad that Gul imagined himself to be leading turned out to be under neither his nor the CIA's control. Many different realpolitik interests had brought it to Pakistan, and would, in time, take it away. The Americans wanted to rouse the Muslims of the world against the Soviet Union; the Saudi royal family, which matched American assistance dollar for dollar, wanted its own version of Sunni Islam, Wahhabism, to triumph over the then resurgent Shi'ism of Ayatollah Khomeini of Iran. Pakistan was merely a base for these larger battles, somewhere that CIA operatives could, for a while at least, mingle happily with such rich Arab jihadis as Osama Bin Laden.

After the Soviet withdrawal was decided upon in Geneva in 1987, American interest in both the jihad and Afghanistan dwindled. The CIA promptly scaled back and soon ended its aid to Pakistan and the mujahideen.

Left pretty much to their own devices, the ISI and Gul began to flounder. In 1989, he abandoned his usual mode of guerrilla warfare in Afghanistan, and conceived and supervised what turned out to be a disastrous frontal assault by the mujahideen on the communist-held city of Jalalabad. Four months later, the mujahideen had lost 3,000 men and were nowhere near taking the city. The Afghan communist government in Kabul lasted for another three years, during which period the mujahideen declared jihads against each other.

The divisions between the seven mujahideen parties recognized by the ISI had been deepening since 1979. The rifts between them owed less to ethnic and linguistic differences, and more to the inequitable way in which the ISI had parcelled out the largesse from America and Saudi Arabia. The ISI under Gul was most generous to a particularly brutal mujahideen leader called Gulbuddin Hekmatyar, whose wealth and power depended on the production and smuggling of heroin. The ISI expected Hekmatyar to install a pro-Pakistan government in Kabul after the fall of the communists. But Hekmatyar turned out to be unacceptable to most other mujahideen leaders, especially to those who had fought the Soviets without much help from America or Pakistan.

When the Tajik mujahideen commander, Ahmad Shah Massoud, finally drove out the communist government of Kabul in 1992, a full-scale civil war broke out in Afghanistan. Hekmatyar, backed by the ISI, rocket-bombed Kabul for months. More people died in the city during the fighting in the early 1990s than during the whole of the decade-long jihad against the Russians. Regional powers stepped in once again to bankroll various factions: the Saudis supported the Sunni fundamentalists, Iran backed the Shi'a Hazaras, Tajikistan and Uzbekistan had their own favourites among the Tajiks and Uzbeks.

The ISI still hadn't lost faith in Hekmatyar when in 1994 the student militia of the Taliban suddenly emerged and conquered most of Afghanistan.

These were more than personal or professional misjudgements and failures. The work of Gul and men like him undermined a whole society. Reckless but powerful adventurers pursuing absurd fantasies of a pan-Islamic empire had taken a largely poor and illiterate country to the edge.

Gul himself had done well out of it all. There was the Palladian-fronted house in Rawalpindi, and also a farmhouse. Rumour had it that he owned more properties elsewhere.

And that winter, the winter before September 11, there were still new jihads and jihadis to root for. 'These Americans now accuse Osama Bin Laden of terrorism. Once upon a time they used to call upon him in Peshawar and ask him to recruit more Arabs for the jihad,' said Gul, anxious, like all the jihadis I was to meet in Pakistan, to claim a special intimacy with Bin Laden. 'I met him in Sudan in 1993. Such a wise and intelligent man. So much spirituality on his face. But this is the effect of jihad. It is a very noble state to be in. That's why I look so young, although I am sixty-four years old. Jihad keeps me young, gives me a great purpose in life.'

Gul's enemies in Pakistan—and there were many—scoffed at his Islamic fervour. It was to them another kind of opportunism: a private pipeline to power and to some of the money that flowed in from rich Muslim countries for organizations devoted to Islamic causes. Listening to them you could easily begin to think of jihad as just another racket visited upon a poor backward country. Certainly, renewed faith alone didn't account for the many sectarian groups that had sprung up in the last twenty years, whose exploits—shoot-outs, bomb explosions, arson—dominated the national news.

The Shi'a groups were funded from Iran, the Sunnis from Saudi Arabia and Iraq. After the proxy war in Afghanistan, Pakistan played host to the traditional rivalries of Islam. And the many sects and ideologies of the Islamic world also travelled to it. The Muslim Brotherhood in Egypt influenced the leaders of the Jaamat-I-Islami, the biggest of Pakistan's religious parties—several of its leaders studied at Cairo. The Saudis arrived late, but their open-handed generosity ensured a speedy embrace of Wahhabism among the poorer members of the clergy: many Sunni madrasas, religious schools partly funded with Saudi money, now stand near the borders that Pakistan and Afghanistan share with the Shi'a-majority Iran.

Among these imported Islamic schools, those belonging to the Deobandis are the most powerful, and closest to the Wahhabis. The name comes from a small town near Delhi called Deoband. A madrasa was established there in 1866 as part of the insular Muslim response to British rule in the nineteenth century. It was set up by men who felt that Western-style education of the kind proposed by the British, and embraced by the Hindus, was going to uproot and fracture the Muslim community, and who were convinced that a training in the fundamentals of the Qur'an and the sharia would shield Indian Muslims from the corruptions of the modern world.

In the newspaper office in Peshawar, Jamal said, 'You must go to the Deobandi madrasas. That's where a lot of the Taliban were trained, and also many of those young Pakistani men who go to Afghanistan to fight for the Taliban. You'll find lots of fanatics there.'

I did want to find a few fanatics; I also wanted to travel to Afghanistan. On both fronts, however, my attempts were being thwarted. At the Taliban's chaotic embassy in Islamabad, my visa application, deposited and redeposited several times, seemed as much of an illusion as the existence of an Afghan state or government. It wasn't easy to find the jihadis. The names Jamal sold me—expensively: he said he hadn't been paid his salary and needed the money, and I didn't argue—turned out to be men who had long ago retired. All the leads offered to me by the other English-language journalists I knew came to nothing. I began hovering round the offices of the Urdu publications, many of which were sympathetic to the jihadis. It was at the office of a plump young editor in Islamabad, one of the professional cheerleaders of the jihad and another self-proclaimed friend of Osama Bin Laden, that I ran into Shafiq.

Shafiq looked very old, although he was only in his mid-forties. When the editor introduced him as a veteran of the jihad in Afghanistan, he raised the sleeves of his kurta and displayed a bullet wound in his left arm. He didn't speak much; his Urdu was a low growl—the furtive tone, it turned out, of a fixer. His demands for money were more extravagant than Jamal's; and we were forced to meet early in the morning or late at night, the only times when the spies were off duty. It was difficult to arrange these meetings—he claimed his mobile phone was tapped by the ISI—but he usually had the information I wanted.

It took him some time to come up with a name for Karachi: it wasn't his 'area', he said. And then he said, with the glint in his eyes that always appeared in expectation of money, that he had found someone special for me: an activist of the Sipah-e-Sahaba, one of the most dreaded anti-Shi'a groups in Pakistan whose acronym, SSP, featured often in the daily papers, usually in news reports of attacks by or on Shi'as. He would, he said, using the English words, provide me with 'good material'. All I had to do was shake off the spies and show up at the Deobandi madrasa in Binori Town.

One early morning, when the spies were still asleep, I took a flight from Peshawar to Karachi. I was relieved to find that no strange men in beat-up cars awaited me at the other end. Everywhere on the wide boulevard leading to the city centre there were signs of Karachi's financial eminence, in the billboards, the glass-fronted boutiques and the fancy patisseries. I had expected a meaner place, living up to its reputation as a setting for violent battles between militant groups of Muslim migrants from India and the police. But in this port city, with the spies gone, and the warm sea air and clear light and colonial buildings so much like those of Bombay, I suddenly felt freer than I ever had before in Pakistan.

I felt as a Pakistani visitor to the city might; and it was as a Pakistani journalist from London that I introduced myself to Rahmat. The deception was necessary, Shafiq had told me: my connection to India would throw Rahmat and he would not want to talk. In any case, it gave me a new assurance the evening I went to the Binori Town madrasa. In my salwar-kurta, bought earlier in the day, I could have been any one of the hundreds of young men coming in and out of the evening namaaz.

Rahmat was waiting for me, as Shafiq had said he would, at a small shop selling Afghan caps and Qur'ans just inside the tall gateway to the madrasa. He was younger than I had expected, and his grimy white kurta, worn plastic slippers and dense beard only highlighted his exceptional good looks, his delicate cheekbones and shyly quizzical eyes.

We sat and talked in one of the garishly lit shops and cafes that hemmed in the madrasa. Initially I felt a little disappointed. Shafiq had exaggerated: Rahmat wasn't a student but an odd-job man at the Binori Town madrasa. As for the Sipah-e-Sahaba, he had never belonged to it, though some members of the group had helped him and his family after his brother had been arrested and charged with murdering a Shi'a landlord.

The murder had happened near Rahmat's ancestral village in the Punjab, where his father ran an auto-repair shop. Rahmat had been languishing there, with his parents, four brothers and two sisters, waiting for a job to come his way after his schooling at a local madrasa near the city of Faislabad. Things hadn't been so bad in the 1980s, in the days of Zia-ul-Haq's Islamization, when you could still get a job after a madrasa education. But Rahmat had gone to the madrasa after that time, and had come out of it to join the hundreds of thousands of unemployable young men in Pakistan. Some of his friends had got enough money together to travel to the Gulf, and he had been hoping to follow them. Then one day his brother murdered the landlord.

There had been ongoing difficulties with the landlord, who was a much-hated figure among his tenants, for the mistresses he kept in semi-servitude as well as for his financial crookedness. He had bungled the records of Rahmat's family's ownership of a piece of fertile land. Rahmat's father and his brothers had been powerless to argue. But then he had tried to manipulate the mortgage on Rahmat's father's auto-repair shop. That was what had enraged Rahmat's brother.

Rahmat said, '*Zamindar bada powerful banda tha*, the landlord was a powerful man.' The many relatives of the dead man came in a Pajero and flogged his father in front of the family and destroyed the auto-repair shop. The police ransacked his house a few times and even locked Rahmat up for a few days, although he had been away in the fields with a friend at the time of the murder.

The revolving disco-like lights on the ceiling glistened on Rahmat's perspiring face as he spoke. The shop was busy. It seemed, rather incongruously, part of the celebration of wealth and leisure I had seen elsewhere in the city. The solemn-faced skullcapped visitors to the mosque inside the madrasa were easily outnumbered by the paunchy men in tight jeans and T-shirts striding quickly to the shops and returning to their Mercedes with small mountains of shiny sweetboxes.

Only the men at the mosque in the nearby town helped his family, Ramat said. They employed his teenage brother at their own madrasa; they used their contacts in the police to get the pressure taken off Rahmat's family. Rahmat vaguely understood that they were members of the SSP, and opposed to Shi'as, but he hadn't given it much thought. Then one evening in 1995 one of the SSP men, not much older than Rahmat, who often led the namaaz on Fridays, called for him.

When he arrived at the mosque on his bicycle, he found a small crowd of young men already there, including a few from his village, people who had also been tormented by the now-dead landlord. None of them knew why they had been summoned. Then the man who had called for them came in, accompanied by an Afghan wearing a black turban, and addressed them briefly.

He said that the guest with him had come all the way from Afghanistan where a new jihad had commenced. There were many corrupt men like the landlords of Punjab in Afghanistan: they called themselves mujahideen, as though they were engaged in jihad, but they were worse than bandits and rapists. Now a new force had arisen to vanquish them and establish the law of the Prophet. The soldiers fighting the jihad were young Talibs, students, but Allah was with them.

It was the first time Rahmat had heard about the students—the Taliban. There had been several Afghans at his madrasa, but he had kept away from them. The Afghan refugees had a bad reputation in his part of Pakistan; they were seen as liars and thieves. His father dealt with them all the time in his auto-repair shop. The heavy trucks they drove from Afghanistan damaged the roads, and the drivers were often high on opium.

So when the Afghan man began to speak, Rahmat was sceptical. He spoke Urdu with a heavy Pushtu accent that, Rahmat remembered, made some of the men smile. But the Afghan was serious. He didn't waste much time: he said he had come to ask for volunteers for the jihad in Afghanistan. He couldn't promise much in return, except food and shelter; the way of jihad was not strewn with roses. But it was a holy duty for Muslims, and *shahadat*, martyrdom, was all they could expect from it.

Most of the young men weren't interested. But Rahmat, with a brother in jail and the auto-repair shop—the sole source of his family's income—now gone, couldn't turn away so easily from what the Afghan was offering. His father and his brothers wondered what he was getting into but didn't try to stop him. He went with other young men in a chartered bus to Quetta in Baluchistan. They crossed the border into Afghanistan illegally, at night. On the other side, along with Pushtun Afghans, there were many more Pakistanis. They were taken to a training camp situated in a rocky valley near the border, where there were men from Chechnya, Kashmir and Uzbekistan. There were even Pakistani army officers. It was in this training camp that he had grown his beard, not under any pressure—although men in Afghanistan were required to wear four-inch long beards—but out of his wish to be a good Muslim.

Rahmat had been at the camp for less than two weeks when his group was summoned to the western provinces where the Taliban were fighting to capture the city of Herat. By the time Rahmat got there, it was already under the control of the Taliban. He and his fellow mujahideen were like conquerors in the city. But it was a strange place for them. It was very cold, and the locals spoke Persian, not Urdu or Pushtu; they even looked like Iranians. Even more alien were the young Pushtun men of the Taliban who went around shutting down schools, smashing TVs and VCRs, and tearing up photographs. One of them discovered a semi-nude photo of an Indian film actress in the tent Rahmat shared with eleven or twelve other Pakistanis. There was awkwardness between the Afghan and the Pakistani volunteers for some time after that.

He didn't like the rough ways of the Taliban: they were backward people, he thought. They were cruel to their women and religious minorities and military opponents—someone from his village had been forced to participate in a massacre of civilians from the Shi'a Hazara community in central Afghanistan. He was a bit frightened of them. But he couldn't deny that they had brought peace to Afghanistan, and when the Pakistanis he was with spoke of imposing a similar peace in Pakistan, where there was so much injustice and banditry, it seemed like an attractive idea.

Rahmat didn't stay long in Afghanistan as he was wanted as a witness at the trial of his brother. Back in his village he met up again with the men at the mosque. It was with one of them that he'd gone to the Binori Town madrasa three years before we met. There was some money to be made in doing menial jobs for the students and teachers; he could eat cheaply and he could always find a place to sleep. Things were better here than in the Punjab where his brother was still in jail and his father close to death.

Rahmat had shaken his head when I first asked him if he wanted to eat anything. But when I ordered another plate of halwa, he was quick to reach out and place his hand on the arm of the waiter, startling him slightly. After the food came—an oily plateful of what looked to my furtive, vegetarian eyes like mutton—he became more expansive and his Urdu, studded up to this point with Punjabi slang, became more formal, full of difficult Arabic and Persian words. He spoke of the greatness and necessity of jihad, of how Muslims were being oppressed everywhere, in Kashmir, Afghanistan, Chechnya, Egypt, Palestine, how the Jews in Israel could get away with anything because they were supported by Western powers.

I had heard, and was to hear, a lot of this talk from both the leaders and the foot soldiers of the jihad. You had to be careful neither to dismiss it nor to swallow it whole. It was easy to see through the self-aggrandizement and deceptions of people like Hamid Gul. But the oppression and injustice that Rahmat spoke of were more than just rhetorical flourishes picked up from the teachers at his madrasa and the ISI officers at the training camp in Afghanistan; they were the basis of his own experience of the world.

Rahmat was like the young men of my own class in small-town India in the 1980s and early 1990s—people for whom the world didn't seem to have a place. The idea of religion as redemption, the unquestioning submission to one creed or philosophy—these were the same demands that my own background had made of me, and it had taken some effort, and much luck, to be able to move away from them, to redefine myself as an individual, and to enter into new, more complicated affiliations with the larger world.

Others weren't as lucky: these were people whose frustration and rage over their many deprivations could easily be appropriated into ideological crusades. It was among the young unemployed in India that the Hindu nationalist movement (also largely funded, like the jihad, from abroad—by rich Hindus in the US and UK) found its foot soldiers: the men who formed the mobs, who were in charge of the dirty stuff, of the lynchings and destruction.

Hindu disaffection, however, was of a different order. The young Hindus I knew were frustrated by their exclusion from the middle class; they did not, despite their rhetoric of an Indian golden age, seek to radically change the ways of the world, or hold up alternative visions, as Mahatma Gandhi once had, of what a good and true life was, and could be. Even the most extreme Hindu ideologues did not, in the end, wish, like the jihadis, to challenge or reject the knowledge and power of the West. They were content to take the world as they found it, dominated by the West, and then find a niche for themselves in it: they were above all sly materialists. This pragmatic collaboration with the West is what has produced the new Hindu renaissance of the last 150 years—a regeneration of which the software tycoons of Silicon Valley and the Indian writers in English are related aspects. Gandhi's ambition—to form a society as different as possible from the one in the West—had few takers left in India. Ironically, his distrust and fear of Western modernity was now amplified best by the radical Islamists of Pakistan, where the westernized post-colonial elite—those men from the posh colleges that Hamid Gul despised, who now spoke helplessly of the Talibanization of Pakistan—had discredited itself.

This is why, while India daily moves closer to the West, Pakistan seems much further away from it. It is also why Rahmat, although he believed me to be a Muslim, saw me essentially as an alien, someone far away from him, a resident of London, the city of Sodom and Gomorrah. It's why I was startled when Rahmat looked up from his plate of mutton and rice and asked me if the women in London went around with their legs exposed.

It was a question that came from my own past: the kind of thing I would turn around in my mind, when I was still a boy in isolated towns, with no TV or cinema around to inhibit my imagination. It was unsettling to think how quickly that past had vanished; how dramatically my circumstances had changed. No one before me in my family had ever left India. I now spend a lot of my time in London, and travel to many different parts of the world. I write for American and British newspapers and magazines; depend upon them, in fact, for a living.

Globalization has opened up the West; there is more space in it for people like me—people who would have had to struggle harder for a similar space in their native countries. I still feel myself on the margins, writing about subjects that appear remote from the preoccupations around me, the obsession with food, sex, money, movies and celebrities that is reflected in the weekend papers in Britain. But the first cultural shock has worn off. As an Indian writing in English I am a child, however strange, of the West. England is, after all, the place I have chosen to be; and I have, in time, come to see something brittle and self-righteous in my exasperation with articles about new restaurants and breast implants.

In any case, I spend most of my time in London at my desk and have only a shallow relationship with the world around me. When I first arrived I was unsettled by the devout Muslims I saw in the streets of east London. However, as so often happens, the more money you have the more liberal you grow, the more in tune you are with the cosmopolitan city and its bland middle-class tolerance. In London, experiencing security and stability for the first time in my life, I became someone without a past; and as the months passed the Muslims faded into the promiscuous bustle of gay discos, Balti restaurants, and bagel shops.

But this kind of westernization can be superficial; you can quickly lapse into an older cultural conservatism. In London one evening I stood behind a group of white-haired Hindu women who had just come out of a sari shop. I couldn't help sharing the distaste they felt at the sight of tall English girls in tight black dresses stumbling out of the Vibe Bar on Brick Lane, chased by drunken boys in bright shirts.

Your political loyalties can also be more complicated than those ascribed to you by other people. This explains my unease when I visited the American embassy in Islamabad a few days after meeting Rahmat. The stern experts on the Taliban and Islamic fundamentalism there kept using the words 'us' and 'them' while impressing upon me the urgency of forcing 'those guys', the Taliban, to give up their special guest, Bin Laden. Although I, with my beard and Afghan cap, looked like one of 'them'—the desperate men just outside the embassy's fort-like walls—the Americans had no doubt where I belonged: I was one of 'us', part of a powerful imperial civilization that, in this vulnerable outpost, was denoted by bowling alleys, cocktail bars, and the framed photos of barbecue parties on office walls.

No ambiguities existed for the diplomats: they defended the government they worked for with as much passion and vigour as the jihadis—the 'them' of their vocabulary—spoke of jihad; and they could make you feel that the war they were fighting was also your war, and the side we were all on had both truth and power behind it.

It was hard to demur when you considered the opposition. Far from offering a blueprint for a new civilization or society, the Taliban seemed perversely intent on destroying the few bits and pieces of Afghanistan's cultural heritage that had managed to survive the long war. I was in India when the news of the Taliban's intention to destroy all Buddhist statues in Afghanistan first broke. I still hadn't gone to Afghanistan and I wasn't sure what was going on. I rang a Pakistani journalist in Peshawar. He confirmed some of the theories I had seen in the Pakistani papers on the Internet: the Taliban were frustrated by the sanctions imposed on them by the UN, and wanted to draw international attention to the plight of Afghans facing drought and starvation. There was a struggle going on between the hardliners and moderates within the Taliban, and this time the former had won.

The journalist wasn't sure about the statues. The huge Buddhas in Bamiyan had been around for centuries; they could not be removed. But the museum in Kabul, which held the best representatives of Indo-Greek sculpture, had been looted long ago, first by the mujahideen who took over the city after the fall of the communist regime in 1992, and then by the Taliban in 1996. There was not much left there. For years now, statues had been smuggled out of Afghanistan and transported as far as New York and Tokyo, although you could still find an occasional example in the bazaars of Peshawar.

Pankaj Mishra

As it happened, I had already seen some of these statues in a house
in an upper-class suburb of Peshawar. They belonged to General
Naseerullah Babur, another of Pakistan's powerful military men, and
Benazir Bhutto's 'favourite uncle'. He wouldn't say how he had got
hold of the statues—which were displayed in glass cases in his living
room and many of which I recognized from photographs—and only
mumbled something about finding them during excavations. But it
wasn't hard to guess; and later I discovered that the manner in which
he had acquired the statues was as much of an open secret as his
original sponsorship of the Taliban.

Babur's connection with Afghanistan began when he was
Governor of the North-West Frontier Province in the 1970s. It was
then he first met the Afghan Islamists who later became famous
names in the jihad, and introduced them to American diplomats in
Islamabad.

He was also responsible for suppressing a particularly savage civil
war in Karachi between local Sindhis and Muslim migrants from
India. As Babur told me his stories, his broad Pushtun face often
cracked into a childlike smile. He came over as the retired man who
has made his little pile a bit dubiously but is nevertheless eager to
establish his role in great events; or like the brave Pushtun of legend,
as an admiring taxi driver described him to me, who travelled around
Karachi during the worst violence in an open, unescorted jeep.

In 1993 Benazir Bhutto came back into power, three years after
being overthrown by the ISI and Hamid Gul, and Babur became
Minister for the Interior in her government. Afghanistan was close
to collapse. Its roads, bridges, schools, orchards and irrigation
systems lay in ruins. Even more disastrous was the moral breakdown
that had taken place in the years after the Soviet withdrawal in 1989.
The law-enforcement systems of a modern state had barely existed
outside the cities at any time in the country's history; now civil war
and the displacement of millions of people had undermined the tribal
and religious codes that served in their place. Warlords and gangsters
flourished in the vacuum. Gulbuddin Hekmatyar, the mujahid
favoured by the ISI, had already branched off into heroin
manufacturing and smuggling; many other mujahideen commanders
took to smuggling and highway robbery. Men with guns stood at
improvised checkposts on all major roads. The situation was

108

particularly bad in the Pushtun-majority provinces of southern Afghanistan, where commanders raped young boys and women and plundered at will.

One day in 1994, in a village near Kandahar, a Pushtun man in his thirties called Mohammed Omar heard about two women who had been abducted and raped by local commanders. Like many young Pushtuns from his village, Omar, the son of landless peasants, had participated in the jihad against local and foreign communists. He had been wounded several times and had lost his right eye. After the Soviet withdrawal he had gone back to teaching at his village madrasa. He was deeply aggrieved by the anarchy around him, and often talked to his friends in the village about how they could bring it to an end and establish the law of the Qur'an. The rapes finally moved him to action. He went to the local madrasas and raised a band of thirty students for a rescue mission. The students got hold of about sixteen rifles. They went and freed the women and hanged the commanders from the barrel of a tank. A few months later, there was another incident in which two commanders fought a gun battle in the streets of Kandahar over a boy both wished to rape. Once again, Omar showed up with his students, freed the boy and executed the commanders.

These were the stories Rahmat heard in his mosque in the Punjab; Babur heard the same stories in Islamabad. The fame of the Taliban grew quickly. Afghans everywhere began appealing to them for protection from the warlords. Soon requests for help—along with large cash donations—came to the Taliban from the traders and smugglers who needed peace and open roads in southern Afghanistan for the transport of goods to Iran and the central Asian republics.

Babur had long been looking into the possibility of building new roads, and oil and gas pipelines, through Afghanistan to reach the central Asian republics of the former Soviet Union. There had been keen interest from multinational oil companies. But Kabul was still being fought over. The ISI, which both Babur and Bhutto distrusted, insisted on supporting Hekmatyar, who was not a leader who could impose the stability that was needed to conduct business in Afghanistan. The only other route to central Asia went through southern Afghanistan, but that route was infested with bandits.

Babur thought up a plan of rebuilding the road from Pakistan to

Herat in north-western Afghanistan with funding from international agencies. In October 1994 he took a group of Western and Chinese diplomats on an exploratory trip to Herat. Later that month, Babur attempted something riskier: he arranged for thirty Pakistani trucks to drive through Afghanistan to the capital of Turkmenistan, Ashkhabad.

Babur told me that he was advised against the trip. The commanders who controlled the roads in southern Afghanistan were reportedly very angry with him. They hadn't been told about the diplomats' visit and they assumed Babur was supporting the Taliban, who just a few days previously had captured a massive arsenal built up during the days when the CIA sent arms to the mujahideen.

Babur said, 'I went ahead. It was an experiment. I thought, let's see what happens.'

A few miles outside Kandahar, the convoy was stopped by local commanders. They ordered the Pakistani drivers to park in a nearby village. There were some Pakistani army officers on the convoy, but they were outnumbered and did not resist. Instead they relayed the commanders' demands to their superiors in Islamabad: money, a share of the goods in the convoy, and a promise to stop supporting the Taliban.

For three days, Pakistani officials in Islamabad wondered what to do. A commando operation to rescue the convoy was discussed and finally dropped. Then Babur asked the Taliban to help.

The students carried out an assault on the village where the convoy was parked, and chased out the commanders and their men. That same evening they attacked Kandahar and after two days of fighting conquered the city and expelled the remaining warlords from the area.

This was the beginning of the military campaign that brought almost all of Afghanistan under Taliban control in the space of just two years. Early in 1995, they took Herat; a year later, they were in Kabul. They didn't do it all by themselves: thousands of Pakistanis like Rahmat volunteered to fight with them; bribes raised from shippers and smugglers neutralized most of the warlords; and Babur put considerable Pakistani expertise at the Taliban's disposal.

He sent Pakistani engineers to replace the phone system, to repair Kandahar airport and to improve the roads; and although Babur wouldn't deny or confirm it to me, and only broke into his impish smile again, Pakistani army regulars fought alongside the Taliban and high-ranking officers planned their campaigns. Babur himself closely monitored the capture of Kabul in 1996, from which he carried away, like the invaders of the past, his own booty: the statues of the Buddha and Bodhisattva that now adorned his living room.

Five years later, the 'boys', as Babur called the Taliban, had grown more ambitious. They weren't content, as in the old days, to expel the warlords and institute a kind of rough and ready justice. They now wanted to create the purest Islamic society in the world. Their leaders called themselves mullahs, although few of them had the necessary educational qualifications—Mohammed Omar had in fact gone a step further and anointed himself Amir-ul-Momineem, Commander of the Faithful. They designed a new flag for Afghanistan. Men from the Department of Prevention of Vice and Promotion of Virtue went around checking the length of beards and beating up women without male escorts.

Babur disapproved of their restrictions on women. But they no longer turned to men like Babur for advice. They had their own supporters: the mullahs of rural Afghanistan, and the jihadis, Islamist politicians and ISI officers of Pakistan.

And they had their sympathizers: Ishrat was one of them, although he hadn't lived in Afghanistan since 1981, when as a sixteen-year-old refugee he made the long journey from the southern province of Helmand to Pakistan. He went to a local school in Peshawar during the anti-Soviet jihad and picked up enough English to be able to act as a guide and interpreter to foreign journalists. Ishrat was, Shafiq told me, the best person to take to Afghanistan; his English was excellent and he knew his way around not only the police and customs men, but also the potentially troublesome tribals in the border areas.

'You must write the truth,' he kept saying, 'and see things in context. Don't be influenced by what you read in the Western media.' There was, he said, nothing unprecedented about the Taliban's restrictions on women, their harshness towards petty criminals or their religious strictures: the tribal system that had ruled the lives of the majority of Afghans had always been severe.

Ishrat was a short man. The beard hanging from his small face seemed very long and the salwar-kurtas he wore were always too big for his thin body. In his admiration for the Taliban there seemed to me to be something of the fascination that the physically unprepossessing have for demonstrations of brute power and strength.

He made me uneasy, but I was stuck with him. And there was a discomfiting kernel of truth in his wildest assertions. Ishrat was obsessed with the attention given by the West to the destruction of the giant Buddhas in Bamiyan. 'Why do Western people care so much about old Buddhist statues no one worships? Why are they not writing front page articles about the millions of starving and dying people in Afghanistan? They want to give money for the statues and take them to their museums, but what about human beings?'

I wasn't sure of my own feelings. I had visited the refugee camps near Peshawar where families huddled under tiny plastic tents on exposed flat ground, next to narrow lanes muddied with soapy water and urine. I had read the alarming NGO reports about famine and mass starvation in Afghanistan. I knew about the UN's failure to fundraise even $221m as humanitarian aid for Afghanistan.

I had also just started writing a book about the Buddha, and had been reading with some fascination about the way merchant caravans had travelled with his ideas from North India to central Asia. In Pakistan, I'd visited some of the sites where the merchants had built great monasteries. I hadn't been much interested in Bamiyan: the giant statues looked ugly in the photographs, and there was Robert Byron's testimony from the early 1930s about them lacking 'even the dignity of labour'. Nevertheless, their antiquity gave them a kind of poise—for fifteen centuries, standing quietly in a broad mountain valley, they had withstood the change of seasons and religions. The news of their defacement appalled me, but then, as the days passed, I got tired of the outrage and scorn. There seemed something too easy and glib about the demonizing of the Taliban. In India, the loudest protests had come from the same Hindu nationalists who had demolished the Babri mosque in Ayodhya in 1992. In the angry editorials in the British papers, the Taliban once again appeared as particularly vicious barbarians from the Middle Ages instead of the very recent product of the West's unthoughtful meddling in a remote and not well-understood society. At least this was how they increasingly seemed to me. So when Ishrat said, 'It is all hypocrisy, the Western people are afraid of Islam, they want to protect the statues, but they had never heard of these statues, they don't know anything about Afghanistan, they are not interested in whether people live or die there,' I kept quiet.

In Afghanistan, Ishrat was always eager to bring my attention to the Taliban's successes. 'You have heard of the Afridis? Pushtun tribe people. They controlled the drug business. Poppy grown in Afghanistan, turned into heroin in Pakistan and then smuggled out to Europe and America through Iran and Karachi. No one was writing about that. American's favourite mujahideen, Hekmatyar, was running dozens of heroin laboratories. Now Taliban has banned poppy, the smugglers are angry at them, but they say heroin is against Islam. They lose money because of their faith. But still no one is writing. They all talk about Osama Bin Laden. But who is Bin Laden? He is America's man, America made him who he is.'

Ishrat's garrulousness made him assertive. He wanted me to go to Jalalabad and talk to Hindus and Sikhs who would confirm his account of the great peace and stability brought to the country by the Taliban. But that wasn't what I wanted to do. I told him I wanted to go to the villages.

'What will you do in the villages?' Ishrat said. 'There is nothing there.' I thought he was resisting me because his contacts were all in the cities. But in the end he backed down and said he knew someone I could talk to.

He kept up his pro-Taliban propaganda in the taxi on the way to a village near Jalalabad. Pointing to an ancient-looking cassette of Indian film music on the dashboard, he said, 'See, Afghans can listen to music. All you Western journalists are saying Taliban banned music.' But then a checkpost approached in the distance. The taxi driver reached for the cassette and stuffed it quickly into the pocket of his frayed jacket before the boys with black turbans and Kalashnikovs could strut over to the car and put their tender-skinned faces through the window and utter severe-sounding questions.

Ishrat was quiet after that. The sun rose higher and the light steadily grew harsh, draining colour even out of the roadside tents of the nomads. There was little traffic: a few big trucks that the straggly families by the road would try to wave down—Ishrat identified them as Pakistan-bound refugees from the Tajik-majority northern provinces—and more frequently, Toyota pickups, fast and dangerous on the broken road, with black-turbaned men holding Kalashnikovs crammed uncomfortably in the back.

The Toyotas—famously the vehicles with which the Taliban had achieved their military victory in Herat—kicked up swaying clouds of dust that were then quietly absorbed into the stubborn white haze. There was more dust once we turned off the road to Jalalabad, and the car began to rock and shudder down a rutted dirt path. The dust blew in through the rolled-up windows and settled in a film on the battered brown leather of the car seats; it powdered the beards of Ishrat and the taxi driver; it blotted out the occasional groups of children and chador-draped women carrying dung cakes on their heads; and it scared off the scrawny goats sitting in the narrow shade of the mud wall before which we suddenly stopped.

A low wooden door opened and a tall man with a long white beard came out and embraced Ishrat. His quick quizzical glance at me modulated into a smile as Ishrat spoke to him in Pushtu and explained my presence.

The man took me through the empty hay-littered courtyard to what seemed like a special room for visitors. He said very little either to Ishrat or to me. He brought me water in a shallow trough and indicated a place in the courtyard—before a furrowed drain that ran around the compound—where I could wash my face and hands. He returned shortly afterwards with some green tea. The tea tasted slightly of dust, and made the bone china cup—an unexpected thing in the bare room—seem as if it had been sitting unused for a long time.

I felt expectant; also slightly exhausted by the drive and by my nervousness of the Taliban men in the Toyotas. Ishrat hadn't promised much in the car. He had told me the name of our host— Faiz. He had filled me in on Faiz's involvement in the anti-Soviet jihad, and the injuries—always glamorous items in these accounts of the mujahideen—he had sustained during a mortar attack by the communists.

It was of that life that Faiz spoke to me intermittently that afternoon and evening in the cool bare room, Ishrat translating, the driver looking on blankly. He spoke not as a man who thought himself successful would, with pride or nostalgia. He spoke—leaning against the wall, his knees drawn up, narrow eyes wandering around the room—with the neutral air of a man who had lived his life in the only way he could.

He could barely remember his childhood, when his father owned a few cows and goats. But he spoke vividly of the time in the 1970s when the desert-like area around him was irrigated with Soviet assistance, and orange and olive orchards came up on the previously uncultivable land. His family was one of the beneficiaries. There had been brief moment of relative prosperity: that was when the house we were sitting in was built, and Faiz's elder brother was sent to Kabul to be educated.

Trouble happened very soon afterwards. Faiz couldn't remember the date, but his brother in Kabul was probably killed in 1978, during the purges that followed the communist coup. He was suspected of being an Islamist, although he was only a student and kept away from politics.

The communists came to the province, rounded up and killed a few mullahs, and arrested anyone they suspected of being counter-revolutionary. Then the Russians arrived.

Ishrat, translating and embellishing at the same time, told me of the Afghan rage and contempt for foreign invaders, and how every Afghan spontaneously joined the uprising against the Russians. But this didn't match what he translated immediately afterwards: how Faiz had stayed away from the young men in the province who went to fight the Russians. He was married by then, with a young son and the orchards to look after.

But then the bombing began, from the Russian helicopters, in response to guerrilla attacks on communist convoys. Many of the cultivated fields near the highway to Kabul were mined, and once the canals were destroyed it became harder and harder to keep the orchards going.

Faiz's parents, on their way to Jalalabad for a wedding, were killed when the bus they were travelling on was hit by a stray mortar. There were other tragedies. His son turned out to be 'insane'—Ishrat used the Urdu word, 'Paagal'—and Faiz took him to various shrines, including a well-known one near Jalalabad which was famed for curing insanity, and made him wear various amulets. But none of these helped.

Faiz's two brothers were already with the mujahideen when he began fighting alongside them. It wasn't a full-time job. He joined specific expeditions, mostly ambushes of government convoys. He was home the rest of the time, taking care of his diminishing farmland.

It was Ishrat who volunteered the information, in Urdu, while Faiz looked on uncomprehendingly, that Faiz had earned a reputation as a brave man very early in the war. It was why he had been smuggled across the border and into a hospital in Peshawar after he suffered serious abdominal injuries during a mortar attack on his position in the mountains around Jalalabad.

Pakistan—where he met Ishrat—was a revelation for Faiz. It was where he first saw how the jihad against the communists had turned into a big business. Some of the so-called leaders of the Afghan mujahideen, living in grand villas in Hayatabad, were not even known to him by name. But there they were, handling the disbursement of arms and aid to the refugees and the mujahideen. They made him think with pity and rage about the young men he was fighting with—people who started out with just a few .303 rifles among them until they managed to ambush an arms convoy and equip themselves with the latest Soviet equipment.

By the time Faiz got back to Afghanistan, the jihad against the Russians was almost over. A local mujahideen commander was already ruling over his province, and so peace came quickly and lasted longer in his part of Afghanistan. White men from UN agencies came to repair the irrigation canals; many of the destroyed orchards and fields were replanted.

Faiz wasn't one of the lucky farmers. None of the canals close to him were repaired. He had to go back to where his father had started out. He made a living out of selling the milk of the few cows and goats he had left over from the days of the jihad; he also made a bit of money by working as a labourer.

This was at a time when great wealth was being created all around him. Most of the restored fields grew poppy, under orders from the mujahideen commander, who lived in a mansion and maintained a private army. He wasn't as bad as the warlords in Helmand province; he wasn't a bandit or rapist. In fact, he was quite helpful to people who had fought in the jihad. But everyone knew he was involved in smuggling and drugs: the big business Faiz had seen in Pakistan had come to Afghanistan. Flights came to Jalalabad from Dubai loaded with colour TV sets that were then smuggled into Pakistan on big trucks. The opium went out to labs in southern Afghanistan and then, as heroin, to Iran.

This was why Faiz had first thought well of the Taliban when they came up from the south and chased out the commander. He didn't mind their severity; only people in the cities chafed at their restrictions on women. But they didn't alter the essential things. The smuggling continued. Poppy cultivation had stopped only recently, and he knew of people who were still at it. A few well-connected merchants and traders in Jalalabad grew rich. Most other people became poorer; his two brothers had to leave with their families for Pakistan where they worked as truck drivers. And there was the harassment. Young men showed up at his house trying to draft his son into the war against the Tajiks in the north, and had to be persuaded that he was unfit to be a soldier. He also didn't like their dependence on Arab and Pakistani jihadis, many of whom he saw in the province. Foreigners had done enough damage in Afghanistan; it was time for them to leave the country and its people alone.

Dismay appeared on Ishrat's face as he translated this, and a brief argument broke out between him and Faiz. I couldn't follow most of it, and I didn't trust the account I got from Ishrat who claimed to be arguing that the Arabs and Pakistanis helping the Taliban were fellow Muslims, and not infidels like the Russians and Americans.

I had wondered all afternoon about that emptiness of the big-seeming house, the absence of Faiz's wife and his son. I now saw two emaciated cows stumbling into the courtyard, followed by a thin stubble-faced man with a stick: this was Faiz's 'insane' son, explained Ishrat. He tethered the cows to an iron picket and then walked out of sight. A little later, I heard pots and pans being shuffled in an adjacent room and then I saw a chador-clad figure move briskly across the courtyard to throw some hay before the cows, and then swiftly retreat. She had been there all through the afternoon, possibly sleeping or lying down silently on the ground.

I asked Ishrat if it was possible to talk to her for a few minutes.

He was quick to pick up on the hesitation in my voice. 'Why do you want to talk to her?' he asked.

I didn't have to respond. Faiz, who had gone out, came back into the room at that very moment. The lantern he held filled the room with the smell of kerosene. Ishrat explained my request to him in Pushtu. I saw his face tense.

The answer was no. Ishrat said, speaking once again on his own, that local custom did not permit strange men to talk to women. Faiz interrupted him and said that he could convey my question to his wife and bring back her reply.

It was better than nothing, so I asked the obvious question about life for women under the Taliban. It took a while for Ishrat to translate this, and I wasn't sure if he had done so accurately until the answer came back with a slightly more relaxed Faiz.

Faiz laughed as he spoke, and even Ishrat smiled as he translated. The thing she disliked most about Taliban rule was when she had to travel by bus to the nearby towns. The roads were bad; the buses were few; and the journeys were worst for the women who were forced to sit squashed at the back, separate from the men in the front of the bus.

The light outside the room grew softer; it was in the grey-blue dusk that Ishrat and Faiz went out to offer namaaz. I watched them from the room: two silently vigorous figures on the scruffy floor of the courtyard, bending and straightening up almost in unison, expressing a common faith, but so apart in their experiences: Ishrat, the fixer for foreign journalists in Peshawar, in touch with and amplifying ever-new ideologies and passions, and Faiz the retired fighter, all his previous disappointments and griefs bleached by his present struggles for survival, by the bare house and courtyard, and the greater blankness outside.

That kind of steady grinding-down of individual lives seems to go on all the time in places like Afghanistan and Pakistan. A few days after that evening with Faiz and Ishrat I was in Peshawar and heard about Jamal from one of the other men I'd met at the offices of *The Frontier Post*. Terrible things had happened to Jamal and the paper. A few days after my visit, a letter had come in by email. It started innocuously enough but then went on to insult Prophet Mohammed in the grossest terms. Jamal approved it for publication without reading it through to the end. No one else noticed before it was pounced upon by one of the fundamentalist organizations who were always waiting to undermine the English-language press. A mob came and set fire to the press. The police arrested several journalists; the editor managed to escape the police and went into hiding with his fellow tribesmen somewhere near the Khyber Pass. Most of the journalists had now been released but Jamal was in prison, awaiting trial for blasphemy.

The punishment for blasphemy in Pakistan was death. But Jamal was already close to dying. The journalist was surprised to learn that I didn't know—hadn't guessed from his dull yellow eyes—about Jamal's heroin addiction. It had begun soon after he arrived in Peshawar and got to know some drug dealers; he had been in and out of several hospitals.

No one could do anything for him now, the journalist said. I was shocked at his callousness at first, and then I felt guilty. In London I had received a couple of emails from Jamal about the book he wanted to write. I hadn't responded, as the book seemed to me a doomed idea.

The journalist, who himself had only just escaped the fury of the fundamentalists, was only being truthful, and I didn't feel that I could offer to help. I was a Hindu and an Indian. How could I get involved with an assassin, a heroin-addict and a blasphemer in Pakistan?

'They are all such fanatics here!' Jamal had said at our first meeting and I had been grateful for the sentiment then. But I had felt myself change during the weeks in Pakistan, after I recovered from the first few days of instinctive fear. There had been an unexpected moment towards the end of my stay. I had gone to see a Moghul mosque in Peshawar. The spies hadn't followed me into the courtyard, where a few men sat in the late afternoon sun, and I felt I was alone until I saw an old man sleeping in one dark corner. He was obviously an Afghan refugee. His long white beard and sharp features made me think he was from Herat, or the western provinces close to Iran. His head, resting on a silk-wrapped bundle, displayed the fine profile of monks and wayfarers in Persian and Moghul miniatures; and watching him in the decaying old building—where the inlaid tiles were all faded or chipped, the broad-blade fans swayed dangerously as they spun—I suddenly felt myself pulled centuries back. I had a sense, fleeting but vivid and exhilarating, of the greatness of the old global civilization of Islam, of the splendour of once-famous and now devastated cities—Herat, Balkh, Baghdad—of the whole life and world the religion had once created.

That world was now in turmoil; it had been broken into by the invincible modern civilization of the West. From the outside it seemed capable only of producing fanaticisms of the kind that had crushed Jamal, and it was hard not to be repelled by it.

'The foreigners should leave us alone,' Faiz had said, 'we will find our own way.' But countless men had tried and failed, many societies had been exposed to new kinds of pain, and it still wasn't clear what that way could be.

I had thought Jamal an ally, someone on my side. But I belonged to another, more fortunate world. The American diplomats in Islamabad had guessed correctly: I already had my side chosen for me. Jamal's fate was tied to the faceless people on the other side—people who were persecutors as much as victims. I couldn't see how things, given the way they were now, could work out for them. They could be cruel and unreasonable—'fanatics'. And yet I wanted them to flourish. I wanted them to have as much dignity and freedom as I had been allowed, even though I increasingly doubted whether the kind of life I lived was what they longed for, or could be content with.

□

GRANTA

YOUTH

J. M. Coetzee

It is late, past midnight. In the faded blue sleeping-bag he has brought from South Africa, he is lying on the sofa in his friend Paul's bedsitter in Belsize Park. On the other side of the room, in the proper bed, Paul has begun to snore. Through a gap in the curtain glares a night sky of sodium orange tinged with violet. Though he has covered his feet with a cushion, they remain icy. No matter: he is in London.

There are two, perhaps three places in the world where life can be lived at its fullest intensity: London, Paris, perhaps Vienna. Paris comes first: city of love, city of art. But to live in Paris one must have gone to the kind of upper-class school that teaches French. As for Vienna, Vienna is for Jews coming back to reclaim their birthright: logical positivism, twelve-tone music, psychoanalysis. That leaves London, where South Africans do not need to carry papers and where people speak English. London may be stony, labyrinthine, and cold, but behind its forbidding walls men and women are at work writing books, painting paintings, composing music. One passes them every day in the street without guessing their secret, because of the famous and admirable British reserve.

For a half-share of the bedsitter, which consists of a single room and an annex with a gas stove and cold-water sink (the bathroom and toilet upstairs serve the whole house), he pays Paul two pounds a week. His entire savings, which he has brought with him from South Africa, amount to eighty-four pounds. He must find a job at once.

He visits the offices of the London County Council and enters his name on a list of relief teachers, teachers ready to fill vacancies at short notice. He is sent for an interview to a secondary modern school in Barnet at the far end of the Northern Line. His degree is in mathematics and English. The headmaster wants him to teach social studies; in addition, to supervise swimming two afternoons a week.

'But I can't swim,' he objects.

'Then you'll have to learn, won't you?' says the headmaster.

He leaves the school premises with a copy of the social studies textbook under his arm. He has the weekend to prepare for his first class. By the time he gets to the station he is cursing himself for accepting the job. But he is too much of a coward to go back and say he has changed his mind. From the post office in Belsize Park he mails the book back, with a note: 'Unforeseen eventualities make it impossible for me to take up my duties. Please accept my sincerest apologies.'

An advertisement in the *Guardian* takes him on a trip to Rothamsted, the agricultural station outside London where Halsted and MacIntyre, authors of *The Design of Statistical Experiments*, one of his university textbooks, used to work. The interview, preceded by a tour of the station's gardens and greenhouses, goes well. The post he has applied for is that of Junior Experimental Officer. The duties of a J.E.O., he learns, consist in laying out grids for test plantings, recording yields under different regimens, then analysing the data on the station's computer, all under the direction of one of the Senior Officers. The actual agricultural work is done by gardeners supervised by Agricultural Officers; he will not be expected to get his hands dirty.

A few days later a letter arrives confirming that he is being offered the job, at a salary of £600 a year. He cannot contain his joy. What a coup! To work at Rothamsted! People in South Africa will not believe it!

There is one catch. The letter ends: 'Accommodation can be arranged in the village or on the council housing estate.' He writes back: he accepts the offer, he says, but would prefer to go on living in London. He will commute to Rothamsted.

In reply he receives a telephone call from the personnel office. Commuting will not be practicable, he is told. What he is being offered is not a desk job with regular hours. On some mornings he will have to start work very early; at other times he will have to work late, or over weekends. Like other officers, he will therefore have to reside within reach of the station. Will he reconsider his position and communicate a final decision?

His triumph is dashed. What is the point of coming all the way from Cape Town to London if he is to be quartered on a housing estate miles outside the city, getting up at the crack of dawn to measure the height of bean plants? He wants to join Rothamsted, wants to find a use for the mathematics he has laboured over for years, but he also wants to go to poetry readings, meet writers and painters, have love affairs. How can he ever make the people at Rothamsted—men in tweed jackets smoking pipes, women with stringy hair and owlish glasses—understand that? How can he bring out words like *love, poetry* before them?

Yet how can he turn the offer down? He is within inches of having a real job, and in England too. He need only say one word—*Yes*—and he will be able to write to his mother giving her the news she is waiting to hear, namely that her son is earning a good salary doing something respectable. Then she in turn will be able to telephone his father's sisters and announce, 'John is working as a scientist in England.' *That* will finally put an end to their carping and sneering. A scientist: what could be more solid than that?

Solidity is what he has always lacked. Solidity is his Achilles heel. Of cleverness he has enough (though not as much as his mother thinks, and as he himself once thought); solid he has never been. Rothamsted would give him, if not solidity, not at once, then at least a title, an office, a shell. Junior Experimental Officer, then one day Experimental Officer, Senior Experimental Officer: surely behind so eminently respectable a shield, in private, in secrecy, he will be able to go on with the work of transmuting experience into art, the work for which he was brought into the world.

That is the argument for the agricultural station. The argument against the agricultural station is that it is not in London, city of romance.

He writes to Rothamsted. On mature reflection, he says, taking into consideration all circumstances, he thinks it best to decline.

The newspapers are full of advertisements for computer programmers. A degree in science is recommended but not required. He has heard of computer programming but has no clear idea of what it is. He has never laid eyes on a computer, except in cartoons, where computers appear as box-like objects spitting out scrolls of paper. There are no computers in South Africa that he knows of.

He responds to the advertisement by IBM, IBM being the biggest and best, and goes for an interview wearing the black suit he bought before he left Cape Town. The IBM interviewer, a man in his thirties, wears a black suit of his own, but of smarter, leaner cut.

The first thing the interviewer wants to know is whether he has left South Africa for good.

He has, he replies.

Why, asks the interviewer?

'Because the country is heading for revolution,' he replies.

There is a silence. *Revolution*: not the right word, perhaps, for the halls of IBM.

'And when would you say,' says the interviewer, 'that this revolution will take place?'

He has his answer ready. 'Five years.' That is what everyone has said since Sharpeville. Sharpeville signalled the beginning of the end for the white regime, the *increasingly desperate* white regime.

After the interview he is given an IQ test. He has always enjoyed IQ tests, always done well at them. Generally he is better at tests, quizzes, examinations than at real life.

Within days IBM offers him a position as a trainee programmer. If he does well in his training course, and then passes his probationary period, he will become first a Programmer proper, then one day a Senior Programmer. He will commence his career at IBM's data-processing bureau in Newman Street, off Oxford Street in the heart of the West End. The hours will be nine to five. His initial salary will be £700 a year.

He accepts the terms without hesitation.

The same day he passes a placard in the London Underground, a job advertisement. Applications are invited for the position of trainee station foreman, at a salary of £700 a year. Minimum educational requirement: a school certificate. Minimum age: twenty-one.

Are all jobs in England paid equally, he wonders? If so, what is the point of having a degree?

In his programming course he finds himself in the company of two other trainees—a rather attractive girl from New Zealand and a young Londoner with a spotty face—and a dozen or so IBM clients, businessmen. By rights he ought to be the best of the lot, he and perhaps the girl from New Zealand, who also has a mathematics degree; but in fact he struggles to understand what is going on and does badly in the written exercises. At the end of the first week they write a test, which he barely scrapes through. The instructor is not pleased with him and does not hesitate to express his displeasure. He is in the world of business, and in the world of business, he discovers, one does not need to be polite.

There is something about programming that flummoxes him, yet that even the businessmen in the class have no trouble with. In his naivety he had imagined that computer programming would be about ways of translating symbolic logic and set theory into digital codes. Instead the talk is all about inventories and outflows, about Customer A and Customer B. What are inventories and outflows, and what have they to do with mathematics? He might as well be a clerk sorting cards into batches; he might as well be a trainee station foreman.

At the end of the third week he writes his final test, passes in undistinguished fashion, and graduates to Newman Street, where he is allocated a desk in a room with nine other young programmers. All the office furniture is grey. In the desk drawer he finds paper, a ruler, pencils, a pencil sharpener, and a little appointments book with a black plastic cover. On the cover, in solid capitals, is the word THINK. On the supervisor's desk, in his cubicle off the main office, is a sign reading THINK. THINK is the motto of IBM. What is special about IBM, he is given to understand, is that it is unrelentingly committed to thinking. It is up to employees to think at all times, and thus to live up to the ideal of IBM's founder Thomas J. Watson. Employees who do not think do not belong in IBM, which is the aristocrat of the business machine world. At its headquarters in White Plains, New York, IBM has laboratories in which more cutting-edge research in computer science is performed than in all the universities of the world together. Scientists in White Plains are paid better than university professors, and provided with everything they can conceivably need. All they are required to do in return is think.

Though the hours at the Newman Street bureau are nine to five, he soon discovers that it is frowned upon for male employees to leave the premises promptly at five. Female employees with families to take care of may leave at five without reproach; men are expected to work until at least six. When there is a rush job they may have to work all night, with a break to go to a pub for a bite. Since he dislikes pubs, he simply works straight through. He rarely gets home before ten o'clock.

He is in England, in London; he has a job, a proper job, better than mere teaching, for which he is being paid a salary. He has escaped South Africa. Everything is going well, he has attained his first goal, he ought to be happy. In fact, as the weeks pass, he finds himself more and more miserable. He has attacks of panic, which he beats off with difficulty. In the office there is nothing to rest the eye on but flat metallic surfaces. Under the shadowless glare of the neon lighting, he feels his very soul to be under attack. The building, a featureless block of concrete and glass, seems to give off a gas, odourless, colourless, that finds its way into his blood and numbs him. IBM, he can swear, is killing him, turning him into a zombie.

Yet he cannot give up. Barnet Hill Secondary Modern, Rothamsted, IBM: he dare not fail for a third time. Failing would be too much like his father. Through the grey, heartless agency of IBM the real world is testing him. He must steel himself to endure.

His refuge from IBM is the cinema. At the Everyman in Hampstead his eyes are opened to films from all over the world, made by directors whose names are quite new to him. He goes to the whole of an Antonioni season. In a film called *L'Eclisse* a woman wanders through the streets of a sunstruck, deserted city. She is disturbed, anguished. What she is anguished about he cannot quite define; her face reveals nothing.

The woman is Monica Vitti. With her perfect legs and sensual lips and abstracted look, Monica Vitti haunts him; he falls in love with her. He has dreams in which he, of all men in the world, is singled out to be her comfort and solace. There is a tap at his door. Monica Vitti stands before him, a finger raised to her lips to signal silence. He steps forward, enfolds her in his arms. Time ceases; he and Monica Vitti are one.

But is he truly the lover Monica Vitti seeks? Will he be any better than the men in her films at stilling her anguish? He is not sure. Even if he found a room for the two of them, a secret retreat in some quiet, fogbound quarter of London, he suspects she would still, at three in the morning, slip out of bed and sit at the table under the glare of a single lamp, brooding, prey to anguish.

The anguish with which Monica Vitti and other of Antonioni's characters are burdened is of a kind he is quite unfamiliar with. In fact it is not anguish at all but something more profound: Angst.

He would like to have a taste of Angst, if only to know what it is like. But, try though he may, he cannot find anything in his heart that he can recognize as Angst. Angst seems to be a European, a properly European, thing; it has yet to find its way to England, to say nothing of England's colonies.

In an article in the *Observer* the Angst of the European cinema is explained as stemming from a fear of nuclear annihilation; also from uncertainty following the death of God. He is not convinced. He cannot believe that what sends Monica Vitti out into the streets of Palermo under the angry red ball of the sun, when she could just as well stay behind in the cool of a hotel room and be made love to by a man, is the hydrogen bomb or a failure on God's part to speak to her. Whatever the true explanation, it must be more complicated than that.

Angst gnaws at Bergman's people too. It is the cause of their irremediable solitariness. Regarding Bergman's Angst, however, the *Observer* recommends that it not be taken too seriously. It smells of pretentiousness, says the *Observer*; it is an affectation not unconnected with long Nordic winters, nights of excessive drinking, hangovers.

Even newspapers that are supposed to be liberal—the *Guardian*, the *Observer*—are hostile, he is beginning to find, to the life of the mind. Faced with something deep and serious, they are quick to sneer, to brush it off with a witticism. Only in tiny enclaves like the Third Programme is new art—American poetry, electronic music, abstract expressionism—taken seriously. Modern England is turning out to be a disturbingly philistine country, little different from the England of W. H. Henley and the Pomp and Circumstance marches that Ezra Pound was fulminating against in 1912.

What then is he doing in England? Was it a huge mistake to have come here? Is it too late to move? Would Paris, city of artists, be more congenial, if somehow he could master French? And what of Stockholm? Spiritually he would feel at home in Stockholm, he suspects. But what about Swedish? And what would he do for a living?

At IBM he has to keep his fantasies of Monica Vitti to himself, and the rest of his arty pretensions too. For reasons that are not clear to him, he has been adopted as a chum by a fellow programmer named Bill Briggs. Bill Briggs is short and pimply; he has a girlfriend named Cynthia whom he is going to marry; he is looking forward to making the down payment on a terrace house in Wimbledon.

Whereas the other programmers speak with unplaceable grammar-school accents and start the day by flipping to the financial pages of the *Telegraph* to check the share prices, Bill Briggs has a marked London accent and stores his money in a building society account.

Despite his social origins, there is no reason why Bill Briggs should not succeed in IBM. IBM is an American company, impatient of Britain's class hierarchy. That is the strength of IBM: men of all kinds can get to the top because all that matters to IBM is loyalty and hard, concentrated work. Bill Briggs is hardworking, and unquestioningly loyal to IBM. Furthermore, Bill Briggs seems to have a grasp of the larger goals of IBM and of its Newman Street data-processing centre, which is more than can be said of him.

IBM employees are provided with booklets of luncheon vouchers. For a three-and-sixpenny voucher one can get a quite decent meal. His own inclination is toward the Lyons brasserie on Tottenham Court Road, where one can visit the salad bar as often as one likes. But Schmidt's in Charlotte Street is the preferred haunt of the IBM programmers. So with Bill Briggs he goes to Schmidt's and eats Wiener Schnitzel or jugged hare. For variety they sometimes go to the Athena on Goodge Street for moussaka. After lunch, if it is not raining, they take a brief stroll around the streets before returning to their desks.

The range of subjects that he and Bill Briggs have tacitly agreed not to broach in their conversations is so wide that he is surprised there is anything left. They do not discuss their desires or larger aspirations. They are silent on their personal lives, on their families and their upbringing, on politics and religion and the arts. Football would be acceptable were it not for the fact that he knows nothing about the English clubs. So they are left with the weather, train strikes, house prices, and IBM: IBM's plans for the future, IBM's customers and those customers' plans, who said what at IBM.

It makes for dreary conversation, but there is an obverse to it. A bare two months ago he was an ignorant provincial stepping ashore into the drizzle of Southampton docks. Now here he is in the heart of London town, indistinguishable in his black uniform from any other London office-worker, exchanging opinions on everyday subjects with a full-blooded Londoner, successfully negotiating all the conversational proprieties. Soon, if his progress continues and he is careful with his vowels, no one will be sparing him a second glance. In a crowd he will pass as a Londoner, perhaps even, in due course, as an Englishman.

Now that he has an income, he is able to rent a room of his own in a house off Archway Road in north London. The room is on the second floor, with a view over a water reservoir. It has a gas heater and a little alcove with a gas cooker and shelves for food and crockery. In a corner is the meter: you put in a shilling and get a shilling's supply of gas.

His diet is unvarying: apples, oat porridge, bread and cheese, and spiced sausages called chipolatas, which he fries over the cooker. He prefers chipolatas to real sausages because they do not need to be refrigerated. Nor do they ooze grease when they fry. He suspects there is lots of potato flour mixed in with the ground meat. But potato flour is not bad for one.

Since he leaves early in the mornings and comes home late, he rarely lays eyes on the other lodgers. A routine soon sets in. He spends Saturdays in bookshops, galleries, museums, cinemas. On Sundays he reads the *Observer* in his room, then goes to a film or for a walk on the Heath.

Saturday and Sunday evenings are the worst. Then the loneliness that he usually manages to keep at bay sweeps over him, loneliness indistinguishable from the low, grey, wet weather of London or from the iron-hard cold of the pavements. He can feel his face turning stiff and stupid with muteness; even IBM and its formulaic exchanges are better than this silence.

His hope is that from the featureless crowds amidst which he moves there will emerge a woman who will respond to his glance, glide wordlessly to his side, return with him (still wordless—what could their first word be?—it is unimaginable) to his bedsitter, make love to him, vanish into the darkness, reappear the next night (he will be sitting over his books, there will be a tap at the door), again embrace him, again, on the stroke of midnight, vanish, and so forth, thereby transforming his life and releasing a torrent of pent-up verse on the pattern of Rilke's *Sonnets to Orpheus*.

The plan at the back of his mind when he came to England, in so far as he had a plan, had been to find a job and save money.

When he had enough money he would give up the job and devote himself to writing. When his savings ran out he would find a new job, and so forth.

He soon discovers how naive that plan is. His salary at IBM, before deductions, is sixty pounds a month, of which he can save at most ten. A year of labour will earn him two months of freedom; much of that free time will be eaten up in searching for the next job.

Furthermore, he learns, he is not at liberty to change employers at will. New regulations governing aliens in England specify that each change of employment be approved by the Home Office. It is forbidden to be footloose: if he resigns from IBM he must promptly find other work or else leave the country.

He has been with IBM long enough by now to be habituated to the routine. Yet still he finds the work-day hard to get through. Though he and his fellow programmers are continually urged, at meetings, in memos, to remember they are the cutting edge of the data-processing profession, he feels like a bored clerk in Dickens sitting on a stool, copying musty documents.

The sole interruptions to the tedium of the day come at eleven and three-thirty, when the tea lady arrives with her trolley to slap down a cup of strong English tea before each of them ('There you go, love'). Only when the five o'clock flurry is past—the secretaries and punch operators leave on the dot, no question of overtime with them—and the evening deepens is he free to leave his desk, wander around, relax. The machine room downstairs, dominated by the huge memory cabinets of the 7090, is more often than not empty; he can run programs on the little 1401 computer, even, surreptitiously, play games on it.

At such times he finds his job not just bearable but pleasing. He would not mind spending all night in the bureau, running programs of his own devising until he grows dozy, then brushing his teeth in the toilet and spreading a sleeping-bag under his desk. It would be better than catching the last train and trudging up Archway Road to his lonely room. But such irregular behaviour would be frowned on by IBM.

He makes friends with one of the punch operators. Her name is Rhoda; she is somewhat thick-legged but has an attractively silky olive complexion. She takes her work seriously; sometimes he stands in the doorway watching her, bent over her keyboard. She is aware of him watching but does not seem to mind.

He never gets to talk to Rhoda about anything beyond work. Her English, with its triphthongs and glottal stops, is not easy to follow. She is a native in a way that his fellow programmers, with their grammar-school backgrounds, are not; the life she leads outside work hours is a closed book to him.

He had prepared himself, when he arrived in the country, for the famous British coldness of temperament. But the girls at IBM, he finds, are not like that at all. They have a cosy sensuality of their own, the sensuality of animals brought up together in the same steamy den, familiar with each other's body habits. Though they cannot compete in glamour with the Swedes and Italians, he is attracted to these English girls, to their equability and humorousness. He would like to get to know Rhoda better. But how? She belongs to a foreign tribe. The barriers he would have to work his way past, to say nothing of the conventions of tribal courtship, baffle and dishearten him.

The efficiency of the Newman Street operation is measured by the use it makes of the 7090. The 7090 is the heart of the bureau, the reason for its existence. When the 7090 is not running its time is called idle time. Idle time is inefficient, and inefficiency is a sin. The ultimate goal of the bureau is to keep the 7090 running all day and all night; the most valued clients are those who occupy the 7090 for hours on end. Such clients are the fief of the senior programmers; he has nothing to do with them.

One day, however, one of the serious clients runs into difficulties with his data cards, and he is assigned to help him. The client is a Mr Pomfret, a little man in a rumpled suit and glasses. He comes to London each Thursday from somewhere in the north of England, bringing boxes and boxes of punched cards; he has a regular six-hour booking on the 7090, starting at midnight. From gossip in the office he learns that the cards contain wind tunnel data for a new British bomber, the TSR-2, being developed for the RAF.

Mr Pomfret's problem, and the problem of Mr Pomfret's colleagues back north, is that the results of the last two weeks' runs are anomalous. They make no sense. Either the test data are faulty or there is something wrong with the design of the plane. His assignment is to reread Mr Pomfret's cards on the auxiliary machine, the 1401, carrying out checks to determine whether any have been mispunched. He works past midnight. Batch by batch he passes Mr Pomfret's cards through the card-reader. In the end he is able to report there is nothing wrong with the punching. The results were indeed anomalous; the problem is real.

The problem is real. In the most incidental, the most minor way, he has joined the TSR-2, project, become part of the British defence effort; he has furthered British plans to bomb Moscow. Is this what he came to England for: to participate in evil, an evil in which there is no reward, not even the most imaginary? Where is the romance in staying up all night so that Mr Pomfret the aeronautical engineer, with his soft and rather helpless air and his suitcase full of cards, can catch the first train north so as to get to the lab in time for his Friday-morning meeting?

He mentions in a letter to his mother that he has been working on wind tunnel data for the TSR-2 but his mother has not the faintest idea what the TSR-2 is.

The wind tunnel tests come to an end. Mr Pomfret's visits to London cease. He watches the papers for further news of the TSR-2, but there is nothing. The TSR-2 seems to have gone into limbo.

Now that it is too late, he wonders what would have happened if, while the TSR-2 cards were in his hands, he had surreptitiously doctored the data on them. Would the whole bomber project have been thrown into confusion, or would the engineers in the north have detected his meddling? On the one hand, he would like to do his bit to save Russia from being bombed. On the other, has he a moral right to enjoy British hospitality while sabotaging their air force? And anyhow, how would the Russians ever get to know that an obscure sympathizer in an IBM office in London had won them a few days' breathing space in the Cold War?

He does not see what the British have against the Russians. Britain and Russia have been on the same side in all the wars he knows of since 1854. The Russians have never threatened to invade Britain. Why then are the British siding with the Americans, who behave like bullies in Europe as all over the world? It is not as though the British actually like the Americans. Newspaper cartoonists are always taking digs at American tourists, with their cigars and pot bellies and flowered Hawaiian shirts and the fistfuls of dollars they brandish. In his opinion, the British ought to take their lead from the French and get out of NATO, leaving the Americans and their new chums the West Germans to pursue their grudge against Russia.

The newspapers are full of CND, the Campaign for Nuclear Disarmament. The pictures they print of weedy men and plain girls with ratty hair waving placards and shouting slogans do not predispose him to like CND. On the other hand, Khrushchev has just carried out a tactical masterstroke: he has built Russian missile-pods in Cuba to counteract the American missiles that ring Russia. Now Kennedy is threatening to bombard Russia unless the Russian missiles are removed from Cuba. This is what CND is agitating against: a nuclear strike in which American bases in Britain would participate. He cannot but approve of its stand.

American spy-planes take pictures of Russian freighters crossing the Atlantic on their way to Cuba. The freighters are carrying more missiles, say the Americans. In the pictures the missiles—vague shapes under tarpaulins—are circled in white. In his view, the shapes could just as well be lifeboats. He is surprised that the papers don't question the American story.

Wake up! clamours CND: *we are on the brink of nuclear annihilation.* Might it be true, he wonders? Is everyone going to perish, himself included?

He goes to a big CND rally on Trafalgar Square, taking care to stay on the fringes as a way of signalling that he is only an onlooker. It is the first mass meeting he has ever been to: fist-shaking and slogan-chanting, the whipping up of passion in general, repel him. Only love and art are, in his opinion, worthy of giving oneself to without reserve.

The rally is the culmination of a fifty-mile march by CND stalwarts that started a week ago outside Aldermaston, the British atomic weapons station. For days the *Guardian* has been carrying pictures of sodden marchers on the road. Now, on Trafalgar Square, the mood is dark. As he listens to the speeches it becomes clear that these people, or some of them, do indeed believe what they say. They believe that London is going to be bombed; they believe they are all going to die.

Are they right? If they are, it seems vastly unfair: unfair to the Russians, unfair to the people of London, but unfair most of all to him, having to be incinerated as a consequence of American bellicosity.

J. M. Coetzee

He thinks of young Nikolai Rostov on the battlefield of Austerlitz, watching like a hypnotized rabbit as the French grenadiers come charging at him with their grim bayonets. *How can they want to kill me*, he protests to himself—*me, whom everyone is so fond of!*

From the frying pan into the fire! What an irony! Having escaped the Afrikaners who want to press-gang him into their army and the blacks who want to drive him into the sea, to find himself on an island that is shortly to be turned to cinders! What kind of world is this in which he lives? Where can one turn to be free of the fury of politics? Only Sweden seems to be above the fray. Should he throw up everything and catch the next boat to Stockholm? Does one have to speak Swedish to get into Sweden? Does Sweden need computer programmers? Does Sweden even have computers?

The rally ends. He goes back to his room. He ought to be reading *The Golden Bowl* or working on his poems, but what would be the point, what is the point of anything?

Then a few days later the crisis is suddenly over. In the face of Kennedy's threats, Khrushchev capitulates. The freighters are ordered to turn back. The missiles already in Cuba are disarmed. The Russians produce a form of words to explain their action, but they have clearly been humiliated. From this episode in history only the Cubans emerge with credit. Undaunted, the Cubans vow that, missiles or not, they will defend their revolution to the last drop of blood. He approves of the Cubans, and of Fidel Castro. At least Fidel is not a coward.

'After careful consideration I have reached the conclusion...' 'After much soul-searching I have come to the conclusion...'

He has been in the service of IBM for over a year: winter, spring, summer, autumn, another winter, and now the beginning of another spring. Even inside the Newman Street bureau, a box-like building with sealed windows, he can feel the suave change in the air. He cannot go on like this. He cannot sacrifice any more of his life to the principle that human beings should have to labour in misery for their bread, a principle he seems to adhere to though he has no idea where he picked it up. He cannot forever be demonstrating to his mother in Cape Town that he has made a solid life for himself and therefore that she can stop worrying about him. Usually he does not know his own mind, does not care to know his own mind. To know one's own mind too well spells, in his view, the death of the creative spark. But in this case he cannot afford to drift on in his usual haze of indecision. He must leave IBM. He must get out, no matter how much it will cost in humiliation.

Over the past year his handwriting has, beyond his control, been growing smaller, smaller and more secretive. Now, sitting at his desk, writing what will be the announcement of his resignation, he tries consciously to make the letters larger, the loops fatter and more confident-seeming.

'After lengthy reflection,' he writes at last, 'I have reached the conclusion that my future does not lie with IBM. In terms of my contract I therefore wish to tender one month's notice.'

He signs the letter, seals it, addresses it to Dr B. L. McIver, Manager, Programming Division, and drops it discreetly in the tray marked INTERNAL. No one in the office gives him a glance. He takes his seat again.

Until three o'clock, when the mail is next collected, there is time for second thoughts, time to slip the letter out of the tray and tear it up. Once the letter is delivered, however, the die will be cast. By tomorrow the news will have spread through the building: one of McIver's people, one of the programmers on the second floor, the South African, has resigned. No one will want to be seen speaking to him. He will be sent to Coventry. That is how it is at IBM. No false sentiment. He will be marked as a quitter, a loser, unclean.

At three o'clock the woman comes around for the mail. He bends over his papers, his heart thumping.

Half an hour later he is summoned to McIver's office. McIver is in a cold fury. 'What is this?' he says, indicating the letter that lies open on the desk.

'I have decided to resign.'

'Why?'

He had guessed McIver would take it badly. McIver is the one who interviewed him for the job, who accepted and approved him, who swallowed the story that he was just an ordinary bloke from the colonies planning a career in computers. McIver has his own bosses, to whom he will have to explain his mistake.

McIver is a tall man. He dresses sleekly, speaks with an Oxford accent. He has no interest in programming as a science or skill or

J. M. Coetzee

craft or whatever it is. He is simply a manager. That is what he is
good at: allotting tasks to people, managing their time, driving them,
getting his money's worth out of them.

'Why?' says McIver again, impatiently.

'I don't find working for IBM very satisfying at a human level. I
don't find it fulfilling.'

'Go on.'

'I was hoping for something more.'

'And what may that be?'

'I was hoping for friendships.'

'You find the atmosphere unfriendly?'

'No, not unfriendly, not at all. People have been very kind. But
being friendly is not the same thing as friendship.'

He had hoped the letter would be allowed to be his last word.
But that hope was naive. He should have realized they would take
it as nothing but the first shot in a war.

'What else? If there is something else on your mind, this is your
chance to bring it out.'

'Nothing else.'

'Nothing else. I see. You are missing friendships. You haven't
found friends.'

'Yes, that's right. I'm not blaming anyone. The fault is probably
my own.'

'And for that you want to resign.'

'Yes.'

Now that the words are out they sound stupid, and they are
stupid. He is being manoeuvred into saying stupid things. But he
should have expected that. That is how they will make him pay for
rejecting them and the job they have given him, a job with IBM, the
market leader. Like a beginner in chess, pushed into corners and
mated in ten moves, in eight moves, in seven moves. A lesson in
domination. Well, let them do it. Let them play their moves, and let
him play his stupid, easily foreseen, easily forestalled return moves,
until they are bored with the game and let him go.

With a brusque gesture McIver terminates the interview. That, for
the moment, is that. He is free to return to his desk. For once there
is not even the obligation to work late. He can leave the building at
five, win the evening for himself.

The next morning, through McIver's secretary—McIver himself sweeps past him, not returning his greeting—he is instructed to report without delay to IBM Head Office in the City, to the Personnel Department.

The man in Personnel who hears his case has clearly had recounted to him the complaint about the friendships IBM has failed to supply. A folder lies open on the desk before him; as the interrogation proceeds, he ticks off points. How long has he been unhappy in his work? Did he at any stage discuss his unhappiness with his superior? If not, why not? Have his colleagues at Newman Street been positively unfriendly? No? Then would he expand on his complaint?

Each time the words *friend*, *friendship*, *friendly* are spoken, the odder they sound. If you are looking for friends, he can imagine the man saying, join a club, play skittles, fly model planes, collect stamps. Why expect your employer, IBM, International Business Machines, manufacturer of electronic calculators and computers, to provide them for you?

And of course the man is right. What right has he to complain, in this country above all, where everyone is so cool to everyone else? Is that not what he admires the English for: their emotional restraint?

Confused and stumbling, he expands on his complaint. His expansion is as obscure to the Personnel man as the complaint itself. *Misapprehension*: that is the word the man is hunting for. *Employee was under a misapprehension*: that would be an appropriate formulation. But he does not feel like being helpful. Let them find their own way of pigeonholing him.

What the man is particularly keen to find out is what he will do next. Is his talk about lack of friendship merely a cover for a move from IBM to one of IBM's competitors in the field of business machines? Have promises been made to him, have inducements been offered?

He could not be more earnest in his denials. He does not have another job lined up, with a rival or anyone else. He has not been interviewed. He is leaving IBM simply to get out of IBM. He wants to be free, that is all. The more he talks, the sillier he sounds, the more out of place in the world of business. But at least he is not saying, 'I am leaving IBM in order to become a poet.' That secret, at least, is still his own. □

NFT50 *bfi*

JOIN THE NATIONAL FILM THEATRE

Taxi Driver

Man with a Movie Camera

Metropolis

Amélie

AND RECEIVE A TICKET TO SEE ONE FILM ABSOLUTELY FREE*

Other benefits include: reduced price tickets for you and up to three guests*, illustrated monthly programme mailings, advance priority booking and much more.

CALL 020 7815 1374
Annual membership costs just £20 (£13 concessions)

Celebrating 50 years of the National Film Theatre on the South Bank London SE1

Background: Sid & Nancy   *Excludes RLFF   Waterloo   www.bfi.org.uk/nft

GRANTA

THE HABIT
Francis Spufford

Prince Caspian

C. S. LEWIS

A Puffin Book

The Habit

'**I** can always tell when you're reading somewhere in the house,' my mother used to say. 'There's a special silence, a *reading* silence.' I never heard it, this extra degree of hush that somehow travelled through walls and ceilings to announce that my seven-year-old self had become about as absent as a present person could be. The silence went both ways. As my concentration on the story in my hands took hold, all sounds faded away. My ears closed. Flat on my front with my chin on my hands or curled in a chair like a prawn, I'd be gone. I didn't hear doorbells ring, I didn't hear supper time called, I didn't notice footsteps approaching of the adult who'd come to retrieve me. They had to shout 'Francis!' near my head or, laughing, 'Chocolate!'

I laughed too. Reading catatonically wasn't something I chose to do, it just happened, and I was happy for it to be my funny characteristic in the family, a trademark oddity my parents were affectionate towards. Though I never framed the thought then, stopping my ears with fiction was non-negotiable. There were things to block out.

I was three when my sister Bridget was born. She was a small baby. Instead of following the nice upward graph of weight gain and turning into a rosy, compact toddler, she puked and thinned out. Instead of hitting the developmental milestones, and sitting up, and crawling, she just lay there. Her bones started to show through. By the time she was a few months old it was clear that something was wrong, but it took the doctors quite a while to come up with a diagnosis, because the odds were so long against the particular biological booby prize she had won. My parents were not related by blood. They came from different parts of the country. They had nothing obvious in common physically, except height and short-sightedness, and a certain earnest bearing. When she was twenty, my mother had disconcerted the male students who wanted to seduce her by not knowing the rules of the game: not so much resisting, as failing to notice that there was something to resist. At the same age my father had been frequently mistaken for a curate, which will happen if you go into a pub in a steel town when you're on an industrial-archaeology field trip, and order yourself a half pint of lemonade to drink. But it turned out that they shared something else. Lost and unnoticed somewhere on the braid of their DNA, both carried an identical sequence of Gs, As, Ts and Cs. The sequence was recessive—it produced no symptoms in the carrier, and it would remain inactive if they had a child with anyone who didn't also have it. Put together two carriers, on the other hand, and each time a sperm fertilized an egg you rolled a dice. I was lucky: I inherited the trait only in the same passive form that my parents had. Bridget wasn't. In her the sequence activated, and made her unable to process an amino acid called cystine. Instead of waste cystine being flushed out of her tissues, it accumulated, as crystals. It accumulated fastest of all in the organs which were supposed to act as filters, her kidneys. There were only about twenty other living sufferers in Britain, only a few hundred in the world: and most of them were found in a cluster in the Appalachians, where hillbillies had been upping the odds by marrying their cousins for generation after generation. It was a ridiculously rare disease, a disaster it was almost absurd to be afflicted by, like being struck by a meteorite. By the time that the Great Ormond Street Children's Hospital in London made the connection between Bridget's failure to thrive and the condition called 'cystinosis' that appeared in the obscure footnotes of medical literature, she had one kidney already defunct, and the other about to give in. It was the autumn of 1967. Only a little time before, she'd have died right then. But the hospital had an experimental therapy that might offer her a few years of life. They offered a plan that would keep her on, but not over, the brink of starvation. My parents threw themselves into doing what was necessary. They crawled out of bed hourly during the night to adjust the tube that fed sugar-water, drop by drop, up Bridget's nose, down her throat past her gag reflex, and straight into her stomach. They coaxed her into taking a daily fistful of pills. They did the four-hour return rail journey to London again and again. They ran a large overdraft. They were brave. Family photographs from the time show them grey-skinned with fatigue, but always smiling, always determinedly broadcasting the message that this was all right, this was manageable, this could be sustained.

I was much too young to take in the causes and effects. I remember being asked which name I liked better, Bridget or Sophie, just after she was born; then nothing until, a year or so later, a generic scene of all four of us in my parents' bed on a Sunday morning, me playing with a drift of red and white Lego pieces, Bridget already well into the routine of existing with a fingertip grasp on the medical precipice. What I could see was that she was emaciated. Her legs dangled out of her frocks like strings. In her, the round family face we all shared became a neat little billiard ball very tightly stretched with skin, a sweet little death's-head. She could talk long before she could walk. The sugar-water was the staple part of her diet, leaving her faintly nauseated a lot of the time, but it was important to tempt her to put aside the sick feeling, when she could, and to eat a little bit, a very little bit, of protein. My parents weighed out minuscule delicacies on a pair of white scales so small they would have made a more natural part of a drug dealer's equipment. 'Look, Bridget,' they said—'how about a quarter of an ounce of chicken?' They drafted Bridget's imaginary friend, Ben, and gave him a new passion for hiding the silver key to the sewing machine case at the bottom of pipkins of cold milk; a key which would only be revealed if all the milk was drunk.

And what I understood about Bridget's fragility made the whole world fragile. It was compounded by my mother, in her early thirties, developing osteoporosis, the brittle-bone condition women don't usually get till after the menopause. Bridget sat on rugs at family picnics, looking as if a breath of wind would blow her away; my mother sported ever-changing plaster casts as she collected fractures. Arm casts, leg casts, a complete upper-body cast. Whatever my life had been like before Bridget was born, it was over: cause for a sibling envy so fierce that I didn't dare show it, or even feel it much, in case it cracked the thinned skeleton of what was left.

It hurt to look at Bridget's situation face on, and I shied away from it. Consequently, although she was a familiar presence, I never really got to know her very well as an individual human proposition. Other people always praised her sense of humour. They seemed to see someone using a dry wit to cope. What wit, I thought? I never found her jokes funny. The ho-ho-ho-ing that greeted them struck me as forced; more than that, as a handy get-out for the people who laughed. It was like the famous put-down she had apparently come up with when I was six or so, and she was three, still rug-bound, and entirely dependent on verbal comebacks. 'You,' she was supposed to have said, crushingly, 'are a little piece of fluff'—and

Francis Spufford

immediately this had been adopted into the family myth as evidence that Bridget could take care of herself, oh yes. I distrusted it for that very reason. In truth, I don't know now whether her jokes were funny or not. I wish I could remember more of them. I dismissed them a priori, on principle. I could never believe in a self-possession large enough to encompass the ruin I perceived: therefore, she had none. I just saw raw vulnerability.

So when I read stories obsessively as a child I was striking a kind of deal that allowed me to turn away. Sometime in childhood I made a bargain that limited, so I thought, the power over me that real experience had, the real experience which comes to us in act and incident and through the proximate, continuous existence of those we love. All right, I said, I'll let a quantity of *that* stream over me, if I can have a balancing portion of *this*, the other kind of experience, which is controlled, and repeatable, and comes off the page. I learned to pump up the artificial realities of fiction from page to mind at a pressure that equalized with the pressure of the world, so that (in theory) the moment I actually lived in could never fill me completely, whatever was happening.

Thirty years have gone by since then. My life has changed, and so has the content of my reading. But the bargain holds. Still, when I reach for a book, I am reaching for an equilibrium. I am reading to banish pity, and brittle bones. I am reading to evade guilt, and avoid consequences, and to limit time's hold on me.

One January day when I was four, the au pair from Denmark who was helping out my parents while my sister was in hospital, took me for a walk in the Keele woods, near where we lived. She'd been reading me the chapter in *Winnie-the-Pooh* where Pooh and Piglet go round and round the spinney in the snow, trying to catch the Woozle. 'Let's go and find Piglet,' she said. The woods were under snow as well, that day. The snow was deep and powdery on the paths, and the trees were smoothed, white masses bowed under the weight of winter, like melted candles. We passed through a zone of little fir trees near the bottom of the steps down into the woods, leaving behind a trail of big footprints and a trail of little ones. (It's not a coincidence that Pooh and Piglet walking together

146

in Ernest Shepard's illustrations have exactly the relative sizes of an adult and child going hand in hand.) And there, perched on the hollow stump of an oak, was Piglet, wearing a small red scarf just like in the pictures. The soft toy versions of the Disney characters did not exist yet. She had sewn him herself from grey and white cotton ticking. It was wonderful.

Looking back, I see that moment almost as the first step in a seduction. As a ten-year-old, as a teenager, as an adult, I've always wanted life to be more storylike; I've always reached out for treats, set-ups, situations that can be coaxed by charm and by the right kind of suggestively narrative talk into yielding something like the deliberate richness of an invented scene. Friends and lovers have known me as someone willing to say aloud sentences they thought could only exist on the page, in the hope that real time could be arranged and embroidered. I'd like words to be magic; or magnetic, attracting the events they name. Perhaps I first saw the chance of that when we found Piglet in the snow.

But at four I was only a hearer of stories. It isn't until we're reading stories privately, on our own account, that story's full seducing power can be felt. For the voice that tells us a story aloud is always more than a carrier wave bringing us the meaning; it's a companion through the events of the story, ensuring that the feelings it stirs in us are held within the circle of attachment connecting the adult reading to the child listening. To hear a story is a social act. Social rules, social promises, social bonds sustain us during it. It is only when we read it stumblingly for ourselves that we feel the full force of the story's challenge.

I learned to read around my sixth birthday. I was making a dinosaur in school from crêpe bandage and toilet rolls when I started to feel as if an invisible pump was inflating my head from the inside. My face became a cluster of bumps, my feet dangled limp and too far away to control. The teacher carried me home on her shoulders. I gripped the dinosaur in one hand. It was still wet with green and purple poster paint. After that things turned delirious. I had mumps; and one by one my sister, my mother and my father all caught it from me. The house stayed convalescent in feeling till the last of us was better. It was a long quiet time of curtains closed during the day, and wan slow-moving adults, and bedsheets that seemed as big as the world when you lay in them, each wrinkle a canyon. On my sixth birthday my class came up the road and sang 'Happy Birthday to You' in the front garden. It was too nice. I hid behind the curtain in my dressing gown and would not show myself at the upstairs window. Perhaps, for the very first time in my life, I was impatient to be done with a human encounter and to get back to my book. When I caught the mumps, I couldn't read; when I went back to school again, I could. The first page of *The Hobbit* was a thicket of symbols, to be decoded one at a time and joined hesitantly together. Primary schools in Britain now sometimes send home a photocopy of a page of Russian or Arabic to remind parents of that initial state when writing was a wall of spiky unknowns, an excluding briar hedge. By the time I reached *The Hobbit*'s last page, though, writing had softened, and lost the outlines of the printed alphabet, and become a transparent liquid, first viscous and sluggish, like a jelly of meaning, then ever thinner and more mobile, flowing faster and faster, until it reached me at the speed of thinking and I could not entirely distinguish the suggestions it was making from my own thoughts. I had undergone the acceleration into the written word that you also experience as a change in the medium. In fact, writing had ceased to be a thing—an object in the world—and become a medium, a substance you look through.

I. N. In. *A.* In a. *H, o, l, e.* In a hole. *I, n, t, h, e, g, r, o, u, n, d.* In a hole in the ground. *L-i-v-e-d-a-h-o-b-b-i-t.* In a hole in the ground lived a hobbit... And then I never stopped again.

The reading flowed, when I was six with the yellow hardback copy of *The Hobbit* in my hands; and the pictures came. I went to the door of the hobbit hole with Bilbo as he let in more and more dwarves attracted by the sign Gandalf had scratched there in the glossy green paint. I jogged along with him on his pony out of the Shire, away from raspberry jam and crumpets, and towards dragons. In *The Lord of the Rings*, this journey would become a transit from a little, naive space of comfort and tended fields into a dangerous world that besieged it. This time, it was only the natural progression of a story outwards from home. Bilbo's life in Bag End was like real life, or at any rate like a bachelor fantasy of it, in which fifty is only just grown up, and the highest felicities are a pipe and convivial male company. The further away from Bag End Bilbo went, the more purely he inhabited the world of adventure, and even of epic. But Bilbo went on sounding like himself, chatty, fussy, scared, resourceful, prosy: ordinary. 'Dear me! Dear me! I am sure this is all very uncomfortable.' He took me to the mountains, and the caverns, and the hollow halls that the dwarves had sung about back at Bag End, in a kind of promise that the book kept. I was ordinary too; if Bilbo could be there, so could I. Tolkien made him more extravagantly cowardly than I thought of myself as being. 'Then he fell flat on the floor, and kept on calling out "struck by lightning, struck by lightning!" over and over again; and that was all they could get out of him for a long time.' The angle from which Tolkien looked at Bilbo set a limit on how scary events in *The Hobbit* could be. Nothing too awful could happen to someone like Bilbo, even if the goblins did set fire to the tree he was hiding in, and sing about skin cracking, eyes glazing, fat melting and bones blackening.

I find now, rereading *The Hobbit*, that Tolkien described few things in the detail I remember. His was a speedy, storyteller's art. It made a few precise suggestions, supplied a few nodal adjectives from which the web of an imagined world could grow in a child's mind, and didn't linger. I made the pictures. I was lucky that my first book put me in the hands of a writer with such a conscious and decided idea of what a reader's imagination needed. Tolkien had trained himself on the hard nugget-like specifics of Anglo-Saxon and Viking poetry, with its names for things that were almost spells, and its metaphors that were almost riddles. At six I had no idea that the sea had once been the whale-path, or that Tolkien had any predecessors when he had Bilbo boast to Smaug that he was 'the clue-finder, the web-cutter, the stinging fly'. What I did know explicitly was that while Tolkien's words were authoritative, his occasional black-and-white drawings in the text only counted as suggestions that I was free to accept or refuse. What Middle-earth looked like was my business. Illustrations—I decided—were limitations. I had not been able to picture Bilbo's face, but I was comfortable with that. It seemed that he existed in a story-space in which it was not necessary that the points of Tolkien's description of a hobbit (round stomach, bright clothes, hairy feet, clever fingers, good-natured expression) should coalesce into one definite image; and in that, Bilbo was like my parents and my sister, whose ultimately-familiar faces I found wouldn't come either when I shut my eyes and tried to summon them in the brown and purple dark behind my eyelids. No: the natural destiny of a story was to be a rich, unresolved swirl in my visual cortex, and any illustrator who tried to pin it down was taking a liberty.

At the same time, I couldn't read quite a lot of the words in *The Hobbit*. I had accelerated into reading faster than my understanding had grown. If I press my memory for the sensation of reading the second half of the book, when I was flying through the story, I remember, simultaneous with the new liquid smoothness, a constant flicker of incomprehensibility. There were holes in the text corresponding to the parts I couldn't understand. Words like *prophesying*, *rekindled* and *adornment* had never been spoken in my hearing. No one had ever told me aloud to *behold* something, and I didn't know that *vessels* could be cups and bowls as well as ships. I could say these words over, and shape my mouth around their big sounds. I could enjoy them. They were obviously the special vocabulary that was apt for the slaying of dragons and the fighting of armies: words that conjured the sound of trumpets. But for all the meaning I obtained from them, they might as well not have been printed. When I speeded up, and my reading became fluent, it was partly because I had learned how to ignore such words efficiently. I methodically left out chunks. I marked them to be sorted out later, by slower and more patient mental processes; I allowed each one to brace a blank space of greater or lesser size in its sentence; I grabbed the gist, which seemed to survive even in sentences that were mostly hole; and I sped on.

Now that I hardly ever spell out a word I do not know, and the things that puzzle me in books do not lie in individual words but in the author's assumption of shared knowledge about the human heart (never my strong point), I still have, like everybody, words in my vocabulary that are relics of that time. The words we learned exclusively from books are the ones we pronounce differently from everyone else. Or, if we force ourselves to say them the public way, secretly we believe the proper pronunciation is our own, deduced from the page and not corrected by hearing the word aloud until it was too late to alter its sound. The classic is 'misled', said not as *mis-led* but as *myzled*—the past tense of a verb, 'to misle', which somehow never comes up in the present tense. In fact, misled never misled me. One of mine is 'grimace'. You probably think it's pronounced *grimuss*, but I know different. It's *grim-ace* to rhyme with 'face'. I'm sorry, but on this point, the entire English-speaking human race except me is wrong.

I began my reading in a kind of hopeful springtime for children's writing. I was born in 1964, so I grew up in a golden age comparable to the present heyday of J. K. Rowling and Philip Pullman, or to the great Edwardian decade when E. Nesbit, Kipling and Kenneth Grahame were all publishing at once. An equally amazing generation of talent was at work as the 1960s ended and the 1970s began. William Mayne was making dialogue sing; Peter Dickinson was writing the *Changes* trilogy; Alan Garner was reintroducing myth into the bloodstream of daily life; Jill Paton Walsh was showing that children's perceptions could be just as angular and uncompromising as those of adults; Joan Aiken had begun her Dido Twite series of comic fantasies; Penelope Farmer was being unearthly with *Charlotte Sometimes*; Diana Wynne Jones's gift for wild invention was hitting its stride; Rosemary Sutcliff was just adding the final uprights to her colonnade of Romano-British historical novels; Leon Garfield was reinventing the eighteenth century as a scene for inky Gothic intrigue. The list went on and on. There was activity everywhere, a new potential classic every few months.

Unifying this lucky concurrence of good books, and making them seem for a while like contributions to a single intelligible project, was a temporary cultural consensus: a consensus both about what children were, and about where we all were in history. Dr Spock's great manual for liberal, middle class child-rearing had come out at the beginning of the Sixties, and had helped deconstruct the last lingering remnants of the idea that a child was clay to be moulded by benevolent adult authority. The new orthodoxy took it for granted that a child was a resourceful individual, neither ickily good nor reeking of original sin. And the wider world was seen as a place in which a permanent step forward towards enlightenment had taken place as well. The books my generation were offered took it for granted that poverty, disease and prejudice essentially belonged in the past. Post-war society had ended them. As the 1970s went on, these assumptions would lose their credibility. Gender roles were about to be shaken up; the voices that a white, liberal consensus consigned to the margins of consciousness were about to be asserted as hostile witnesses to its nature. People were about to lose their certainty that liberal solutions worked. Evil would revert to being an unsolved problem. But it hadn't happened yet; and till it did, the collective gaze of children's stories swept confidently across past and future, and across all the international varieties of the progressive, orange-juice-drinking present, from Australia to Sweden, from Holland to the broad, clean suburbs of America.

For me, walking up the road aged seven or eight to spend my pocket money on a paperback, the outward sign of this unity was the dominance of Puffin Books. In Britain, almost everything written for children passed into the one paperback imprint. On the shelves of the children's section in a bookshop, practically all the stock would be identically neat soft-covered octavos, in different colours, with different cover art, but always with the same sans-serif type on the spine, and the same little logo of an upstanding puffin. Everything cost about the same. For 17½p—then 25p and then 40p as the 1970s inflation took hold—you could have any of the new books, or any of the children's classics, from the old ones like the *The Wind in the Willows* or *Alice* to the ones that were only a couple of decades into their classichood, like the Narnia books. (C. S. Lewis had died the year before I was born, most unfairly making sure I would never meet him.) To a British reading child in the Sixties or the Seventies, how securely authoritative Puffins seemed, with the long trustworthy descriptions of the story inside the front cover, always written by the same arbiter, the Puffin editor Kaye Webb, and their astonishingly precise recommendation to 'girls of eleven and above, and sensitive boys'. It was as if Puffin were part of the administration of the world. They were the department of the welfare state responsible for the distribution of narrative.

Bookshops were nice, but the real home of the massed possibilities of story was the public library. Before I discovered it, my life beyond home encompassed only the university—the solitary rooms

The Habit

I found my parents working in. My father's office in the Chancellor's Building smelled of floor polish, and the butterscotches he sucked when he was concentrating. It was a modernist box, whose glass and concrete he'd fitted out with the old desk and the heraldic panels he had brought with him from Cambridge, pouring the spirit of the history he studied into the future he believed in: the civilized welfare state that educated all its talented sons and daughters. The past flowed into the future without any break for him, because the student revolution and the counterculture had happened while his attention was elsewhere. Princess Margaret had come to a University of Keele function in 1965 or thereabouts and made a beeline for my parents, the youngest people in the room, hoping they would be groovy. 'Do you know anything about pop music?' she asked. 'No,' they said, embarrassed. And it was true. As a teenager I would test them with pictures of Elvis, unable to believe that two people who had been young in the Fifties could really fail to recognize him. I gave them clues. Memphis? No. Blue suede shoes? No. Rock 'n' roll? 'Ah yes,' said my father proudly—'the music with the very strong *beat*!'

Keele University ran a free bus service for the cleaners who came up from the towns of the Potteries to Keele Park to wax the floors of the university departments and clean the students' rooms. Anyone could use it, and from when I was about seven or so, I regularly rode the bus down the hill on my own to visit the library in Newcastle-under-Lyme. The bus turned out of the park gates, and suddenly, instead of being inside the small horizon of the campus, cupped on the hilltop round its lakes and woods, the view opened on to a long valley full of housing estates and pit winding-gear and factories. In the fields sloping down to the town, bullocks nosed at blackberry bushes on rainy mornings. Rooks cawed in the trees. At night the valley twinkled with sodium lights. Beyond the new roundabout at the foot of Keele Bank, the weirdly centreless conurbation of the Potteries began, as large as a city altogether, but never as concentrated. There were five small-town provincial High Streets, five sets of Victorian civic architecture. Newcastle's core was red sandstone, scorched by nineteenth-century industrial soot.

As I first remember it, it still had a cattle market, and one of those courtly antique grocery emporiums smelling of cheese and coffee beans, where the money my parents paid over for food in neat waxed-paper

Francis Spufford

packages vanished into the ceiling up pneumatic tubes, and the change came jingling down other tubes into round brass dishes the size of an ashtray. But both those hold-outs from the past had vanished by the time I was taking myself to the library. The shops along the Ironmarket had posters of Slade, 10cc and the Osmonds for sale. When I bought a packet of Sweet Cigarettes for 4p in decimal currency there was a cigarette card of the space race inside. Down Bridge Street there was an Indian restaurant where I had been with my dad and adventurously eaten a biriani. When my Coke came, there'd been a slice of lemon floating in it. Amazing sophistication!

The town seemed just as glamorous to me as the parkland up the hill, only with a different orientation, a different job to do in my imagination. For a long time, just as I set any wild scene in Keele woods, whenever I read a story set somewhere urban, I borrowed Newcastle in my mind's eye as the setting. Newcastle figured as London, as Paris; tweaked with columns, it was Rome, with a few pointy bits on the roofs it was Chinese. Later, when I read *To Kill a Mockingbird*, I made it into the Deep South.

The library was a brand-new concrete and glass block at the end of the Ironmarket. In the window, leaflets about passing your driving test were stapled to a corkboard, and there was a poster, put up well in advance, encouraging you to PLANT A TREE IN SEVENTY-THREE. To get to the children's section, you turned sharp left inside and down the stairs into a long basement room lit by the blue-white of fluorescent tubes. The issue desk was at the far end, next to the floor-level picture books and coloured stools for the tinies; two or three wire twirlers of paperbacks tried to tempt you on your way out, like the chocolates for impulse purchasers at supermarket checkouts, but at that time library budgets ran to hardbacks as a matter of course, and, anyway, paperbacks were for owning yourself. The library's true treasure was the A–Z Children's Hardback Fiction, running the whole length of the right-hand wall on metal shelves arranged in big U-shaped bays. Every book had its dustwrapper sealed on to the cover in heavy-duty plastic, soup-proof, thumb-proof, spaghetti-hoop-proof. Every book bore a yellow Dewey Decimal code number on a sticker on the spine. I approached them slowly, not with reverence exactly, but with the feeling that the riches in the room needed to be handled with some kind of grateful attention to their ordered abundance. Also, I knew that once I'd chosen my four books, the multiple possibilities of the library would shrink down to that finite handful. I hated to be hurried out of the great, free bazaar.

Books, it seemed to me, could vary more than virtually anything else that went around in the world under one name. They infused me with incompatible, incomparable emotions. Arthur Ransome's *Swallows and Amazons* series, for example, idylls of meticulous detail, instructive about semaphore and surveying and gold refining. They let me try out a counter-life for size: a wonderful alternative to my own small, dreamy, medically-unlucky family of four. Ransome's brothers and sisters were robust. They milled around. The parents waved the adventurers off at the dock on page one, and no intense spotlight of anxiety fell on anyone. They reminded me of my cousins in Cambridgeshire, who messed about in canoes on Fen rivers. The stories blended with the life I imagined my cousins had. Without having to feel disloyal, I could experiment, reading Arthur Ransome, with the idea of belonging to that other version of family life that existed over at my aunt and uncle's house, with its dinghy in the garage, and its big Pyrex pots of stew and mounds of boiled potatoes at meal times instead of our Elizabeth David-inspired experiments with risotto and pasta.

When I made my choice, I knew that I could have melancholy under my arm on the way to the bus stop; or laughter; or fear; or enchantment. Or longing. I didn't just want to see in books what I saw anyway in the world around me, even if it was perceived and understood and articulated from angles I could never have achieved; I wanted to see things I never saw in life. More than I wanted books to do anything else, I wanted them to take me away. I wanted exodus.

Exodus: and not least from school. I had two friends, but they played soccer most break times, leaving me at a loose end in a playground that never seemed to be intelligible the way a story was. There was no narrator. I would banish my uncertainty by walking around and around the white line at the edge. Pace, pace, pace, corner; pace, pace, pace, corner, looking neither to right nor to left until the whistle blew. I abolished loneliness, I abolished school, by thinking myself into the schools I had read about. From Angela Brazil and the Chalet School books, through to the unexpected rebirth of the genre at Hogwarts in the Harry Potter books—where a new atmosphere, both magical and democratic, still does not displace such key features as the sneering rich boy, and the contest for the house cup—school stories explore what are essentially autonomous towns of children. As a perceptive critic of Harry Potter pointed out, what makes the school setting liberating is that school rules are always arbitrary rules, externally imposed. You can break them, when you get into scrapes, without feeling any guilt, or without it affecting the loyalty to the institution that even unruly characters feel, right down from Angela Brazil to Joanne Rowling. Harry loves Hogwarts. The rules of conduct that really count are worked out by the children themselves, and exist inside the school rules like a live body inside a suit of armour. School stories are about children judging each other, deciding about each other, getting along with each other. The adults whose decisions would be emotionally decisive— parents—are deliberately absent.

Soon my parents were absent too. At the age of ten I was sent away to boarding school, a choir school, my parents having discovered the miserable miles I was covering round the playground. At first I hated the way that even sleeping wasn't private. You were in bed, but the bed wasn't truly your bed, the sheets weren't your sheets. I pulled the covers over me as if they were the bedroom door I hadn't got, but it never entirely worked. The pocket of warmth you made as you curled up was still an ambiguous, only semi-boundaried zone. Rustles and snuffles and coughs came from the beds four feet to the left, and four feet to the right. You could hear the world that had rung electric bells at you all day, and called you by your surname, and required you to be on your guard all the time, still going on; and though the oblivion that came when your mind's grip on your surroundings softened, and frayed, and parted, was truly private, sleep being a kingdom whose doors opened equally everywhere, it never seemed to last for more than a moment before morning came and the long cycle of the school day began again. Boarding school was a town of children, just as the stories said, but what the stories hadn't told me was how strange it would feel, at first, to live for weeks at a time with boys' social hierarchies omnipresent and the deep connections of family nowhere.

The Habit

It took three years, but I got used to it eventually. I found the compensations in boarding school, from having teachers who seemed actually pleased when I knew things, to the astonishing comfort of fitting in. I had, not just a few best friends, but a role I could play. Other boys knew what I was when they saw me coming, and had a workable set of expectations about it. It turned out that school—this school, anyway—had an actual niche for someone bookish who was willing to play bookish, and live up to the images of cleverness that were current in our shared world of comics, and war films, and TV programmes. I could be Brains in *Thunderbirds*, I could be Q in *Live and Let Die*. I could be the officer there invariably was on the escape committee at Stalag Luft 17 who wore glasses and came up with cunning plans. In short, I could be a Prof. It was a mask, but it felt as if it bore a friendly relationship to my face.

And beneath these satisfactions, I had a feeling as if a long-tied private knot had been loosened. My family's unending medical crisis had gone into lovely, unexpected remission. The prediction had been that Bridget would die by the time she was eight or so, but by chance she had survived long enough for medicine to move on. They still couldn't do anything about the cystinosis itself. Cystine crystals were still forming, an accident happening in every one of her cells. But transplant surgery had arrived, by 1975, pioneered as a solution to quite different diseases but perhaps adaptable to her problem. The doctors thought that a transplanted kidney could probably be protected by careful management from going the way of her own; maybe it would give her more life; maybe it could even give a semblance of an ordinary life. So in the year that she was eight and I was eleven, her medical notes, by now a mass of paper it took a trolley to move, were transferred to the kidney unit at Guy's Hospital, and to save time looking for a compatible kidney my father donated her one of his. He and Bridget were trundled into theatre together on two gurneys. They disappeared through the red rubber doors: my mother took me to spend the afternoon in a little stamp dealer's shop under Waterloo Bridge. I should have been terrified, with two of the three people I loved most going under the knife at once, but I had cultivated blind faith in doctors as an essential fear-limiting tool, and I don't remember being afraid during that long, edgy afternoon, nor noticing what my mother was feeling either. I remember the stamps. They were the ordinary pre-decimal British definitives, in strips, in little glassine envelopes. The Queen on them was a young woman, her black-and-white photograph an oval island on a rectangle of pale, clear colour. The halfpenny stamp was orange, the penny blue, the thruppence purple.

The operation had its costs. My father's hair turned white at forty-one. The steroids they pumped into Bridget to stop her body rejecting the kidney made her bloat up, turning her abruptly from a very thin person into a very fat one, so drastic and irreversible a transformation that for the rest of her life it was hard to find more than occasional reminders of the person she had been before, in a glimpse of the back of her neck, for example, always slender even when she was most enpudgified. But it seemed to work. Suddenly, for the first time, Bridget could walk distances, and eat normal food. The crated bottles of sugar-water faded out of her life, leaving nothing behind but a hatred for sweet things, and a counterbalancing taste for vicious little salad dressings, heavy on the pepper and the tabasco. Suddenly her life had no fixed expiration date any more. The year after the transplant, she stumped to the top of a Scottish mountain. It was a small mountain, but it was a mountain. The wind on the summit blew her tartan cape around her ears, but she herself was anchored: solid enough, decisively enough there in the flesh that there was no danger of the wind blowing her away. Gravity had hold of her. I didn't have to see her any more as thistledown, or bird bones, or a crushable paper sculpture. Something in me that had been vigilant for years, relaxed.

I wish I'd been brave enough as a teenager to try the experiment of facing the emotions that all this left pooled in the sump of my psyche. Books might have helped here, too: they can be instruments of hope and discovery, after all, as well as of escape. But I wasn't. It's not that the story of my life as a reader from thirteen onward has followed one grim line of evasion. I hoped. I discovered. But when it came to it, whenever fear presented itself to me and asked to be addressed, I always turned back to books as the medium into which I was used to pouring my troublesome emotions.

Bridget died when she was twenty-two, of cystine deposits in the brain, the one organ that can't be transplanted. 'I'm sick of living at the frontiers of medical knowledge,' she said soon before the end. She lingered long enough for my father to read her the whole of *The Lord of the Rings*, aloud.

I still go into bookshops when things go wrong. And as I walk down the aisles, I remember that in every novel there are reverses, that all plots twist and turn, that sadness and happiness are just the materials authors use, in arrangements I know very well; and at that thought the books seem to kindle into a kind of dim life all around me, each one unfolding its particular nature into my awareness without urgency, without haste, as if a column of grey, insubstantial smoke were rising from it, softening the air, filling it with words and actions which are all provisional, which could all be changed for others, according to taste. Among these drifting pillars, the true story of my life looks no different; it is just a story among stories, and after I have been reading for a while, I can hardly tell any more which is my own. □

Celebrating
Women's Writing

SPIT-LIT
FESTIVAL
3-10 March
2002

presented by **Alternative Arts**

**Readings, Talks, Discussions, Performances,
Interviews, Signings, Exhibitions, Workshops**

SPITALFIELDS, LONDON E1

Free Programmes and Bookings
020 7247 2584

LONDON ARTS

*City*SIDE regeneration

SPITALFIELDS
MARKET
COMMUNITY
TRUST

CORPORATION
OF LONDON

Tower Hamlets

'In its blend of memoirs, photojournalism and reportage, and in its championing of contemporary realist fiction, Granta has its face pressed firmly against the window, determined to witness the world.' *Observer* 1. New American Writing 2. The Portage to San Cristobal of A.H. 3. The End of the English Novel 4. Beyond the Crisis 5. The Modern Common Wind 6. A Literature for Politics 7. Best of Young British Novelists (I) 8. Dirty Realism 9. John Berger, 'Boris' 10. Travel Writing 11. Milan Kundera: Greetings from Prague 12. The Rolling Stones 13. After the Revolution 14. Autobiography 15. James Fenton, 'The Fall of Saigon' 16. Science 17. Graham Greene,'While Waiting for a War' 18. James Fenton, 'The Snap Revolution' 19. More Dirt 20. In Trouble Again: A Special Issue of Travel Writing 21. The Story-Teller 22. With Your Tongue Down My Throat 23. Home 24. Inside Intelligence 25. The Murderee 26. Travel 27. Death 28. Birthday Special! 29. New World 30. New Europe! 31. The General 32. History 33. What Went Wrong? 34. Death of a Harvard Man 35. The Unbearable Peace 36. Vargas Llosa 37. The Family 38. We're So Happy! 39. The Body 40. The Womanizer 41. Biography 42. Krauts! 43. Best of Young British Novelists (II) 44. The Last Place on Earth 45. Gazza Agonistes 46. Crime 47. Losers 48. Africa 49. Money 50. Fifty! 51. Big Men (and L.A. Women) 52. Food 53. News: Scoops, Lies and Videotape 54. Best of Young American Novelists 55. Children: Blind, Bitter Happiness 56. What Happened To Us? Britain's Valedictory Realism 57. India: the Golden Jubilee 58. Ambition 59. France 60. Unbelievable: Unlikely Ends, Fateful Escapes and the Fascism of Flowers 61. The Sea 62. What Young Men Do 63. Beasts 64. Russia: The Wild East 65. London: The Lives of the City 66. Truth + Lies 67. Women and Children First 68. Love Stories 69. The Assassin 70. Australia: The New, New World 71. Shrinks 72. Overreachers 73. Necessary Journeys 74. Confessions of a Middle-Aged Ecstacy Eater 75. Brief Encounters 76. Music 77. What We Think Of America 78. FREE ISSUE! *See overleaf...*

FREE ISSUE OFFER

Every issue of Granta features outstanding new fiction, memoir, reportage and photography. Every issue of Granta is a handsome, illustrated paperback of at least 256 pages—because the writing itself endures. Every issue of Granta is special. That's why it's published only four times a year: to keep it that way.

So why not subscribe? It's excellent value for money: you save up to £38 on the bookshop price of £8.99 an issue—and get Granta delivered to you at home. **Or give Granta to a friend?** A Granta subscription makes an unusual, thoughtful and lasting gift.

YOU SAVE 25% (£9) with a one year (four-issue) subscription for £26.95. In other words, you get a Granta—free.

YOU SAVE 30% (£22) with a two year (eight-issue) subscription for £50.

YOU SAVE 38% (£38) with a three year (twelve-issue) subscription for £70.

G R A N T A

✂ . . . .

I'D LIKE TO SUBSCRIBE FOR MYSELF, FOR: ◯ 1 year (4 issues) at just £26.95 (25% off)
◯ 2 years (8 issues) at just £50 (30% off)
◯ 3 years (12 issues) at just £70 (35% off)

BEGIN MY SUBSCRIPTION WITH ◯ this issue ◯ the next issue

I'D LIKE TO GIVE A SUBSCRIPTION, FOR: ◯ 1 year (4 issues) at just £26.95 (25% off)
◯ 2 years (8 issues) at just £50 (30% off)
◯ 3 years (12 issues) at just £70 (35% off)

BEGIN THE SUBSCRIPTION WITH ◯ this issue ◯ the next issue

MY DETAILS (please supply even if ordering a gift): Mr/Ms/Mrs/Miss

_____Country_____Postcode_____
02BBG771
GIFT RECIPIENT'S DETAILS (if applicable): Mr/Ms/Mrs/Miss_____

_____Country_____Postcode_____

TOTAL AMOUNT* £_____ paid by ◯ £ cheque, enclosed (to 'Granta') ◯ Visa/Mastercard/AmEx:

card no: ___ ___ ___ ___ ___ ___ ___ ___ ___ ___ ___ ___ ___ ___ ___ ___

expires: ___ ___ / ___ ___   signature:_____

* POSTAGE. The prices stated include UK postage. For the rest of Europe, please add £8 (per year). For the rest of the world, please add £15 (per year). DATA PROTECTION. Please tick here if you would prefer not to receive occasional mailings from other compatible organizations. ◯

➠ POST ('Freepost' in the UK) to: Granta, 'Freepost', 2/3 Hanover Yard, Noel Road, London N1 8BR PHONE/FAX: tel 44 (0)20 7704 0470, fax 44 (0)20 7704 0474 EMAIL: subs@granta.com

GRANTA

AUTUMN IN AFGHANISTAN
Thomas Dworzak

The grave of Northern Alliance leader Ahmad Shah Massoud, Panjshir Valley, September 2001

Taliban prisoners in a Northern Alliance prison, near Bohab, September 2001

Northern Alliance soldiers training near Dasht-e Qal'eh, Takhar province, October 2001

Northern Alliance camp near the front-line village of Chagatai, October 2001

An internal displacement camp for Afghans fleeing Taliban-held areas, Novobad, October 2001

The village of Dasht-e Qal'eh, Takhar province, October 2001

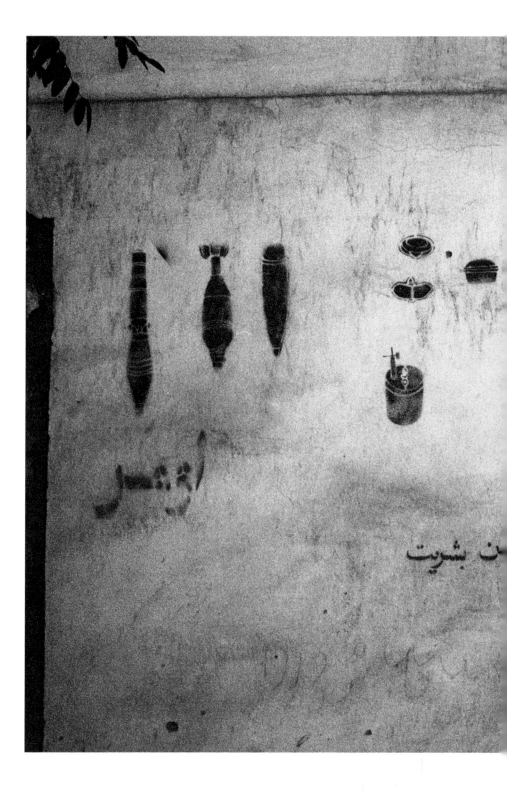

Stencils to teach mine awareness on a wall in Feyzabad, Badakhshan province, October 2001

A destroyed Soviet tank in the Panjshir Valley, September 2001

Displaced mother and child on the outskirts of Dasht-e Qal'eh, November 2001

US B52s bomb Taliban positions near the Kokcha river, November 2001

Taliban prisoners and Northern Alliance soldiers on the road to Kunduz, November 2001

Northern Alliance soldiers playing football, near the Chagatai front line, November 2001

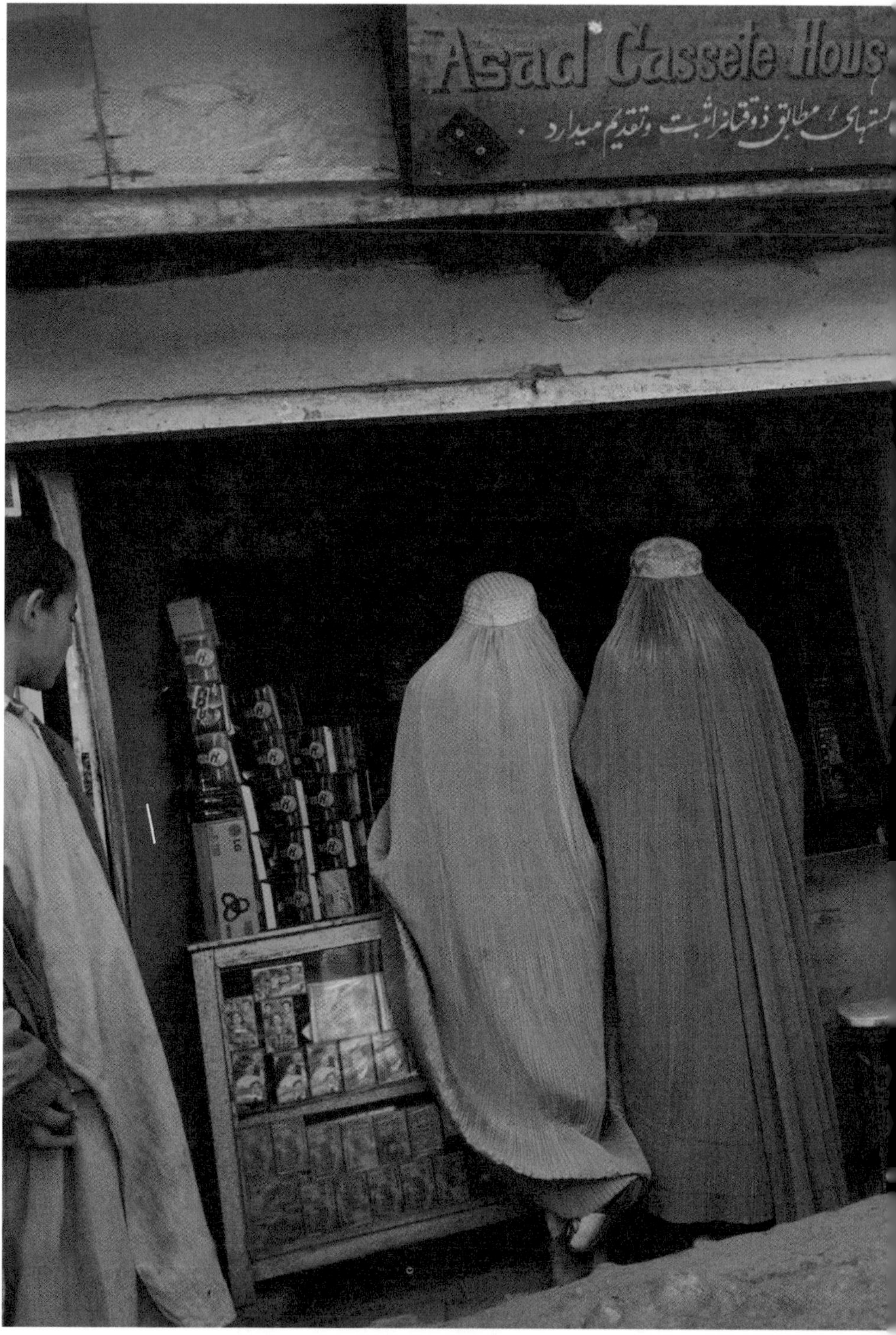
Asad Cassete Hous

Women at a cassette store in the market at Feyzabad, October 2001

Soldiers from the United Front/Northern Alliance near the Kala Kata front line, November 2001

The Old City of Kabul, December 2001

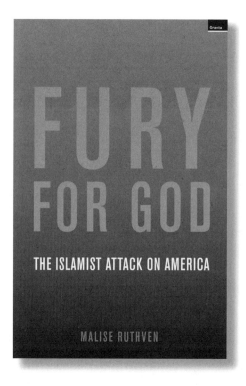

GRANTA

HAVE YOU DECIDED TO LOVE ME YET?

Blake Morrison

Have You Decided to Love Me Yet?

Crownhill, Plymouth
20.1.43
Dear Agnes (Gennie in future),
Just a line to let you know the shocking type is still alive. I am
sorry you couldn't turn up at the station to see him off. It was
really very selfish of him to suggest it. He would have left a poor
defenceless Gennie in the dark in the city of Manchester.

How are you? Still busy I suppose. I have been very busy since
getting back here and look like being an hell of a sight busier shortly.
They are going to make me take a sick parade six miles away from
here at 08.30. I shall probably be the sick one.

I have only had one night out since I got back so I think I am
behaving very well, don't you. I suppose you, on the other hand,
are carrying on as usual.
Love, Arthur

Hope Hospital, Pendleton, Salford 6
27.1.43
Dear Arthur,
Thanks so much for your letter received last week. Was rather
surprised to hear from you in spite of the fact that you did say
you would write some time!

Life here has been peaceful since you left, everyone being very
respectable. I did not like the crack in your letter about my
'carrying on as usual'—I have not even been 'smoking and
drinking'. Actually you are one up on me by having had a night
out—it is probably more than that now.

I was in Lancaster yesterday, at the Assizes, but did not have to
go in the witness box—they all pleaded guilty and the abortionist
got 6 months...

If you think my effort deserves an answer do write again.
Agnes.

One minute she's posing in her gown and mortar board, the next
she's on the boat. It's what you do if you're young and Irish:
get away as quickly as you can. America was her first thought. But,
with her schooling and her medical degree, she needn't go that far.
England's crisis is her opportunity. With so many of their own called

up, they're crying out for doctors—even Irish girl doctors like Agnes O'Shea. Summer of '42. My mother—not yet my mother—is on her way. She stands by the rail, as millions have before: dreamer, chancer, economic migrant. Dun Laoghaire grows tiny in her wake. Herring gulls wheel above like smudgy angels. On the far side of the water lies Hope.

'I hear in Ireland you can qualify in six months,' he teases. 'Three months,' she replies, 'if you're a girl.'

Glass in one hand, cigarette in the other, he reminds her of someone—her father, she realizes with a sinking heart. She has heard the nurses talk about Arthur Morrison. He's a wild one, they say— a drinker, prankster and flirt. Can this man at the bar be the same Arthur? The winged blue uniform's not bad, but she'd imagined someone tall and dashing. Still, he's attentive—buys her a drink, offers a ciggie, flirts, and nervously asks for a dance. His feet are all over the place, either from beer or unfamiliarity with the foxtrot. His hands on her waist are uncertain, too, which reassures her: she's been warned about English wolves. In any case, the dancing's quickly over, an air-raid siren (the usual false alarm) bringing the evening to a premature close. They say goodnight casually. No kiss. No great loss, either, if he thinks as little of women doctors as he pretends.

Next morning he turns up on her ward. 'Just passing through,' he says, but she doubts it, all the more so when he invites her for coffee. They sit in the bleak canteen, exchanging gossip and war news. Their own war is only just starting: he's been in Coastal Command, and she at her English hospital, for under three months.

'Why Plymouth?' she asks.

'For training,' he says. 'Till I'm posted overseas.'

'Where will that be?'

'They've not said,' he says, but talks of where he'd like to go, she—in a teasing send-up of a send-off—polishing his brass buttons for him while he speaks. Anyone watching would say the two of them had taken a shine to each other. They linger over their undrunk coffees. But once he leaves, she's so busy on the wards she barely gives him a second thought.

Just before Christmas there's another party—a bigger one this time, in the canteen. Two young Irish nurses insist she accompany them, 'to save us from the wolves', and they share a bottle of sherry in her room. Swigging from teacups, they bemoan the hopelessness of the men at Hope Hospital, not a patch on those back home. The sound of a band playing hits them long before they reach the party:

In shady shoals, English soles do it.
Goldfish, in the privacy of bowls, do it.
Let's do it, let's fall in love.

At the makeshift bar stand a trio of blue and khaki uniforms— forces doctors home on leave. She doesn't recognize him at first. But the small one, barrel-chested, pint in hand, is undeniably Arthur.

'Ah, the Irishwoman,' he says.

'Irish*women*,' she corrects him. 'We're taking over.'

'Arthur Morrison,' he nods to her two companions. 'I used to work here.'

'But why are you here tonight?' she says, more rudely than she means.

'They're still sodding about with my posting.'

He gets one in, which she knows is a mistake. 'My head's not made for gin,' she tells him, as he buys a second and third. Somehow her glass is always full. Does that mean she's drinking or not drinking? Slow down, she tells herself. But everything seems to happen so fast.

'I bet Mike's been flirting with you,' says Arthur.

'I'm a woman, aren't I? There'd be something wrong if he didn't.'

'I've been flirting too. A girl in Plymouth called Terry. Nothing serious, but she's a stunner.'

Nothing serious, but she finds she's annoyed with him. And at the way he watches how she'll react. And at his smile, when he sees her displeasure. Well, it looks like a smile. Her vision's all skew-whiff. It could be a frown.

'Ter-ry,' she says, hovering on the syllables, 'funny name for a girl.'

'Jealous?' he asks.

'Why would I be jealous?'

'She's hoping we'll get engaged.'

'That'll be nice for you.'

'But I'm holding out. Fancy a dance?'

'I don't feel like it.'

From his look, she'd say he was keen on her. Or is he merely playing games? She can't decide. Stuff him—he can have his Terry, what does she care? He makes do with a nurse, while she, turning her back on the dance floor, talks to Guffy, the Hope anaesthetist, whose halitosis is legendary—they say he puts patients under by breathing on them. Amazed at her attentions, Guffy buys her another—no, no, she mustn't but she does. Next thing, she's dancing with him. Grateful for the support, she rests her hand on his arm, then drapes herself on his shoulder. The two Irish nurses smile encouragingly as she drifts past. Over his shoulder, she grimaces back. Love and romance? With Guffy? They've got to be joking.

Back at the bar, short of dance partners, Arthur is pretending not to watch. Though he hardly knows her, he can tell she's been drinking too much. Guffy! He's tempted to leave her to it. But when Moriarty, or is it Coward, says, 'Arthur, you should rescue her,' he walks across and cuts in, brusque as an old stag: 'Care for a dance?' Unprotesting, she slips into his arms. This time the song's more upbeat, though you wouldn't know it from the way she leans on him. She'd let him kiss her, if he tried. Why doesn't he try? Is he thinking of Terry? They're cheek to cheek, nothing could be more natural. But when she draws back and catches his eye, it slips away from hers, as though embarrassed. By what? Her wooziness? Other people watching? It's a relief when the smoochy numbers stop and the music turns loud and fast. They uncouple and join a wider circle for the finale—left leg in, right leg in, a whole crowd of them hokey-cokeying: 'That's what it's all about.' There are cries for more when the band stops and the band is happy to oblige. But she's tired, and the rumbustiousness is too much. Together, they sit out the encore, he with a pint of best, she with a glass of lukewarm water.

At midnight the lights come on. She should be off now, the two nurses are waiting, but he won't let her go. They stand there playing for time while everyone drifts out, distant doors slamming under the stars. 'You're cold,' he says, feeling her fingers, taking her hand in his. 'Shall we find a fire?' Strong black coffee would be more like it, but they head for the doctors' sitting room, which is warm, tatty and (as they'd hoped) completely empty. From the battered sofa they stare into the flickering coals. And what might have ended in nothing becomes what this is about.

Have You Decided to Love Me Yet?

*Have I ever really impressed on you just what effect your cleaning
my buttons had one morning in October 42? How I then forgot
about you (almost) till next time I came on leave? And how I
nonchalantly approached you? And that first night when everyone
left us and you sat on the couch with me in front of a dying fire,
and then kissed me for devilment despite what you had heard?*

So he would recall it for her later. The fateful first kiss. The night
from which everything followed. But I shouldn't overdo it. The
buttons, the fire, the kiss, the sofa and (as he'd keep reminding her)
the alcohol: they mean a lot to me because without them I'd never
have been born. But in the sum of things this wasn't a cataclysmic
event. The two of them might have met other people. They might
have had other children. For them life would have been different,
and for me it wouldn't have happened, but none of us would have
known what we were missing and the century would have panned
out much the same.

Still, let me ask the question. What were the odds of my parents
meeting? Quite short odds: both were doctors, and about the same
age, and medicine, like most professions, is a small world. Quite long
odds: they came from different countries, and there was a war on.
They met through work, at a hospital—but not really, because he
left before she arrived and only returned for a brief visit. They met
at a party, and were attracted to each other—but he was half-engaged
to a woman in Plymouth, and she had various admirers, one a family
friend. He was too short and boozy for her taste; she wasn't blonde
or bosomy enough for his. She felt ambivalent about England and
didn't know how long she'd stay. He felt ambivalent about female
doctors—liked having pretty girls around, but was more relaxed with
nurses. Both had things going for them—the promise of careers
ahead. But wherever it was they were going, chances were it
wouldn't be the same place.

What were the odds they'd meet again that Christmas (which they
did, several times, mostly in pubs) after kissing on the sofa? So-so.
He was home for ten days and wanted to see her, but recoiled at the
memory of her staggering about the dance floor with Guffy. She liked
the way he kissed, but thought him priggish (she hadn't been *that*
drunk) and anyway he'd soon be overseas. And when they said

Blake Morrison

goodbye in the new year and promised to write, what were the odds they'd keep that promise? Fifty-fifty at best. It was an 'I'll call you', no more. Even if honoured, it might have come to nothing soon enough. They weren't in love yet, and in the first flush of 1943 neither knew where they stood.

In late January, nonetheless, they did exchange letters—he mildly teasing her for failing to see him off from the station in Manchester, she regaling him with recent trials she had endured (including a court trial in Lancaster, that of an abortionist). The letters were circumspect. But there were phone calls, too, late at night, after a drink or two. He had broken things off with Terry, he told her. 'What you get up to in Plymouth is your business,' she said. For all she knew, he and Terry could be going stronger than ever. Still, his telling her it was over seemed significant—even more so in early February, when (his posting delayed) he invited her to meet his parents the following weekend.

What were the odds of him inviting her home, just weeks after they'd met? Most Englishmen, she had found, saw their homes as fortresses—dark castles to retreat inside, not (as in Ireland) open hearths for drink and craic. In six months at Hope no one had asked her back even for tea. So she was flattered by the invitation. But worried by it, too. What did it mean, in England, to be taken to meet a man's parents? Was it the prelude to something else? Would it be casual? What should she wear? What if his family took against her? What were his parents expecting? Did they even know of her existence? The more she thought about it, the more she fretted. She'd have liked to discuss it with someone. But who could she ask?

What were the chances of them meeting, dancing, kissing and—within weeks—going home to his parents? And the relationship then lasting, despite their being separated? And them lasting, when friends and relations were being killed? And all their differences being resolved, so they could marry? Infinitesimal. And yet the thing was inevitable. As love does, for any two people, it happened inexorably, against all odds.

Cherry Trees, St Mary's Ave, Northwood, 6.3.43
Dear Gennie,
I'm pretty prompt in writing, aren't I. You'll see the reason shortly…

Have You Decided to Love Me Yet?

A gnes is her name. But 'Gennie' is how he thinks of her, and it's with 'Dear Gennie' that his letters begin. Another woman might be troubled that he can't bring himself to use her Christian name. But she has told him she loathes it as much as he does. A third-century virgin martyr, traditionally depicted holding a lamb: to this Agnes, the associations are undesirable. Lambs mean sheep, and sheep mean the skins heaped up in her father's wool yard—the world she has left behind. So although she signs herself Agnes, religiously, and won't adopt Gennie (not even when his sister calls her it too), she's prepared to contemplate a change. In May 1943, she offers him Oonagh: 'I just remembered it the other day—it's the Irish for Agnes (pronounced Una here, but in Ireland Oona). What do you think?' Not much, it seems: he doesn't take it up, nor does she feel enough of an Oonagh to insist.

The name problem nags away for ages. They are still trying to deliver and baptize her nine months later. 'We forgot the christening, didn't we,' she writes in February 1944 after a weekend together, 'Have you thought of it since?' He has, he replies, but 'can't think of the right name yet. Don't like Sherry. Haven't you some suggestions? Something short and catchy but not too boyish like Bobby, which doesn't fit you. What about Billie? Quite sweet. Anyway, your turn now, pet.' In a PS, he adds: 'What about Kim for a nickname? KIM.' Bobby, Billie, Kim: does she notice that these names are also men's names? If so, doesn't she find his androgyny odd? Is the laddish 'Terry' (his sweetheart in Plymouth) a coinage too, his version of Teresa? No less perturbing is his use of 'pet', which is what his Daddy calls his Mummy and what he (his father's son) calls his new love. Yet she doesn't react to his names and endearments, except to complain 'the christening is going very badly... Wish I had been given a decent name.' Eventually she signs off with a '?' in place of Agnes, as though uncertain who she is. Ten days later, after another weekend together, accepting his suggestion, she ends her letter 'Kim'. Reborn, rechristened, reinvented, she will be Kim for the rest of her life.

Was this my mother's first mistake, a capitulation that set the trend for several more? It's *Pygmalion* revisited, Eliza transformed by Henry Higgins so she can take her place in the English bourgeoisie. (In time the accent faded, too. With an Irish gardener she employed later in life, Mr Kelly, she would sometimes revert to Kerry brogue. But throughout her middle years, no one would have known where she came from.) Arthur was behaving like a bully. If she'd told him 'Get lost—it's Agnes or nothing', he'd have moaned and nagged but finally come round. Her going along with the rechristening plan—indeed reminding him when they failed to discuss it—proves she was ready to ditch her identity. It was part of cutting the cord with Ireland.

Names are important. Once married and no longer an O'Shea, she became Dr A. Morrison, which was confusing, indeed effacing, since my father's title was the same. He tried to help out, by calling himself Dr A. B. Morrison. But for simplicity's sake patients preferred to know her as the Lady Doctor, and a few even called her the Mrs Doctor, to distinguish her from the Mr. At home, there were confusions, too. She'd grown up calling her parents Mammie and Daddie. But he called his Mummy and Daddy, and it was this 'normal' English use that triumphed. To us she was Mummy, whether she liked it or not (after a time I didn't like it, preferring Mum or the prolier 'our Mam'). By us I mean not just my sister Gill and me but my father, who called her Mummy even when we weren't there—and even when his own mother was still alive.

His wife he knew as Mummy; his mistress—Beaty, the woman he was obsessed with for a decade—he called Auntie, while Terry was the name he later gave our family labrador. A psychoanalyst might want to make something of this. But it's my mother who interests me here—the slipperiness of her names and her desire to be someone new.

Cherry Trees, St Mary's Ave, Northwood, 6.3.43
Dear Gennie,
I'm pretty prompt in writing, aren't I. You'll see the reason shortly. I arrived in London by 7pm, and at Northwood by 8. Transport (with two WAAFs) to Cherry Trees, owned by a W/cdr Truss (easily remembered name), who is overseas. Mrs Truss is very pleasant, as is her daugher (18, attractive—pity I'm not staying long). Continued to HQ, about a mile away, where I learnt from Aur/Cdr Biggs (Principal Medical Officer) that I was to go to Iceland for at least a year—flying soon. Had a few beers and a game of snooker.

Now to the point. I think I ought to be able to get Sunday off.

Have You Decided to Love Me Yet?

Will you come down? You see I mightn't see you for a very long time after that and shan't be here next time you have a weekend off. I should finish at 7pm so could be in London...
HELL
I was just called down then—I am leaving now, well in 3 hours, for a couple of weeks in Belfast, so have to pack again. This is too bad. I will ring from Belfast. Look after yourself, pet.

His posting to Iceland involves her in some strange shenanigans. To stop his parents worrying about the journey, he decides not to tell them he's going. He swears her to secrecy—only she must know he's on his way, he'll cable them once he's safely there. It's a mark of how things have moved on that she allows herself to be embroiled in his devices. Yet the letters are still comparatively formal. These are only their first exchanges ('of fire', I nearly added, but no fire is visible). Anything could happen. They could lose touch or be killed or forget each other's faces. 'Will you please send me a photo?' he asks. 'Most blokes have their beds surrounded by photos of their wives (funny thing that, by the by—nearly all the men here are married), and I can't be content with nude drawings, etc.' Soon she is making a similar request, for 'that photo of you as a child sitting on the front steps with your sister Mary, the one your Mammie has on the dining-room mantelpiece.' He sends love and kisses at the end of each letter—thirteen xs, his lucky number. But he's not sure of her. 'Have you decided to love me yet?' he asks: HYDTLMY? To which she doesn't respond. She's thinking it over, but no, not yet.

April is bitter in Iceland. The RAF camp, just outside Reykjavik, is marshy and bleak. The roads are a mass of potholes and laval mud, virtually impossible for the lumbering old Albion ambulances to negotiate. The wind howls and they get all sorts of weather in a day. But he has a bedroom to himself (a perk of being a Medical Officer), they feed exceedingly well (with eggs every morning), there's a bath with hot water in Station Sick Quarters (SSQ as it's known) and a batman to each hut to make the beds. Beer is 9d, whisky 6d and gin 3d: not bad. Cigarettes are 6d for twenty. Reyki itself is modern if crude, with a swimming baths and four cinemas. The blokes in the squadron are a decent crowd. As for the girls, he tells her, 'they seem rather similar and pale-faced. Still, they will probably look pretty good when one's been in this place for a year.'

With no patients to see after eleven in the morning and little paperwork to do, he throws himself into improving his Nissen, which he shares with seven other men. He builds a cupboard, with a shelved door that becomes a writing table. He lines the walls of his bedroom with blankets and plugs the rat holes. He devises a system for heating water, by hanging a petrol tin on the side of the coke stove. He'd be happier doing a proper job, but these ones keep him out of mischief. And it's not as if the pilots are seeing any more action than he is. The role of Coastal Command in Iceland is threefold: reconnaissance (recce-ing from Reyki), convoy work (ensuring a safe passage to and from Britain for American ships and planes), and hunting down German U-boats. 'Aircraft can no more eliminate the U-boat than a crow can fight a mole,' the German naval commander Doenitz claims, and in the early years of the war he seems to be right. But longer-range Allied aircraft and improved radar devices have begun to turn the tide. Inhospitable Iceland may be, but prangs aside it isn't especially dangerous. As an RAF doctor, Arthur is aware of the common conditions affecting pilots—anoxia, aero-embolism, fatigue, frostbite and flash burns. He knows about LMF, too—lack of moral fibre—and on the rare occasions when he comes across it is understanding: who wouldn't be rigid with fear in a heavy plane on an icy runway? Who wouldn't shit his pants with a German fighter on his tail? But in Iceland the main problem is depression: with the monotonous surroundings and long nights, it is (so the official medical history of the war records) 'a place where boredom, low spirits and loss of enthusiasm for work are quickly felt'. Luckily, once spring arrives at last and hostilities are stepped up (in May sixty U-boats are sighted and seven sunk), the depression afflicting aircrews recedes and Arthur starts to enjoy the perks of the place: hot springs, fresh salmon and pollack, bars and cafes. Everyone says he's looking tired, but that's only his 'subocular oedema' (bags under the eyes, in common parlance). He gets ten hours' sleep a night—and dreams of his girlfriend back in Salford.

She, at Hope, is finding herself busier than before. She has to cope with a spate of emergency admissions—not bombing casualties, but pneumonia cases—so many that every spare bed is taken and adults are sent to the children's ward. 'The sisters are kicking up,' she tells

Arthur, 'but Brown says the pneumonias must be put somewhere. I got on to him for admitting an inoperable cancer to my ward but he just said "He'll only last two weeks". Fortunately he only lasted two days. They've had to open another ward, one with eighty beds for chronic females, but it's not relieved the pressure at all.'

The work doesn't get to her; the chaos does. One day Reswick, her immediate boss, snaps at her in theatre for not passing him a scalpel quickly enough (who does he think she is—a nurse? his bloody servant?). She goes straight to Brown, the big chief, and says she wants to leave. He persuades her not to hand in her notice—yet—and urges her to take a bit of holiday. She also sees something of a boy called Tom, whom she knew back in Kerry and who happens to be over in Manchester. She takes him to the hospital sports day, where they're taken for a married couple. As she tells Arthur: 'Tom told me that when he was home everyone he met asked was it true he was engaged to me—even his mother. Don't know how the rumour started, but it's very much in the air. Even Grimmy [the resident surgeon] said a patient had told him Dr O'Shea and her husband were observed at the sports.' Arthur isn't best pleased to hear this. But at least she's still writing to him. It's when she goes home to Ireland for three weeks that the trouble starts.

Iceland, Ireland. Just a single letter separating them. But that August it becomes a massive gulf.

KIM TO ARTHUR
Eire, 12.8.43
Arrived here a few days ago. Terrible journey over (Irish trains are as packed as English) and the weather is awful. Despite that, my younger sister, who still lives at home, has promised me a real holiday. It seems some of the Irish Army are on manoeuvres nearby and she has met all the officers. She says they are nice lads and have shown her a very good time. Like me, they will be staying on till the end of the month.

Everybody keeps asking if I'm engaged. I suppose they must have heard the Tom rumours. My policy is to laugh and keep them guessing.

No other news of interest. Not in good form for letter writing today so must finish. How's Iceland?

Blake Morrison

ARTHUR TO KIM
Same as usual, 2.9.43
How's Ireland? (Or are you back?) Received your letter dated
Aug 3 a bit since. Would have replied sooner but life has been one
long round of drunken parties. Hope you are behaving yourself.
Before your holiday you seemed to be slipping—with your
'husband' at the sports and about to have a party. I see this Tom
is talking about your engagement already. I wonder what your
next letter will have in it.
    I went out to a local beauty spot the other day—pretty bloody
day and pretty bloody beauty spot, but I was with one of the
lads.
    Well, that's all for now.

KIM TO ARTHUR
Hope, 3.9.43
Should really have written long before now but since I came back
from hols I've been lazy. Arrived here a week ago feeling
thoroughly miserable, having had an immensely enjoyable time in
Ireland. Too much smoking and drinking, maybe, but as people
kept on reminding me I was supposed to be having a holiday.
Even had a hangover on the crossing back to Holyhead, after the
previous night in Dublin. Got here to find a party going on. I was
very glad of it. Everyone—about 12 of them—was gloriously
tight.
    That's all the news of interest.

ARTHUR TO KIM
Iceland, 12.9.43
My letter of Sept 2nd will have crossed with yours of the 3rd, but
by now you'll have had it. You are, as I said, slipping. You put
'Eire' on your one tiny letter from home, as if the address was a
secret. It hurts my pride but I don't know what to feel or think—
whether to be glad or sorry. Two things are evident. One is that
when on holiday you have difficulty writing and don't seem to
connect me in any way with the life that is yours. The other is
that you bring Tom in again, and everybody says it's time you
were engaged.

Have You Decided to Love Me Yet?

Well, pet, as I said, I don't know what to feel. Is it that you're worried what to do and afraid of hurting me (incidentally, don't be—I'm too hardened nowadays for anything to upset me)? Or are you realizing what an hell of a lot of difficulty it would mean if you did decide to love me? Maybe that's why you say you've more than one reason for wanting to get away from Manchester. Really, I don't know what I want you to do. But surely we could stay friends even if you marry Tom—or if I marry someone. Or could we? I don't know—nor do I know if I want to marry you, or if you want to marry me. I'm only trying to say what we said that night in the bed and again on the grass at the edge of the wood. We were still happy when we finished talking then, weren't we, and we decided to wait till our next meeting to see what to do.

Reading this through, I'm not sure whether to post it or tear it up. It might make you decide not to stay on after October. But on the other hand I am really just the same as I always was and want you to remain a very sincere friend even if we decide not to be anything more.

Well, that's that. I'm going to get drunk tonight.

Was that it, then? Had love begun to fade, eleven months on? Would my parents become mere friends and I fail to be born seven years later? I felt like Tristram Shandy, hovering over my own conception, willing myself into existence against the odds. Or like the Michael J. Fox character in *Back to the Future*, rocketed back through time to the agonies of his parents' courtship. I could imagine my father's reassuring voice: 'Just relax, lad. No future in worrying.' It was true. I knew the ending. I kept telling myself: it's OK, things will work out, this is just a counter-plot before the happy denouement. But trapped inside my parents' present tense I began to panic. No future... It was dark in there. I couldn't see the light ahead.

My mother was 'slipping'—slipping away from him (and me). She always had that slipperiness. Could change her name, could change her nature. In photographs he keeps the same face, a little more lined as the years pass, but forever smiling and unmistakably him. Whereas she wears a series of masks: Agnes, Kim, Mummy, the Mrs Doctor and countless more; short-haired and long, wide-hipped and narrow, gawky, elegant, morose, beatific, shy, introverted, happy, sad, each new mask different from the last. The 'real her' can't be identified and may not exist. No wonder he didn't feel sure of her. What was there to feel sure of? The lack of letters from her that August was symptomatic of a deeper absence. The hole in the middle. The space he couldn't enter. The portal that wouldn't admit him (or me).

As she slipped, so he began slipping too. Took out local girls. Got drunk with the boys. Wondered if it—she, them, the thing they had together—was worth the effort of seriousness. They'd known each other less than a year, most of it spent apart; was marriage a realistic proposition? Perhaps the gulf was too wide. He knew almost nothing about her family, and she'd avoided filling him in—wouldn't give her address or put a name to her younger sister. Better to keep some distance: that seemed to be her message. To which he responded with talk of friendship.

How seriously did he mean it? And what was it they'd said 'that night in the bed and again on the grass at the edge of the wood'? Since they'd agreed to wait till their next meeting before deciding what to do, why couldn't they stick to that? I felt frustrated by their vacillations. I'd expected to follow them to the altar, but here they were divorcing. I'd come to find my mother, but here I was losing her all over again.

Some of their problems were due to the vagaries of the post, which gave their conversation an odd staccato rhythm. They kept missing each other. He'd get an affectionate letter from her, feel jaunty, and say something complacent or insensitive in reply. She'd receive this when touchy or depressed and feel diminished and taken for granted and come back with something sarcastic. By which time he'd have sent her several more letters, but be suffering from 'flu or feeling browned off, and get angry and go silent on her. Meanwhile she, having been cheered by his intervening letters, would have written a warm and loving reply and be baffled by his failure to respond— had she been too amorous? too candid? too pushy? Well, the bastard could stuff it, she'd decide—just at the point of getting his next letter which, being cheerful and loving again, would soften her and prompt her to send a loving reply, which would then prompt him (in a glow of pleasure at receiving it) to say something jaunty or complacent and insensitive, making her feel taken for granted... And so it would all start again, the endless, circling switchback of love.

Not everything was out of sync. Sometimes, checking dates, they'd find they'd dreamed strange dreams on the same night, or had sore throats or fits of laughter on the same day, or experienced premonitions or 'feelings' which proved correct. Her letters, he told her, were as prophetic as *Old Moore's Almanac*. 'You are already a Mrs Moore,' he wrote on one occasion, 'and I hope it won't be long before the "ore" is altered to "rrison".' I found it funny and heartening to read such stuff. Perhaps this was why my father had kept the letters: because he hoped I (or others) would be touched by them. Even the tiffs and rifts were touchingly comical. Later in life, he liked to tell a joke, about a man whose lawnmower is broken and who goes to the next door neighbour in hope of borrowing his. As he waits on the step for the door to open, the man thinks of all the objections the neighbour might raise: that his mower is brand new and can't be risked on anyone else's lawn, that the last time he lent someone something it came back broken, that he now has a rule never to borrow or lend, that there's a perfectly good mower repair shop down the road, etc. When the door finally opens, he's so incensed by these imagined replies he tells the neighbour: 'You can keep your bloody mower, you arsehole.' I thought of this joke while reading my parents' war letters: in many, one of them races ahead and becomes upset that the other (suddenly cruel, cold, selfish, manipulative and untrustworthy) must be feeling x or thinking y. The second-guessing was mostly wrong—and a reminder that we never know what's going on in another person's head. It all struck me as very funny.

Funny in retrospect, that is. In August 1943 my parents were short on jokes and hopes for the future. The war looked set to last, and even when it ended the prospects for them were uncertain. They became, as they admitted, 'brittle and impersonal'. The tone of their correspondence was dutiful. The heart and heat of it began to go out.

S he can afford to be distant with him, because her work at Hope has become more interesting: a sudden vacancy brings promotion to a post as surgeon. At twenty-six, she looks five years younger. A child wielding a knife—it's just as well the patients are anaesthetized. As RSO (Resident Surgical Officer), she's responsible for anything and everything, but most cases are straightforward enough—though it doesn't seem that way in the first twenty-four hours, with two strangulated hernias in the morning and at night 'two filthy appendices—one gangrenous and oh so hard to get at, the other perfed and a shocking mess'. As well as her own work, she acts as an assistant to visiting surgeons: 'earned a very easy £1.1.0. this morning, assisting Mr Buckley with a private patient—excision of a cyst on a breast, which takes about 5–10 minutes.' But running the show herself is preferable. Battlefield heroics? Man's work? A dangerous frontline activity, requiring strong arms and a stronger stomach? Not at all. It's about precision. Cleanliness, too: the scrub beforehand under a flowing tap—nails, palms, arms up to the elbow, each finger, minutely, in turn. Small hands are an asset. There are a few old lags, the heirs of barbers, who hack in and yank about, but it's a tender science. The weaponry is less like a soldier's than a carpenter's: knife, bone chisel, metacarpal saw, mallet, clamp, hook, tongs, surgical clip. As for the reek and goo assaulting the senses, they barely impinge. You hold the scalpel like a pen, forefinger along the top, the blade at ninety degrees to the skin. A single, clean stroke is best for parting flesh—no bevelling, or the sewing up afterwards will be harder. The intimacy is alarming. There you are inside the body of a stranger who's drugged and unable to move. Which is to make it sound like rape, when it's the opposite: a kindly invasion, ending in cure. Work on the wards is a slow cycle of despair. In theatre, you can be quick and effective. She thinks of it as a kind of nunhood: the bleeding victim; the attendant worshippers with only their eyes showing; the discipline, the concentration, the self-transcendence. You can lose yourself while cutting. In time, as her confidence grows, she finds she has a knack for it. Keeps her nerve, in a crisis. Has a cool temperament, under the lights. A steady hand, too. Begins to feel this is how she wants to spend her life.

Arthur is meanwhile discovering how he doesn't want to spend his. Being educated and middle class, with minimal medical duties, he's asked to do some cutting of a different kind: censorship. It's a matter of reading through chaps' letters home and excising sensitive material with a pen or scissors. By 'sensitive' is meant anything that might help the enemy if intercepted: details of manoeuvres, technical know-how, and any suggestion of poor morale. But the only sensitive material he encounters is men pining for the girlfriend or missus. He expects to feel like a voyeur, but the main sensation is boredom. There are only so many ways a man can tell a woman he loves her, and the lads in Reyki haven't the wit to get beyond 'I'm lonely' or 'I miss you'. His own letters are censored, too, by senior officers in the next camp. With luck they're too lazy to read closely. And he reckons he knows what he can get away with. Still, letters should be private, even in wartime, and he doesn't like the idea of someone prying. Most censors are clots, anyway. One of his squadron had a sentence struck out giving the latitude and longitude of Reyki, as if such info was classified rather than available on any map. 'I ask you!'

In fact—so I found reading them fifty years later—very few of his letters home were censored, though my mother once had a bundle of them confiscated while disembarking at Holyhead from Dublin (seized in haste, they were returned at leisure). Had my parents felt intruded on, they might have resorted to code, but aside from xs and DILYs they didn't. Deciphering the language proved an effort all the same. The wartime slang was easy enough—gen (information), prang (crash), snag (problem) and bull (bureaucracy) were familiar from childhood—but I didn't know about people getting whistled (mildly drunk) or screechers (completely pissed). And though Germans were Jerries, I'd not heard of the Portugese being Pork 'n' Beans. Similarly with abbreviations: TTFN for goodbye (ta-ta for now) and BF for bloody fool were common usage, while SSQ (Station Sick Quarters) and OMO (Overnight Medical Officer) would have been plain to any medic. But was HYDTLMY his own invention? Was BIB (breakfast in bed) hers? There are no four-letter words in their letters, nor even many bloodys: ruddy and blasted serve for disapproval, while expressions of happiness come in several forms: wizard (and wizzo), top notch, A1, bang on, full of beans, box o' birds and happy as a sandboy. A fed-up person is browned off but a brown job is a serviceman (unlike those non-combatants who idle on Civvy Street). Braggarts shoot a line, cowards are windy, slackers refuse to pull their finger out, and someone who's exhausted is shot at. The dead, meanwhile, have simply bought it. RIP.

My father, I now see, took pleasure in self-expression, whereas my mother, who had several different selves to express, found it painful ('you know I'm not much good at saying things'). He should have been a writer, she once told him, but he wasn't enough of one to think words (or the editing of them) a proper vocation. Medicine was what he knew best, and it maddened him to be stuck in Iceland while she was advancing at Hope. When she informed him of her promotion he congratulated her, but the tone was peevish and condescending. 'So you are to be acting RSO?' he writes in early September. 'Ye Gods, what opportunities this war has presented. You must jump at it, you lucky little devil. I shall be embarrassed to talk any sort of medicine with you when I come back—I know so little nowadays. That's if we see each other.' The churlish sod. Her promotion might make him jealous, but it was unkind to attribute her rise to luck (and gender and Irishness) rather than skill. And then to throw in that last sentence: 'That's if we see each other.' Didn't he want to see her? Or did he think, because she'd written only the once in August, she didn't want to see him? He expands on it ten days later, in his intemperate letter of September 12, the one that talks of them marrying others and becoming friends—which says, in effect, let's call the whole thing off. How steady was her hand in surgery that night? His letter must have been very upsetting.

Or would have been, had she read it. But in the event he denied her the opportunity, as he explains when he next writes, on the 16th:

Dear Gennie,
Well, pet, here we go again. Was very disgruntled by the 'note' you scribbled to me from Eire, and wrote a long rude letter in reply. I'm glad I didn't post it but I will keep it to show you when I come home on leave—Nov or Dec probably. I still think there must be something on your mind. Come on, what is it? I hope you're not worrying about the RSO job. I imagine it is more than that.
I had my birthday two days ago—did you remember? I've forgotten what date yours was pet. I've an idea March or May, but I may be miles out.

Had he sent his letter of the 12th, that would have been the end of them. But it went unposted, and four days later he's petting and HYDTLMY-ing her as though nothing had happened. 'Here we go again': well, almost. Whereas before he'd hoped to sweep her off her feet, now he's more tentative, keen to impress on her his understanding of the difficulty they face ('I have thought about it a lot.'). What this difficulty is he doesn't explain. But clearly they agree there is one. They've avoided a final break. But the letters that autumn come more slowly than in the spring.

'Sorry, pet,' runs one of his in November, 'I haven't written for 24 days and the last was, as you say, only a note. I've tried to settle down on several evenings but have got as far as writing the address and then said "hell!" and gone to the flicks or into the club with the lads. Still, it makes us quits.' Ten days later, she replies sarcastically: 'Strange thing happened this morning. I had a letter from you, the first in about 30 days. Thought you had got frostbitten or something. I've not written myself for three weeks, purely out of pique. No mention of coming home for Christmas, either.' The tone isn't romantic agony, only mild scolding. Nor does she bother to say much more, only that 'I'm really enjoying the surgery now I'm not scared of it any more… Just off to do two appendices so I'll finish this.' Not a letter that can have delighted him since she so casually curtails it, as though he came a poor second to her work. Miffed, he doesn't write to her again. Instead he writes to Terry, his old girlfriend, suggesting that when he's next back they spend a weekend together in London.

The relationship seemed to have run out of steam. For six weeks they sent no letters. Despite the evidence (in unopened envelopes) of more to come, I feared the worst. But then in January they broke their silence. And everything changed for good.

KIM TO ARTHUR
Hope, 5.1.44
Hello darling,
How's Davidstow?…

ARTHUR TO KIM
RAF Station, Davidstow Moor, Camelford, North Cornwall, 5.1.44
Hello darling,
HYDTLMY? It was nice to hear from you tonight—what bit I could hear. I went into the film afterwards, then came across here to write to all my girlfriends: one letter in all. I've got a wizzo billet—fire and wash basin in room—private bath with constant

hot water and WC—a light over the bed, too. Did sick parade at 8.45 this morning and have been busy cruising around finding out what's what from the SMO, who's going on leave tomorrow night for three weeks.

Oh yes, one more thing—strictly between you and I. I don't think I shall be here for much more than a month after the SMO gets back—nowhere local but very pleasant although distant. Wish I could take you with me.

KIM TO ARTHUR
Hope, 8.1.44
Your letter arrived this morning and a good thing too—I'd have had a miserable weekend if it hadn't. Did not like the last part of it—any idea where you are going? All sounds very vague. I don't think it would be a good idea for me to come to Davidstow before the 25th. Remember, you have got to live there. Hope you ring tonight. Hope I have a letter on Monday. Hope lots of other things—like you still love me.

ARTHUR TO KIM
Davidstow, 9.1.44
Hell am I busy. That is—I consider myself very busy having led a nice easy-going sort of life for nearly two years. Honestly my ears are sore as hell from using a stethoscope—I'm going to lubricate the ear-pieces tomorrow.

Got your letter of the 5th and noted the concidence in the way we had both started. Mental telepathy or something.

I spoke to the SMO about having his house while he's on leave but he didn't bite saying 'Well, there are lots of places nearer—try the Vicarage or Old Major —'s last billet'. Well, pet, I'll investigate. I think it may be a good thing if you come down before he comes back because you'd be able to sit in SSQ with me—you see it's outside the camp limits and then we could have nearly all day together. I can be on call at the local, too (if there's a phone there and there's no flying on), so will be able to get about quite well. What do you think? By the way, I have breakfast in bed every morning. It's perfect. HYDTLMY?

What did she think? She thought it would be lovely to join him, but doubted he could fix it. No worries, he said, and within days had found her lodgings at a farmhouse: 'Sitting room downstairs and upstairs bedroom with, ahem, a nice double bed but nil else at present. How much? "Well," I was told, "the Polish officer used to pay £1 a week." I tried not to show my amazement and said that was OK.'

She came for a week and stayed a fortnight. Arthur wangled time off camp and endeared himself to the landlady, whom they nicknamed—in their affection—'Auntie'. For two weeks they were alone together, free of family and friends. ('Alone together': the oxymoronic condition which lovers crave.) The only sadness was it ending too soon. He softened the blow by travelling with her to London and catching the night train back.

KIM TO ARTHUR
48 Belsize Ave, Hampstead, 10.2.44
Sorry about my temper before you left—so unnecessary but I expect it was just because I was so very very miserable.
Everything was fine after all—except that you had to get that 1.25am train.
I have mislaid McKay's testimonial, which I need for the interviews. Could you see if I left it at Auntie's?
Did I remember to tell you that I love you very much?

ARTHUR TO KIM
Davidstow, 10.2.44
I cycled down to Auntie's at lunchtime—she seemed very glad to see me and has apparently turned several people away saying that she hoped you were coming down again—so there we are! I couldn't find any trace of McKay's testimonial and she hadn't even emptied the waste paper basket, so—though I'll look through my papers—it doesn't look hopeful. I also mentioned, as agreed, that we hoped she didn't think there was any question of—well, anything. She said 'Very nice of you to tell me but I never had any doubts—she's a nice girl'.

KIM TO ARTHUR
Burndell, Yaptow, Nr Arundel, Sussex, 14.2.44
Feel so restless... I'm having too much time for thinking at the

Blake Morrison

moment. I wept myself sick last night and as a result woke with a rotten headache today. I can't sleep either—there is a chiming clock here which I curse every half hour. The only thing I'm sure about at the moment darling is that I love you. By the way I'm in bed now and feel a bit better. There's no place I'd rather be than Auntie's but please don't ask me to come down again just yet. I'm at the panicky stage again and must try to relax here for a while.

When I'm with you I never seem able to tell you how much I love you. But you know, don't you?

ARTHUR TO KIM
Davidstow, 22.2.44
Paddy, the girl on the phone, and at least two other people have asked me whether I got married whilst on leave. Well!!!

It doesn't look as if I'll get any more leave now before I go as the rest of the boys won't and it would be unfair. But we'll see.

TTFN. DILY. DDYLM?

PS When I was censoring their mail in Iceland, I used to cuss blokes who wrote to their wives or girls every day. The letters always seemed so poor—just said 'darling, I love you' over and over again, with perhaps one or two sensible remarks only. I hope mine don't read like that, darling.

KIM TO ARTHUR
General Hospital, Northampton, 24.2.44
You know, darling, we are falling in love with each other more and more every day. All the time I think about you and wonder where you are and my mind is only half on what I'm doing. And occasionally I have a quiet weep. How long can we go on like this—you feeling more sure things will work out, me feeling less sure? I know that I love you more than anything in the world and that I could be perfectly happy with you—if things were different.

ARTHUR TO KIM
Davidstow, 25.2.44
Helly-ohy My darling, It's 1.30am and I'm pretty whistled and I've just spoken to you on the phone (it cost me 4/- and then I reversed the charges). I wish not just that you were here but that

216

Have You Decided to Love Me Yet?

we were in our own house and this blasted war was over. When we spoke earlier this evening it was as though I'd just rung you at our own home and told you I'd be late as I was going out with the boys so you'd have to bath baby yourself. And when we spoke just now, after I'd got back from Tintagel (20 of us, including three Waafs, but I didn't say a word to them all evening), and after (as the crowd started to dwindle) I asked various different blokes to change all the silver I had in my pocket, and they all said 'You're not going to ring up the girl now, surely,' and then left me alone, and I had my three minutes, and nearly all your three minutes, a trio of them came howling into the room saying 'There's Ol' Doc on the phone—Cummon!', so I said 'Well, darling, there's someone coming, so I'll probably have to ring off,' and you said 'same here' and then as they didn't open the door to the booth I wanted to carry on, but you seemed to get all self-conscious about being heard saying 'darling' and started talking as though to a distant relative, and then rang off. Anyway, I'm sorry, I know I'm a bit whistled (not drunk) and must have sounded it, and I hate speaking to people a bit whistled myself— they never seem able to stick to the point—but I love you a terrible lot, and always shall, even if I throw this away in the morning.

Following day.

Well, I'm sorry for how I was last night. At least the above (which I'll post, not burn) explains it. It's because you have not yet promised to marry me and any sign that you don't want everybody to know how much we love each other shakes my faith in you. Damn stupid—forgive me?

Phone calls are bloody unsatisfactory, aren't they. But I did feel a bit better after ringing and dreamt you let your hair down again, among other things.

How did I feel reading their letters? How would you have felt? I felt excited, guilty, lucky, furtive, amazed. What did I think? I thought it was miraculous to encounter my parents like this—when they weren't my parents, before they married or even knew they'd be together. 'Never put it in writing,' my father liked to say, and yet he had, they both had—and when they died, there were the letters,

217

Blake Morrison

carefully preserved and chronologically ordered, under a makeshift desk in my father's study. Such was the detail—the things they did on particular days, the ideas they had, the emotions they felt—I was more in touch with their past than my own. Whenever I'd thought about them before, even when I was forty, it was as a child in relation to his elders. But the selves they'd now disclosed were twentysomething, younger than me. I felt protective, avuncular, parental. It was like overhearing my children. I wanted the best for them, and shared their pain when things went wrong. Unlike them, in their perpetual present, I knew what the future looked like—when the war would end, and where and how they'd spend the rest of their lives.

At times I felt voyeuristic. Coming across the print of her lips—like a red seal—at the end of one letter, I quickly passed on: here was an intimacy too many. I was equally discomfited finding notes of his on the back of an envelope containing a letter of hers—headlines to himself of various worries which he must address ('miserable beggar', 'all my fault', 'will say no more until I hear from you', 'can't think of breaking it off now'). But it was he who had kept the letters and made me witness to histories I'd not have known. The still, small voice of conscience told me: 'This is none of your business.' But it was my business. Family business. The legacy I'd come into. The love to which I owed my life.

'Too many darlings?' Arthur worries. Too many xxxs and DILYs? Perhaps. But to see my parents cooing and billing like this was strangely comforting. Call me greedy or just pathetic, but I needed the proof that they'd once been in love with each other. As a child I'd never been sure. They shared a house, a medical practice, two children, but they didn't share hugs or kisses. My bedroom lay just down the hall from theirs. I once walked in on them having a cuddle, but was never woken by the sound of lovemaking. Most teenagers, squeamish at the notion of oldster sex, would have been relieved. But I felt worried. My mother, always the gynaecologist, liked to talk about sex, and certain wry remarks implied the marriage had become celibate. They were affectionate—he called her pet, and sometimes pecked her on the cheek—but not passionate. Passion lay elsewhere: in films, on television, beyond the door.

Yet the notion of romantic love was impressed on me from an early age. And reading the letters my parents wrote at the beginning of

1944, I fell in love with love again. ('Falling in Love with Love': a song by Lorenz Hart and Richard Rodgers, written in 1938 and later recorded by Frank Sinatra.) To pore over old letters might seem a morbid occupation. But it was my parents' youth I loved—their passion for life and for each other. I had nothing to do with this passion. It predated me. By the time I existed it did not, or at any rate had hidden all the evidence. I hadn't known they ever felt like this. I had forgotten I could feel like this. Racing heart, dry mouth, butterflies in the stomach, trembling hands: weren't these the symptoms? Oh, and those tidal aches and razors of longing, that make you think you'll surely die. I ran their love through my fingers. It was no more than faded ink on dry paper. But it felt fresh, incurable, alive.

A new year and a new beginning. Those 'Hello darlings' chiming together on January 5. They were back in each other's orbits again, reaffirmed and newly enchanted. Before, they'd only been playing at love, not sure if it was worth the effort. Now they began in earnest. As before, there are gaps between their letters. But the gaps don't mean what they used to mean. It's something I took a while to grasp: that when the letters between them stop, it's because my parents are together. The old lacunae came from boredom, doubt, estrangement, a sense of futility, things going wrong. That phase is over now. Silence hereafter means they're in each other's arms—that things are going right. The gaps are protective, a kind of privacy. They prevent intrusion. I can imagine what it was like when they met at Hope just before Christmas, he (having downed a couple of whiskies with the old man) seeking her out on the ward, she (in the operating theatre) given a message that someone important is asking to see her, he flirting at the nurses' station while he waits, she arriving tetchy and flustered because she thinks it's the registrar or some heart specialist, he wishing she were dressed in something other (or less) than a medical gown, she noticing the bags under his eyes (as heavy as ever), the two of them sharing cigarettes in the corridor, too nervous to touch each other yet immensely happy. But in truth I don't know how it happened. The letters only tell so much—only go so far. I find this frustrating. In love with my parents' love, I want to be there all the time, egging them on. But the letters won't allow it. I can be with them only when they write, and when they write they're not together. There they sit, at a table, on a bed, in a Nissen hut, on the bench of a railway platform, a notepad balanced on a knee, ink flowing through the nib from the hearts they need to empty, intense and intimate—but always separate. It's the essence of letters. Correspondence: a bringing together. But correspondents are absent to each other. When they write, they're in different places. That's the point of them writing. Because they're apart.

There's only one exception. On the back of a sheet of paper dated January 23, 1944, my father has scribbled four questions, and my mother three replies:

1 DYSLM? Yes.
2 HYDTMMY? No.
3 Isn't it nice in bed? Yes.
4 What time are you getting up?

No answer to the last, which is odd, since it's the easiest, or least compromising, question. Perhaps her answer lay in action rather than words: she got up there and then, to prove she wasn't lazy, or because the sun was pouring in, or they'd a walk planned, whatever. Or perhaps some action of his, amatory or otherwise, prevented her from using the pen. No knowing. Still, it's clear they were together during this writing exercise, and the dates put it in Cornwall, at 'Auntie's', the house my father rented so my mother could spend time with him at Davidstow. He was between RAF postings, she between hospitals. The experience transformed their lives.

'Isn't it nice in bed?' Does that mean...? Let me leave that one with you. We can take Auntie's word for it that my mother wasn't that kind of girl. Or accept that two people might share a bed but refrain from having sex, a not unknown phenomenon even now and a common one in wartime (when air-raid shelters and overcrowded lodgings created some strange bedfellows). Or decide that despite what Auntie thought, probably, yes, they had become lovers: there was a war on, they were young and euphoric, the Forties (like the Sixties) loosened many inhibitions about premarital sex, there was no one to stop them, most of us would do the same, it's perfectly natural and they were in love, even if they'd not been in love it would have been natural, let's not be prissy for God's sake, why ever not?

Have You Decided to Love Me Yet?

In my teens, the LPs turning on our record player were ones that I'd bought—the Kinks, the Who, the Beatles. But sometimes my mum would sneak Sinatra on, with his plaints of foolish love and broken hearts. Sadness struck a chord with her, in middle age. She felt nostalgic for Cornwall, spring of '44. For a fortnight, the moon shone between clouds, and love was honey and fire. Never such closeness. Never such innocence again. □

GRANTA

MECCA
Ziauddin Sardar

One

The lean man with a falcon-like face smiled from behind his huge desk. Underneath it his feet were shaking. I smiled back. Our smiles were different. His casual, glibly courteous expression announced indifference. The set civility of my forced facial exertion, the conscripted memory of what a smile might be, said: I don't really believe you.

He repeated the litany: '*Insh'Allah.*' A single phrase, the essence of a world view founded on the proposition of the omniscient omnipotence of One God, yet so capable of expressing an infinity of mood and circumstance that one must always think of the particular significance borne by each utterance of the litany. 'If God so wills,' 'If God is willing,' 'God willing it to be so'—the subtle implications of how the affairs of man stand in relation to the enormous complexity of divine creation in even the simplest of undertakings. The phrase covers all permutations: from positive affirmation of the duty of humans to act, to the spirit-crushing evasion of the same human duty. In the end the phrase merely implies everything takes time because everything bears such an infinite philosophical burden, too much almost for humankind to manage. Today the man behind the desk was in overburdened mode, which suggested the lack of volition to act, as always when I entered this office. 'God willing, I will sort your papers out in a few hours and you can be on your way by tomorrow. No problem, *Insh'Allah.* Why don't you sit down and have some tea?'

Abdul Aziz Al-Turki was the *mudir* of the *idara*: the head of the administration at King Abdul Aziz University in Jeddah. Like most Saudis, he was more polite than frank. Not to accept the invitation to tea might offend, and that was the last thing I wanted.

Al-Turki's desk was brimming over with files. While there were two neatly arranged trays marked IN and OUT on his desk there was no real indication that anything actually left his office. Everything seemed to be permanently IN. The office was always crowded with people. Some, like myself, sat on the conspicuously large sofa—which indicated Al-Turki's importance in the *idara*—drinking tea. Many filed in and out holding pieces of paper that they thrust in front of him. He would take a cursory look, then, depending on mood and occasion and the constructions of God's will, would either sign the papers with a

225

scribble, or just leave them on the desk. A few individuals simply came in to say hello and drink tea. All the while he was reading, scribbling, inviting people to tea, he was talking to someone on the phone. From time to time he would be chatting on two phones while holding a conversation with a third man standing by his desk. It was an immense display of activity for someone who nevertheless managed to suspend all actions well short of decisive conclusion.

The file somewhere on his desk bearing my name contained a very important document: my 'release' papers, the essential documents that would allow me to leave Saudi Arabia for good.

Over the previous few weeks I had spent my time going from office to office collecting signatures. In all, I had collected eighteen signatures. Each testified to some important fact such as, for example, that I was not walking off with the property of my employers, the university. Others witnessed that I was not leaving the country with a library book, that I had collected my last salary and the university did not owe me anything, that I had fulfilled all the requirements of my contract. There were signatures to prove I had not offended anyone during my five years' stay in the country and that I was not leaving behind large arrears in rent. Now all I needed was the final signature from the head of the administration. The ultimate scribble in the long gestation of departure, what was referred to in expatriate idiom as the 'final bird'. Fitzgerald could never have been to Arabia or he would never have rendered Omar Khayyam's thought into 'Lo, the bird is on the wing'. Long seasons pass before the moment when winged migration can begin; this is the order in nature, the flocks wait for the ineffable moment of quickening. Long seasons during which the flocks must patiently roost on their perch. I began to suspect this bird would have to occupy his perch a few days more.

A *farash* came in, holding a set of miniature cups in his left hand, and a traditional brass kettle in his right. Everyone in the room was presented, in a matter-of-fact way, with a glass full of sweet *chai*. As soon as the cup was empty, it was refilled, unless the visitor indicated that he had had enough by tipping the mouth of the cup towards his chest, away from the *farash*. Seeking any decision was a strain on the kidneys, a matter of concentrated bladder control. I sat there stubbornly in front of Al-Turki, drinking cups of tea. Eventually, Al-

Turki looked at me and made a common facial gesture. He raised his chin upwards, and flicked his right hand in a dismissive manner. For emphasis, he made an accompanying derisive sucking dental click. I knew this was a sign of displeasure. *'Insh'Allah, bukra!'* ('God willing, tomorrow!') he said in a matter-of-fact way, a definite statement of indeterminacy. Today God most definitely would not will any action on or for me, tomorrow was another day and who could tell, when foretelling would be heresy, what that day might bring. There was nothing further my attempt at a menacing presence could achieve; it seemed my only option was to leave the office. I was not going to collect my final signature today.

Al-Turki sat comfortably among the top layers of what we, the expatriates, used to call the 'Saudi sandwich'. Actually it was, and remains, a large club sandwich. Like the Bin Ladins, Bughsans and Al-Shaikhs, the Al-Turkis were close to the royals who occupy the top level of the sandwich. One in ten Saudis, in some convoluted way, belongs to the royal family or is related to them by marriage. At the bottom of the sandwich are the *farash*. *Farash* are the true Bedouins: still largely nomadic, they are, on the whole, extremely poor as a result of their refusal to buy into the Saudi system on a permanent basis. *Farash* tend to be caretakers, gatekeepers and tea makers. Every *mudir*, every director of every institution, had a *farash* attached to him: he would serve tea to the guests and guard his master with hawkish eyes. Occasionally, he would disappear for an unspecified period, only to reappear and carry on as if nothing had happened.

Between the two layers of 'Saudi bread' were the expatriates, also arranged in strict hierarchical order. At the top, just underneath the privileged Saudi families, were the Americans, commanding the highest salaries and perks. Underneath the Americans came the Europeans. There was a distinction between ordinary Europeans and European converts, who had a slightly higher status because they proved the superiority of Islam. By logical extension, American converts were almost as good as the members of the privileged families. Below the Europeans came the Egyptians and the Palestinians, who were superior to Pakistanis and Indians because they spoke Arabic. Beneath expatriates from the Indian subcontinent came all the rest of the varied hired help: the Filipinos, contracted either as labourers or as maids; the South Koreans, who built most of the road networks and were confined to their special quarters, and finally the *takrunis*, or blacks, Africans mainly from Ethiopia, Somalia and the Sudan, who came for pilgrimage and stayed, often illegally.

Al-Turki greeted visitors to his office according to their status. As in any society the invisible markings of one's status are obvious to a local, and often perplexingly impenetrable to an outsider. In Al-Turki's office I had plenty of time to observe the delicate gradations of behaviour and to contemplate their meaning. When a Saudi entered, Al-Turki would stand up, walk around his desk, and greet the visitor warmly. He would shake the hands and kiss the tip of the nose of someone who was higher in status than himself. If a visitor had an equal rank, the two men would touch each other with their noses while embracing. For American and European visitors, he would half get out of his chair, lean forward, shake their hands and invite them to take a seat. He would shake the hands of Egyptians and Pakistanis while leaning back in his chair, suggesting it was a chore rather than a pleasure.

I always produced an ambiguous reaction.

To begin with, there was a dichotomy between my British passport, which said I was European, and my 'Hindi' looks, which said I was from the Indian subcontinent. Then there was the obvious fact that we hated each other. Actually, Al-Turki hated not just me, but everyone who worked at the Hajj Research Centre. For him, and the university administration in general, all three words were a problem. Why was the 'Centre' outside the mainstream budget of the university? Why was it necessary to do 'Research' when Saudi Arabia could afford to buy everything? And what did the hajj—the pilgrimage to Mecca—have to do with an institute of learning? It was the province of the Ministry of Hajj, which was doing a very good job, thank you. There was no need for a 'Hajj Research Centre'.

For Al-Turki, and indeed for most Saudis, the centre was a mystery wrapped in an enigma. 'Just what do you do in there?' he would ask at every opportunity. But no explanation could satisfy him. What we did was beyond his comprehension. An even bigger problem was how the centre came to be. There was no royal edict. No ruling from the Ministry of Higher Education. Not even a recommendation from the *Majlis-e-Shura*, the Consultative Council of the university, that such a centre should be established. Yet there it was. It was part and yet not part of the university. Although it was administered by the university, the university had no real say in what it did, how it did it, and who it employed to actually do it.

The Hajj Research Centre was the brainchild of Sami Mohsin Angawi. With his long, flowing hair, which he wore in a ponytail, and his large, enticing eyes, Angawi embodied every western preconception of the 'Sheikh' since the films of Rudolph Valentino. One day, during the winter of 1975, he turned up at my council flat in Hackney, east London, with a man called Bodo Rosh. Angawi had just finished his master's in architecture at the University of Austin, Texas. Rosh was a protégé of the German architect Frei Otto, well known for his innovative tent architecture. Rosh had recently converted to Islam. They brought a slide projector and insisted I watch their show.

It was about Medina, the ancient city of Yathrib, the second holiest city of Islam. Medina is the home of the Prophet's Mosque, the burial place of the Prophet Muhammad. It was in Medina—in Arabic the generic term for 'the city'—that the civilization of Islam was born. 'Despite the fact Medina gave birth to one of the most dynamic and intellectually profound civilizations,' Angawi explained, 'the city itself has always been simple.' Much of the social and commercial life of the city focused around the Prophet's Mosque. The original mosque was built of sun-dried brick. The floor was made of earth and the ceiling constructed of palm fronds covered with mud and supported by pillars of palm wood. The mosque has been rebuilt a number of times over the centuries, added to and made splendid by caliphs and kings. The Ottomans in particular paid a great deal of attention both to the Prophet's Mosque and the city, and Ottoman architecture reflected the beauty, grace and splendour of the holy site. Angawi showed slides of the Salutation Gate, one of the main entrances to the mosque, which was embellished with beautiful ceramics given by Sultan Suleyman the Magnificent at the beginning of the sixteenth century.

'Since the formation of the kingdom of Saudi Arabia,' Angawi said, 'the city has undergone two transformations.' In the time of King Abdul Aziz, it still retained its Ottoman flavour. At the entrance to the city, a splendid inner castle stood as a reminder of the medieval wall that once defended it. Streets were lined with stucco houses ornamented with *mashrabiah*, intricately worked wooden lattices. The Prophet's Mosque was rose-red with Ottoman minarets and magnificent gates surmounted with gold inscriptions by Turkish calligraphers. Between 1948 and 1955, during the reigns of two successive Saudi kings, the mosque was extended by one third and entirely rebuilt in grey stone, in neo-Mamluke style. The two styles clashed somewhat but, during this period of transition, most of the old city was left untouched. Only a few large modern hotels overshadowed the old houses, and here and there occasional car parks appeared as eyesores. Then came the second transformation in June 1973. Angawi became visibly emotional. 'In a matter of days,' he said, commenting on slides of bulldozers demolishing ancient cultural property, 'the whole city was razed to the ground.' No one complained.

Indeed, not many knew what had happened. 'Fourteen hundred years of history and tradition disappeared in a puff of dust,' Rosh added. The slides became a parade of 'modern city' views, with large multi-lane roads, gaudy hotel buildings and hideous new mosques where the elegant old Ottoman mosques had stood. The pictures spoke for themselves.

Angawi made me an offer I could not refuse. 'They will do the same to Mecca,' Angawi said. 'We have about five years to save Mecca,' Rosh intervened. 'We need you to work with us on this cause,' they concluded, their voices filled with urgency and passion. 'There is one more thing,' said Rosh. 'I am looking for a wife and I am told you are about the best person to consult on these matters.'

I was. In my mid-twenties I led a double life. During the week I was active in the 'Islamic movement'. I had just finished my stint as the General Secretary of the Federation of Students' Islamic Societies in UK and Eire (FOSIS). Occasionally, I edited the FOSIS magazine, *The Muslim*. At the time Angawi and Rosh came to see me, I was President of the London Islamic Circle, a discussion group that met at the Central London Mosque in Regent's Park. My diverse Islamist connections meant I knew many 'sisters'. These sisters were of just such an age as to be looking for a husband. Hence my famed ability to provide the answer to the delicate predicament of so many. Matchmaking is traditionally a female preserve, the exercise of immense power dispensed with a strategic understanding of worldly realities and a level of psychological insight that would leave the FBI gasping in admiration. Among transplanted and uprooted communities, however, this traditional maternal work was often supplemented by gadabout youngsters like myself. The traditional verities of what made a good match were a constant in my mother's conversation. I knew what—whom—to look for. And I knew that a European convert with financial prospects was a prized catch. In no time, Bodo Rosh was married.

In the meantime, at the weekends, I took up my other existence as a socialist—one of that special generation of British youth which had been nurtured by the golden age of the welfare state and radicalized by distant revolutions, domestic student protests and the Vietnam War. I was active in the Hackney Citizens' Rights Group and manned an 'advice stall' in the Ridley Road market. Later I got involved with a local social project that helped establish a youth centre called Centreprise. In both facets of my life I met idealistic young men like myself with a burning desire to change the world.

Sami Angawi was offering an opportunity to do just that. After a quarter of a century, one particular phrase still echoes in my mind. 'The main challenge of Mecca and the hajj today,' Angawi said, 'is how to fit the variables into the constants.' For me, that was not just the problem of Mecca and the hajj, but the problem of Islam itself. Besides, no idealistic young Muslim could pass up an opportunity to work on and in Mecca, the holiest city of Islam. My mother would never have spoken to me again had I even contemplated refusal. Angawi mistook the complexity of the emotions which informed my facial expression for hesitation. So he mentioned the size of the salary I could expect. The deal was done there and then. Angawi embraced me, kissing me on my left cheek, then on my right cheek. I pushed him away when he attempted to kiss my nose. When Rosh tried to follow suit, I simply turned away.

Once he had gathered a hand-picked, interdisciplinary bunch of dedicated Muslim intellectuals, Angawi set about establishing the Hajj Research Centre. Besides Rosh, there were three other 'returnees' to Islam: James Ismael Gibson, a British town planner; Peter Endene, a British transport engineer; and Jamil Brownson, an American sociologist. Besides me—a physicist and information scientist—there were two other British Muslims: Zaffar Abbas

Malik, an artist and designer, and Zaki Badawi, our Shariah (Islamic law) expert. The final member of the group was Dr Dabash, an Egyptian veterinary surgeon and our 'sacrifice expert', who specialized in talking in gory detail about scrapie, foot and mouth disease and the plumbing of animal reproduction.

Angawi was a smooth operator of the kind that Sade was later to immortalize in her famous song. To establish the centre he used his considerable charm, his Meccan family connections, and the few contacts he had in the royal family. 'Establish' is perhaps the wrong word. The centre just came into being the day Angawi gathered his nascent team. Everyone knew, or thought they knew, that Angawi had the ear of some powerful prince in the higher echelons of the royal family. And that was enough for the university administration to allow the centre to exist on its margins. Anyway, Angawi always managed to secure the relevant funding. Sackloads of money would arrive mysteriously so we could buy the latest research technology, fly in absurdly overpaid consultants and secure the specialized services of European and American firms.

All this was just too much for Al-Turki, who represented the mainstream Saudi view. He suspected that some of the centre's not-so-permanent members were walking off with suitcases full of cash. Indeed, some were. But he had no way of differentiating between the honest guys and the less scrupulous ones.

I had stayed for five years. Now I wanted to leave. I returned day after day in search of the final signature on my file and I was always told *bukra*, tomorrow. Realizing my file could lie on Al-Turki's desk for months, I decided to intervene in the cycle of the constant indeterminacy of *'Insh'Allah, bukra'* by trying, somehow, to make him interested in my file.

One morning I arrived at Al-Turki's office before sunrise and parked myself as usual on the sofa with a book. He arrived a few minutes later and was surprised to see me so early in the morning. As no one else was in his office, he was forced to direct his ritualistic greetings at me.

'Ahlan. Ahlaaaan. Ahlan wa sahlan,' ('Welcome,') he said.

'Ahlan,' ('Welcome,') I replied.

'Kayfa-l Haal?' ('How are you?') he asked.

'Kayfa-l Haal?' I replied.

'Alhamdulillah. Allah yubaarikfi. Allah yubaarikfi,' ('Allah be Praised. May Allah bless you. May Allah bless you').
'Alhamdulillah. Allah yubaarikfi. Allah yubaarikfi. Allah yubaarikfi.'

He paused as he made himself comfortable in his executive chair and noticed that I had not lifted my face from my book.

'Kayfa sihhat?' ('How is your health?')
'Kayfa sihhat?'
'Alhamdulillah. Allah yubaarikfi. Allah yubaarikfi.'
'Alhamdulillah. Allah yubbarikfi. Allah yubaarikfi.'

I carried on reading without looking at him.

'Esh akhbar?' ('What is the news?') he said.
'Esh akhbar?'
'Alhamdulillah. Allah yubaarikfi. Allah yubaarikfi.'
'Alhamdulillah. Alhamdulillah. Allah yubaarikfi. Allah yubaarikfi.'

He couldn't control himself. He leaned forward, trying to see what I was reading. I shielded the cover from his view.

'What are you reading?' he asked, finally.

'It's Ibn al-Marzuban's *Book of the Superiority of Dogs Over Many of Those Who Wear Clothes,'* I said without looking at him.

'Oh!' He was unsure whether to look surprised or smile. In Arabia, dogs are unclean.

'You know the book?' I continued. 'It is a collection of stories and poetry inspired by a conversation in tenth-century Baghdad between Ibn al-Marzuban and a friend. They contemplate the decline of moral standards and responsibility amongst the Arabs, sigh with nostalgia for the days when things were done punctually and efficiently, and praise the fine qualities displayed by man's best friend, the dog.' I paused, and then added, 'For example, the dog's consistency, intelligence, quick reactions and guarding instinct.

'Let me read a little for you,' I said, taking a side glance at his reaction.

'No, no,' he said, 'no need.'

But I read anyway. And I read aloud in English:

You (O Arabs) have acquired qualities that are inferior to the dog's.
The dog is fashioned to provide help and defence.

He is faithful and keeps to what you would expect him to do,
protecting the whole neighbourhood.
He gives voluntarily, not by compulsion.
He cures you of your anger and rescues you from distress.
If you were like him you would not be like a burning oven on
my heart.

Al-Turki chuckled. 'I like Ibn al-Marzuban's ambiguous use of the
word "many" in the title of his book,' he said. 'At least he concedes
not everyone has acquired qualities which are inferior to the dog's.'
I raised my hand and described a squiggle in the air to imitate a
signature. Al-Turki raised his hand and made inviting gestures with
his palms. I moved to a small chair next to him. He placed his right
arm over my shoulders and whispered in my ear, 'Tell me, brother,
in strictest confidence, how much money you are taking with you.'
'Fifty thousand pounds, cash,' I replied without hesitation. 'This
is what I have saved during my five-year stint at the Centre.'
Al-Turki roared with laughter. 'That's all! Now let me see, where
is your file?'
My feeling of triumph, I imagined, must be such as experienced
by a grand master of chess. Al-Turki started rummaging through
mounds of paperwork. He shuffled a few documents and removed
some files from one end of his desk, placing them at the other. 'It
must be here somewhere,' he muttered. He removed a few more files
from his desk. Then he threw his hands in the air. 'I can't find your
file. It's lost!'
He read the undisguised anger and frustration on my face.
'Malish!' he said. 'Malish—never mind. Stay here for a few more
years. Imagine how much more you can save. Malish.'

Two
I had no choice. I had to start the process of collecting signatures
all over again. I dreaded the thought, particularly as my first
signatory had to be Sami Angawi. He had been more than upset at
my decision to leave the centre. I knew a second request would
provoke another no-holds-barred attempt to change my mind. For
all I knew, Angawi might have asked Al-Turki to lose my file. But I
was determined to leave. With the sole exception of Angawi,

everyone at the centre realized the battle was lost. Mecca had already gone the way of Medina. To remain was not merely to become a permanent victim of an increasingly evident defeat—itself a serious malaise, a wasting sickness of the spirit and aspiration—it risked something far worse. I feared being trapped, confined within the dimensions of our defeat and the new order it was building over our cherished environment, the heart and soul of Islam. What I had witnessed, it seemed to me, was not merely a physical assault on a cultural tradition. It was an ideological onslaught on a spiritual and philosophic richness as delicate and intricate as the *mashrabiah*, the tracery of lattice windows that was so rapidly disappearing. Subtlety and complexity were disappearing from the mental environment at the same rate, crushed by a pathologically reductive brand of Islam that matched the straight lines of the new architecture. If I didn't get out, what was happening to Mecca in the physical world might easily do a similar kind of damage to my own beliefs.

Mecca, the birthplace of the prophet Muhammad, the site of the Holy Ka'ba, is the primary focus of the Muslim world, the symbol of the ethics and values of Islam. It provides Muslims with their sense of direction: five times a day, the faithful turn to face Mecca when they pray. From every point on earth a Muslim seeks orientation towards this central place, the starting point to which they must constantly return on the daily journey through life. It is also the ultimate goal, the embodiment of the spiritual objective to hold a constant course through the vagaries of life. And it isn't just a metaphor, since every Muslim, once in their lifetime, is required to perform the hajj, the pilgrimage to Mecca, if they can afford it. Of all the practical manifestations of Islam, the hajj most potently captures the imagination. Many Muslims save up all their lives in order to embark on the great journey to the Holy Places. In the past—and still today in some parts of the world—people disposed of all their capital, made over their worldly goods and left their affairs as if preparing for death. Not just to raise the necessary funds for the journey, but in order to bring one part of their life to culmination. Taking stock, auditing the achievements of their existence, they liquefied their assets in order to reinvest them in spiritual capital. The pilgrims come not in search of belief, but to express, confirm, rededicate and redouble their belief. Some still cover long distances on foot; some still take years on the journey. Literally, the word 'hajj' signifies an exertion. The hajj is an effort, the Great Effort; the effort, physical as well as mental, that brings the pilgrim to a new level of understanding, a higher spiritual state. When they return to their homes, the pilgrims will be known by the honorific of *hajji* (male) or *hajjah* (female) in recognition of their effort to complete a life of faith. All this makes Mecca much more than a geographical location. It is a sanctuary, a frame of mind, a profound experience. It is the Beginning, the Present and Forever.

On the other hand, what actually, observably happens in Mecca? Where do the pilgrims come from? How do they get there? And how do they behave when they arrive? For our research, we were building a computer model of Mecca and the hajj. Simulations have a voracious appetite for data; and a great deal of our time was spent gathering data. Data of every kind: traffic flows, locations and extent of cultural property, population movements and growth, social and cultural habits of Meccans, public expenditure, imports, demand for skilled labour, numbers of hotel beds—it all went into the computer. But it was during the hajj season that our data-gathering reached fever pitch.

During Dhu'l-Hijja, the twelfth month of the Islamic calendar, when the hajj takes place, the population of Mecca increases five-fold. Half a million local inhabitants play host to two million pilgrims from every corner of the Muslim world—or, more accurately these days, from every corner of the world where Muslims live. Technically, the hajj falls on the ninth, tenth, eleventh and twelfth days of this month and follows a routine established by Prophet Muhammad. But the pilgrims arrive much earlier, and move between ritual points by specified routes at specific times. I would target a group of pilgrims—Pakistanis one year, Nigerians the next—and follow them throughout the entire hajj, observing their behaviour and noting any problems they might encounter. I would watch them as they prepared to enter the holy areas and changed their everyday clothes for the pilgrim garb, *ihram*—two white, unsewn sheets of cloth—and acquired a state of grace. I would follow them to the Sacred Mosque, where they would perform the *tawaf*—walking seven times anticlockwise around the Ka'ba, circumambulating the fixed point that had always given meaning and direction to their

Pilgrims praying before the day of Arafat

Ziauddin Sardar

lives. In this exultant moment men walked with their right shoulders bared to demonstrate their humility, and men and women walked alongside each other, no segregation, no separate lines, mutually engaged in a common quest. After *tawaf* comes *sa'y*. In remembrance of the plight of Hagar, wife of Prophet Abraham, the pilgrims run seven times between the hills of Safa and Marwah, just as she ran desperately seeking water in the desert before God showed her the well of Zamzam. Then it is out of Mecca and to the hill town of Muna, where the pilgrims spend the eighth day of Dhu'l-Hijja.

The hajj proper begins the following day. The Day of Arafat is the supreme moment of the hajj. The pilgrims leave early to cover the five miles that separate Muna from the Plain of Arafat, arriving before midday. When the sun passes the meridian, the ritual of *wquf*, or standing, begins. At the mosque of Al-Namira, before Mount Arafat, the congregation of over two million prays as a single entity. Nothing in the world can match this spectacle or surpass this experience. Here in this valley, the Magnificent, the Beneficent, the Merciful, will send down his forgiveness on those whom He chooses, and they will feel His presence. In this enormous mass of humanity, the pilgrim knows both unity—brotherhood, sisterhood—and the most profound moment of individuality and personal identity. In all this crowd it is 'I', and 'My Lord'. Each pilgrim says simply 'Labaik'—'Here I am'—in the knowledge that each is individually heard, individually known, individually valuable, distinct and particular. 'I was a hidden treasure and I wished to be known.' The pilgrims at Arafat are joined by Muslims everywhere who observe this day as one of the two Eids—the other marks the end of Ramadan—the high points of the Muslim calendar.

Immediately after sunset on the ninth day of Dhu'l-Hijja the *nafrah* begins: the mass exodus of pilgrims from the valley of Arafat towards Muzdalifa. Muzdalifa is an open plain sheltered by parched hills with a sparse growth of thorn bushes. The pilgrims spend the night under the open sky of the roofless mosque, the Sacred Grove, Al Mush'ar al-Haram. On the morning of the tenth day, the pilgrims return to spend three days in Muna. During this second stay in Muna, an animal is sacrificed and the ritual of 'Stoning the Devil' takes place. Three small pebbles are thrown at each of the three masonry pillars marking the different spots where the Devil tried to tempt the Prophet Abraham, a gesture that symbolizes the pilgrims' intention to cast out the evil within. Once these rites are performed the pilgrims conclude their hajj by removing their *ihram* and cutting their hair.

We recorded the hajj in every way we could think of. We measured the influx of pilgrims to the Sacred Mosque, recorded the physical pressure on an individual pilgrim when more than 100,000 of them tried to go round the Ka'ba in unison, and noted how long it took them to go from one ritual point to another. We carried out surveys of the traffic in the holy areas and measured the output of exhaust fume pollution. We studied the accommodation problems of the pilgrims, and examined their health and hygiene. We took aerial photographs and made time-lapse films. Everything went into the computer model; and it began to tell us a few important things.

The dynamics of hajj were more complex than we realized, but so far they had worked. Pilgrims travelled through the geography of the hajj like water flowing in a stream. Groups of pilgrims moved from ritual point to ritual point at their own pace, negotiating their way around mountains and through valleys, arriving at designated places at different moments—but always in time to perform the necessary ritual. Now, however, the physical changes brought about by modern technology were throwing the whole system out of sync. From a sublime spiritual experience, the hajj was becoming a hazardous obstacle course which threatened the physical well-being of the pilgrims.

Angawi spared no effort in communicating what we had discovered. Princes, ministers and influential businessmen arrived at the centre at all hours of the day and night. They would sit intrigued by the time-lapse sequences showing pilgrims behaving like drops of water. They were fascinated by the documentaries focusing on potential and actual disasters: fires, structural collapse at ritual points, the chaos that could happen if one variable, such as traffic, should experience manifold increase. All these meetings ended in exactly the same way. The visitors showed awe and appreciation, often expressing these emotions physically. One common gesture involved a loud kissing sound, accompanied by a movement of the hand away from the lips, with the thumb and the tip of the forefinger pressed together and the other three fingers fanned out upwards. They were all impressed by our technology and what it could do—but not with our results. When the influential visitors looked at our simulations, they would draw a downward line with their index fingers on their cheeks below the eyes to signal the thought: 'Isn't it pretty?' Outside the centre, they would make similar gestures in front of their new Mercedes.

The Saudis approached technology as though it was theology. And in both, complexity and plurality were shunned. God is one, the Prophet is one, *ummah*—the international Muslim community—is one. Just as a plurality of opinions within Islam had led to discord and weakened the *ummah*, so different perspectives on Mecca and diverse solutions to problems of the hajj would lead to complication and disaster. All the problems of the hajj had a single solution: modern technology. If two-lane roads out of Mecca caused congestion, then they should be increased to four, or six or eight lanes. The fact that more lanes produced more congestion was not allowed to figure. Moreover, if Truth was monolithic, then the holy areas should reflect the monolithic nature of Truth.

So everything had to be at the same level.

There was no place in Mecca for history or tradition or culture, the human wellsprings of diversity, even if, according to the Qur'an, these are Divinely created, purposeful endowments of human nature and human society. I remember the fateful day when the old Ottoman library was demolished and the land cleared. Then it was the turn of the traditional houses, the ancient mosques and the old contours of the holy areas—the hills and the valleys. Everything was flattened.

The centre had many enemies but none as formidable as the Bin Ladin group. Originally from Hadramawt in Southern Yemen, the Bin Ladin family had developed a special relationship with the royal family. The family business, established by the patriarch Mohammad bin Ladin in the Thirties, had built palaces and other grand properties for the Saudi monarchs. So pleased were the royals with their efforts that they were given the sole contract not just to renovate the Sacred Mosque in Mecca, but for all construction of a religious nature in the kingdom. And the Bin Ladin group was as zealous in its development work as it was in its religious outlook. The more we issued calls to 'suspend all demolition and construction projects for reconsideration in view of their far-reaching and irrevocable character', the more they demolished.

In 1980 I performed the last of my five hajjs. The previous year, I'd made the hajj on foot with a donkey for my bags. I walked the forty-six miles from Jeddah to Mecca, over the mountains and across the desert, and then walked everywhere to perform my rituals. The purpose of the exercise, a reconnection with tradition, was to show that walking was not only more humane and ecologically sound, it was also safer, and a more direct route to the fulfilment of the spiritual objective that is the hajj. But this year I became a more ordinary pilgrim. I took a pilgrim bus. I sat in the bus for around eleven hours in the burning sun and unbearable heat as it negotiated the few miles from Mecca to Muna through a web of multi-lane roads and coiling junctions, one gridlock after another. I saw the many large cars that took VIPs in insulated luxury from place to place. In the area where the Devils are stoned, which looked like a multi-storey car park, I was nearly crushed to death as a wave of pilgrims came storming down from the top level. Throughout my journey to Muna, Arafat and Muzdalifa, I was coughing and choking on exhaust fumes. Every now and then I would be drenched with DDT from one of the helicopters that constantly hovered over the heads of the pilgrims. While going round the Ka'ba, I was constantly harassed, shooed and beaten with a long stick by the religious police. As I sat in the Sacred Mosque, reconstructed to resemble an underground station complete with escalators, I looked up beyond the Ka'ba. Outside the mosque I could see that a brand new palace, overshadowing the Ka'ba, was about to be completed. Something profound happened at that instant. I knew that I had to leave Saudi Arabia. Now. *This very moment.*

If anyone could help me, it was Abdullah Naseef. In London, where he pursued his postgraduate studies in geology, we had worked together as comrades in the Islamic movement. It was Naseef who had directed Sami Angawi towards my house. And it was Naseef's influence and skill that ensured the survival of the Hajj Research Centre. A slim, elegant figure, he had risen rapidly through the ranks of the university to become its president. He was both my mentor and my best friend. Now I really needed him.

Naseef was normally the first to arrive at the university. So early

Ziauddin Sardar

one morning, immediately after the morning prayer, I parked myself in front of his office. He arrived with a *farash* in tow and looked surprised to see me. My face declared that something was wrong. 'I want to leave,' I said. He smiled knowingly. I was ready to launch into an explanation but he ushered me towards his office in a seamless movement that demonstrated he understood instinctively. I sat on a chair next to him. 'I tried to follow the normal procedure, but...'

He stopped me before I could finish my sentence. 'I know,' he said. 'I know everything.' He made a telephone call, talked animatedly for several minutes, and then looked at me with his broad, generous smile. 'I think I have found a way to get you an exit visa today,' he said. He asked his *farash* to call Shaikh Abdullah.

A few moments later Shaikh Abdullah entered the room and stood with respect and reverence in a corner. I knew Shaikh Abdullah well. A stubby man in his early sixties, with a handsome white beard, he had responsibility for arranging exit and entrance visas for the employees of the university. It was a job Shaikh Abdullah relished: it gave him a lavish sense of importance and power. Every single employee of the university had to pay his respects to the Shaikh at least twice a year. Once to get an exit and entrance visa; and once simply to show that you appreciated him doing what he ought to be doing anyway. Shaikh Abdullah never took less than three weeks to get anyone an exit visa, despite his numerous assistants who were always kept busy. To persuade Shaikh Abdullah to take one's passport required a letter from one's head of department, a completed exit visa form, three photographs and considerable expertise in grovelling. Shaikh Abdullah liked his applicants to grovel; and if you could cry in front of him, the chances you would get your visa within a fortnight were markedly improved. That is, if he hadn't lost your passport. He followed no system that I, as an accredited information scientist familiar with many classificatory techniques, could discern. He stacked passports everywhere: his cabinet, his desk, on table tops. When the going got tough, he would place them on top of his chair and sit on them to show he was overworked. Once a passport was lost in his maze, it was practically impossible to retrieve. I was a frequent visitor to Shaikh Abdullah. He knew I had little patience with him, but also that I had influence in high places that could be brought to bear against him. Whenever

I approached his office, he would hide under his table and indicate to his assistant to tell me the office was closed.

Shaikh Abdullah surveyed the room and let his eyes come to rest on me. His face changed. He murmured my name and thrust his hands over his ears. He did not want to hear what he was about to be told.

Naseef gave him a letter. 'Take this to the *jawazat*,' and pointing towards me, 'make sure you get him an exit visa *today*.'

Shaikh Abdullah looked dazed, as though he had suddenly walked into a wall. 'It cannot be done. It cannot be done,' he murmured. 'I have used every single trick I know to get this man exit visas. It just cannot be done in less than three days.' He looked sheepish.

'It can be done in a day,' said Naseef. 'I will speak to the director of the *jawazat* myself.'

'But…'

Naseef raised his index finger and pointed it in the direction of Shaikh Abdullah. That was a direct command. 'Go now. Straight to the *jawazat*.'

Shaikh Abdullah responded with the 'ready to comply' signal. He pointed to the tip of his nose and then his right eye with his right index finger, which means literally: your command is on my head and in my eye.

Naseef looked at me and smiled. 'You go with him and stay with him till he gets the job done.'

I followed Shaikh Abdullah out of Naseef's office.

Three

Shaikh Abdullah wore a perpetual grin. But now he looked more serious than I had ever seen him. I decided not to try making polite chat and merely followed him in silence. He went to his office, placed Naseef's letter and my passport in a file and informed his assistant he was going to the passport office on a special assignment and would be there for the rest of the day. We drove in Shaikh Abdullah's old pickup truck to the Ministry of the Interior, off the old Airport Street.

At the *jawazat*, the visa section of the Ministry of the Interior, we walked straight into the office of the Director of the Visa Department. Shaikh Abdullah placed the letter, clipped inside the file, in front of him. The Director read the letter carefully, wrote something on it and asked Shaikh Abdullah to take it to a particular window outside the building. The window was actually a small opening in a very large wall. It was about three feet high and two feet wide and protected with five vertical iron bars. Through them, about a dozen individuals were simultaneously trying to pass files and talk to the man inside. My heart sank at the spectacle.

Shaikh Abdullah sensed my dismay and gently tapped me on the shoulder. 'I know my job,' he said confidently. 'Now, stay back and watch.'

He counted off a number of paces from the crowd surrounding the visa window like a fast bowler preparing his run-up. About twenty yards from the crowd he stopped, turned and shouted for the two or three people standing between him and the crowd at the window to move out of the way. He then pulled up the bottom half of his *toupe*, his long white outer garment, and tied it around his waist. Finally he looked at me and grinned, revealing a gold tooth.

Suddenly Shaikh Abdullah yelled '*Ya Allah,*' in a dreadful voice and charged. The people gathered at the window turned in horror, unable to believe what was about to hit them. Shaikh Abdullah jumped on top of the crowd, walked at lightning speed across their heads and shoulders and placed his file right into the hands of the man behind the window. Then he descended elegantly—an effortless dismount—and nonchalantly walked back to stand beside me.

'Never fails,' he said triumphantly.

'I can't believe a man of your age has so much energy and dexterity,' I said in genuine amazement and admiration.

'That's exactly what my wife says,' he replied.

'When performing this incredible manoeuvre, have you ever hit one of those iron bars?'

'Never.'

'What now?'

'*Choia.*' He joined the fingers and the thumb of his right hand and raised them to the level of the chest: '*Choia.*' 'We wait.'

After about half an hour the window was closed. The crowd dispersed. A few loiterers remained but most sought shade elsewhere. Shaikh Abdullah and I squatted under a tree.

The Saudis have developed waiting into an art form. *Choia* is undoubtedly the most common word, and gesture, in the Saudi idiom. It has something to do with the Bedouin notion of time.

Throughout their history, it is said, the Bedouins owned nothing—
other than plenty of time. They enjoyed hanging around, not rushing
to do anything in particular. So waiting has become an essential
ingredient of all Saudi life. Saudis never give a precise time for
anything. When someone says *insh'Allah, bukra*, he will visit you,
he could possibly mean tomorrow, the day after, in a few days, or
sometime in the near future, or any time before eternity begins.
Similarly, rendezvous times are never given in relation to hours or
their divisions but in relation to the five daily prayers. *Bad zuhr*, after
the midday prayer, could mean any time between midday and sunset.
Time, when calibrated in hours, always occurs in round numbers: it
is five o'clock, when it could be twenty minutes before or after five.

In a strangely perverted sense, this notion of time has become
integral to Wahhabism, the revivalist movement founded by
Muhammad ibn Abd al-Wahhab which has become the state creed
of Saudi Arabia. Abd al-Wahhab was born in 1703 in a small town
in Najd, the northern part of the kingdom, and brought up in the
Hanbali sect, the most severe of the four schools of Islamic thought.
Abd al-Wahhab advocated a return to the purity and simple
profundity of the origin of Islam, to the words of the Qur'an and the
code of the *Sunna* (practice of the Prophet). He rejected customs that
had grown up since that time, such as celebrating the Prophet's
birthday or visiting the graves and shrines of saints and divines. Rather
like the Reformation thinkers of Christian Europe, Abd al-Wahhab
set himself against the abuses by which religion pandered to masses
rather than educating or ministering to them. His zeal sent many back
to the purity of Islam as a doctrine of humility and unity motivated
by equality and justice. All kinds of nonconformist Christian
movements have their roots in the same ideals. Saudi Wahhabism also
owes much to the thirteenth-century Muslim political scientist Ibn
Taimiyya. Ibn Taimiyya was concerned, almost exclusively, with the
strength and survival of the Muslim community at a time when Islam,
recovering from the onslaught of the Crusades, was under siege from
the Mongols. He saw dissension amongst Muslims as their main
weakness and sought to ban plurality of interpretation. Everything
had to be found in the Qur'an and the *Sunna*; even theology and
philosophy, Ibn Taimiyya asserted, had no place in Islam. The Qur'an
had to be interpreted literally. When the Qur'an, for example, says

Ziauddin Sardar

God sits on His throne, He sits on His throne, period. No discussion can be entertained on the nature and purpose of the throne. Nothing can be read metaphorically or symbolically.

I learned a great deal about modern Wahhabism from students at Medina university. During the hajj season, we would hire hundreds of these students to help us with our surveys and studies. A few of them were Saudis, but most were from other parts of the Muslim world. Without exception, they were funded by Saudi scholarships and guaranteed badly paid employment from the Saudi treasury when they finished their course. All were being trained to be *dias*—preachers—who would, on graduation, go out to Asia and Africa, as well as Europe and America, to do *dawa*: run mosques, *madrasas* and Islamic centres, to teach and preach. What did they learn? And what were they going to preach? From the *dias*, I discovered that in modern Wahhabism there is only the constant present. There is no past and no notion of different future. But the present exists in an ontological shadow of the past—or specifically, the days of the Prophet Muhammad. The history and culture of Muslim civilization, in all its greatness, complexity and plurality, is totally irrelevant, and to be rejected as deviancy and degeneration. It was hardly surprising, then, that Saudis had no feelings for the cultural property and sacred topology of Mecca.

The students from Medina university were fiercely loyal to their Saudi mentors and their particular school of thought. The Wahhabism they learned was based on tribal loyalty—but the place of traditional *asabiyya* (tribal allegiance) was now taken by Islam. Islam was essentially the territory they defined through their approach to the Qur'an and *Sunna*, occupied by virtue of their education and employment, and of which they were the guardians. Everyone outside this territory was, by definition, a hostile dweller in the domain of *kufr*, or unbelief. But the exterior was not limited to non-Muslims; it included all those Muslims who had not performed the *biya*, or pledge of allegiance to Wahhabism. In the minds of these *dias*, and in Saudi society itself, there is a strict demarcation between the insider and outsider, orthodox and heretic. The students would often tell me that any alliance with the *kuffar* (the unbelievers) was itself *kufr*; one had to shun their employment, advice and friendship, and avoid any display of conviviality with them.

246

In Saudi Arabia, the expatriates were and are treated in this fashion, confined to their specific quarters according to their status. All women, of course, were totally marginalized and their difference emphasized at every juncture. All men in the kingdom dress in white, in crisply ironed *toupes* and jallabiyahs. White is the natural colour for such an extreme climate: it reflects the sun and absorbs very little heat. Women have to be covered from head to toe, by law, in black shrouds that absorb the sun and heat. To wear traditional female Muslim dress, *hijab*, is not enough. They must wear the more extensive *niqab*, the head covering that leaves only a narrow slit for the eyes. The only place in Saudi Arabia where the *niqab* is not seen is inside the Sacred Mosque, where older Islamic conventions dictate that a woman's face should be uncovered.

At first I dismissed the views of the students from Medina as the ranting of over-zealous young men. I also suspected my own observations of Saudi society. As someone brought up and educated in Britain, I thought, I was looking at the Saudis through my own prejudices. What about people like Angawi and Naseef? I had not, and still have not, met more rounded, humane or refined individuals. Naseef's belief in the simple profundity of Wahhabism soared beyond the word 'fundamentalist'. In his own lifestyle and in the way he related to others, Naseef was a sublime minimalist. He radiated subtlety and finesse while being surrounded by clumsiness and ugliness. He operated with a gentle tolerance while all around him a harsh incivility and disdain were becoming the norm in Saudi life. It dawned on me that there were significant differences in Saudi society. Naseef was a Hijazi from the southern part of the kingdom, where Jeddah and Mecca are located. The royal family were Najdis from the north. When King Abdul Aziz, the founder of Saudi Arabia, first entered Jeddah as a triumphant conqueror in 1932, most of the families of the Hijaz came out to greet him. The Bughshans, the Bin Ladins, the Al-Turkis and Al-Shaikhs all came; only the Naseefs declined. The Naseefs were a scholarly family, proud of their cultural inheritance. The old patriarch, Muhammad Naseef, born in 1884, was a celebrated scholar and editor. His house stood at the centre of the *souk* that overlooked the city and contained an impressive library, with thousands of priceless manuscripts and rare books. He entertained visiting scholars from across the world: from Morocco and Sudan, Syria and Iran, India and Malaysia. But he was not favourably inclined to the Najdi king, and therefore the family were marginalized. Much of old Jeddah has gone the way of Mecca. But the Naseef family home, in all its renovated magnificence, with its delicately crafted windows, panels and eaves, was still there. The Naseefs fought tooth and nail to preserve it. In the hot Jeddah summers, when the temperature reaches forty degrees Celsius, it was the coolest place in town. Whenever there was a power cut—in those days an almost daily occurrence—and the air conditioners stopped, I used to walk down to the old town and sit under the tree in front of the Naseef house. In Jeddah, trees were rare. It was the best place to smoke a *sheesha*—the Saudi version of the 'water pipe'.

The true import of Saudi Wahhabism was brought home to me in November 1979, when a group of zealots occupied the Sacred Mosque in Mecca. They accused the Saudi state of many sins: cooperating with Christians; confirming the heresies of the Shias; promoting dissension by permitting more than one interpretation of Islam; introducing television and film into the kingdom; and fetishizing money. Mecca was cut off from the rest of the world, and the mosque was surrounded by both the army and the National Guard, whose main function is to protect the royal family. But before the rebels could be flushed from the mosque—literally so, as it turned out—they had to be formally sentenced to death. The task fell to Sheikh 'Abd al-'Aziz Bin Baz, the chief scholar and the Mufti of the kingdom. Bin Baz was blind and I used to see him often in the Sacred Mosque, performing the circumambulation around the Ka'ba. The spectacle was always the same. A young student, holding him by his left shoulder, would lead him around the Ka'ba, while hordes of admirers and devotees would try to kiss his right hand. Bin Baz would allow them to hold his hand, but the moment they tried to bring their lips to his wrist, he would pull his hand away. The accusations of the rebels against the Saudi state were read out to Bin Baz. He agreed totally with the thesis of the rebels. Yes, he said, a true Wahhabi state should not associate with the unbelievers. Yes, the heresies of the Shias cannot go unchallenged. Yes, more than one interpretation of Islam should not be allowed under any circumstances. Yes, images of all kind were forbidden in Islam, including television and film. And, yes, money should not be fetishized. The only thing that Bin Baz could not agree to was that these things happened in the Saudi kingdom. So the Sacred Mosque was flooded and the rebels were drowned. It seemed to me that the puritan rebels were at least honest, unlike the representatives of the Wahhabite State.

By denying the complexity and diversity of Islamic history and rejecting so many pluralistic interpretations of Islam, Wahhabism has reduced Islam to an arid list of dos and don'ts. In Saudi Arabia, these were enforced with brute force and/or severe social pressure; it amounted to totalitarianism. What horrified me was not simply this realization but that I, as someone who was active in the Islamic movement, who was brought up on the literature of Jamaat-e-Islami and the Muslim Brotherhood, might begin to subscribe to this vision; or even that, unaware, I already did.

At around two in the afternoon, when most offices closed for the day, the *jawazat* window opened. A hand holding a file appeared through the window and flung a file of papers in the air. A man waiting patiently in the shade jumped up, caught the file, opened it to take a quick look, and walked briskly out of the compound with a satisfied look. A few moments later the hand emerged again and the process was repeated. Finally the hand appeared with another file. This time Shaikh Abdullah caught it.

He opened the file and glanced at it. I looked at him anxiously. 'Have I got the exit visa?'

'Well, not quite,' Shaikh Abdullah replied. 'You haven't got the visa but the letter from Dr Naseef has been honoured.'

'What does that mean?'

'I don't know. I have never faced this situation before. But I think you can leave the country tomorrow.'

I took the file from Shaikh Abdullah. There was an official-looking letter attached to my passport. Shaikh Abdullah pointed at the letter and said: 'I think it is an emergency visa. Read it to me.'

'You read it,' I passed the letter to him. 'My Arabic is not good enough.'

'That's what my wife says to me as well.' He handed the letter back.

I asked him, 'Considering all files look the same, and the man behind the window did not indicate anyone or anything, how did you know which file to catch?'

'Are you in charge of the passport section of the university or am I?' Shaikh Abdullah was irritated with the question. 'I can't tell you everything. Now if you take this letter to the airport, you will find they will allow you to leave the country.

'*Khalas*,' he said, stroking his palms and fingers as though he was dusting his hands. '*Khalas*,' he repeated: 'It's over.'

Without waiting for a reply Shaikh Abdullah jumped in his pick-up truck and drove off.

Four

The following day was the first day of Ramadan. The city, indeed all of Saudi Arabia, stays up all night. During this blessed month a whole new lifestyle emerges. The day becomes night. Once the cannon is fired (actually there are twelve cannons fired in unison) to mark the end of *suhur*, or the beginning of the fast, just before dawn, the city goes to sleep. The streets are deserted; offices and shops are closed, opening for only a few hours between ten and one. The city begins to show signs of life just before sunset. By the time the cannons have been fired again, now to announce the *iftar*, which marks the end of the fast, the city becomes vibrant with excitement. The roads are jammed with traffic, and the streets and alleyways are crowded with people shopping for the following day. Offices and shops open again around ten o'clock at night and don't close until two in the morning. Some will do a brisk trade until dawn.

It is truly astonishing how easily and speedily the Saudis adjust to change, to living by night and sleeping by day. The previous Ramadan, after the siege of Mecca, I had started thinking about permanence and change in Islam. I had concluded that the problem was not, as Sami Angawi had put it, about fitting the variables into the constants. The problem was developing a contemporary understanding of the constants. I had started to write a book called *The Future of Muslim Civilization*. It was an attempt to describe what an Islamic society should and could be. Nothing remains 'contemporary' forever, I argued. Islam has to be understood afresh, from epoch to epoch, according to the needs of specific times and places. And as our understanding changes, Islam of one particular epoch might not bear much resemblance—except in devotional matters—to Islam of another epoch. Wahhabism, I concluded, had introduced two metaphysical catastrophes into Islam.

First, by ending any further interpretations of the 'absolute frame of reference'—the Qur'an and the life of Prophet Muhammad—it had removed what cultural theorists call 'agency' from the believers. They had no choice but to obey the *'ulama*. Without the constant struggle of interpretation, Muslim societies are doomed to exist in suspended animation. If everything is a given, nothing new can really be accommodated. The intellect becomes an irrelevant encumbrance, since good behaviour, even wisdom, comprises obedience to a formula.

Second, by assuming that ethics and morality reached their apex with the companions of the Prophet, Wahhabism negates the very idea of evolution in human thought and morality. Indeed, I argued, it set Muslim civilization on a fixed course of perpetual decline. The challenge of our time, I argued, is to work out and implement Muslim values that are clearly and distinctively more appropriate than those worked out by the Companions of the Prophet.

From the perspective of Wahhabism, these were heretical thoughts and I kept them mostly to myself. But now the manuscript was finished. I spent the night checking and making final changes. I typed a false title page and placed the real manuscript between some mundane thoughts about the hajj, just in case they checked at the airport. A small suitcase, containing mostly rare books and manuscripts I had scavenged and rescued, was already packed. A friend had agreed to take my furniture, my stereo and my beloved hammock—I used to lie on it, swinging in the middle of my living room listening alternately to the recitation of the Qur'an and 'Tangerine Dream'. I placed the manuscript of my book and the £50,000 I had saved in a Saudi Airlines shoulder bag, and headed for the airport.

I was at the airport by seven in the morning, hoping to catch the eleven o'clock Saudi Airlines flight to London. Unlike the new King Abdul Aziz Airport, which was twenty miles outside the city, the old Jeddah airport was only a few minutes' drive from where I lived. It couldn't have been more different from the tent-like structure and technological efficiency of its modern counterpart. It was little more than a loosely linked collection of prefabricated sheds. I got there before everyone else; but I had no booking. So I gave the Palestinian man behind the check-in counter a long sob story. My grandmother had died. My uncle had died. Half of my relations over the age of fifty had died. But he wasn't convinced.

'Who else do you want me to kill?'

He looked slightly bemused. 'OK,' he said, 'it's Ramadan and I believe you.' The blessed month has an unfailing hold on Muslim consciousness. People are supposed to be more compassionate then. 'But even in Ramadan we have to eat,' he added, rubbing his thumb and fingertips together. *Falus*, said his gesture. Money. I slipped 500 riyals—more than £100 at the time—into his hand. 'Normally, you would have to go on the waiting list, but considering that your grandmother has died...' He paused for a moment. 'I'll take the risk and give you a seat.'

I thanked him and handed him my passport.

He flicked through the pages. 'You don't seem to have an exit visa.' He looked puzzled.

'I do,' I said. 'I have an emergency exit visa. It's that piece of paper in the passport.'

He looked at the piece of paper, turned it over to examine the passport office stamp and nodded. 'No one has ever left this country on an emergency visa,' he said. 'But still, it's Ramadan.'

While I was digesting the clerk's words, I noticed the porter was putting the wrong labels on my suitcase.

'London, London,' I shouted. 'Not Rome. London, London.'

'Don't shout,' said the porter. 'It's Ramadan.' And he proceeded to put the wrong label on my suitcase and placed it on the conveyor belt.

'Forget the luggage, worry about your exit visa,' said the clerk as he handed me my passport, ticket and boarding pass.

At passport control, two officers sat at separate desks casually stamping passports and collecting exit cards. I filled in an exit card and pushed through the crowd. I handed my passport and the sheet of paper to one of the officers. He looked closely at the paper, taking his time. Eventually he spoke: 'Sorry, I'm not qualified to give exit visas. You'll have to see the *mudir*.'

'Where's his office?' I asked.

The man pointed in an arbitrary way. 'Over there,' he said.

I found my way to the passport section. Three men were sitting inside chatting. I placed my passport and clearance sheet on the table. 'Please,' I said, 'I have an emergency exit visa. I need the director to sign it.'

One officer forced himself to get up. He looked closely at my piece of paper. Then he walked to a desk on which lay a large register. He turned a few pages of the register and checked my name against it. After a few minutes' examination, he closed the register. He initialled the paper and pointed me towards another office.

There, a small man sat behind a very large desk. I put my piece of paper in front of him. He took several minutes to examine it and then signed it at the bottom.

'You will get your final clearance at the Immigration Office in Arrivals,' he told me.

'Arrivals?' The flight was now being called. 'Arrivals? I want an exit visa, not an entrance visa.'

'Don't shout,' said the official. 'It's Ramadan. I know what you want. But you have to follow the procedure. You have to go to the Arrivals. *Khalas.*' Without a word I took the paper from his hand and ran out. I could hear the last call for my flight. I ran from the departure lounge and out of Terminal One. I ran along the old airport road and turned into the Arrivals.

A Bedouin soldier tried to stop me, but I did not wait to argue with him. I ran into the first office I could see.

Inside an elderly man sat on a chair. *'Salaam alaikum,'* I said, and without waiting for an answer I grabbed his beard. I pulled it gently and kissed it wildly. I kissed it on the left side, and then on the right side. I kissed it from the front and under his chin.

The old officer was completely transformed. He looked both embarrassed and concerned.

'Tell me, O Brother, what can I do for you?' he said.

I explained the situation.

'Don't worry,' he said. 'Your paper needs several signatures and I will go with you to collect them. After all, today is the first day of Ramadan.'

We went from office to office collecting signatures. Then the old officer took me back to the Departure Lounge. We ran towards a group of Saudi ground staff.

'Flight SV 172, Flight SV 172!'

Ziauddin Sardar

'Quick,' said one of them, 'get in the coach.'
I jumped in the coach. I was the only passenger. The driver closed the door and made for the plane. I sat anxiously. Halfway through the journey, the coach was stopped.
'Turn back, turn back,' somebody shouted outside.
From the window of the coach I could see the plane still standing on the tarmac. A very long limousine with a Saudi flag whizzed past the coach. A few moments later, a princely-looking Saudi mounted into the plane with his entourage.
'There goes your seat,' said the Filipino coach driver. 'None of the princes stay in the country this time of year. It's Ramadan, you know.'
'Yes,' I said. 'I know. It's Ramadan.'
I arrived the next day in London by British Airways. □